I LOVE YOU, I REALLY DO!
PART TWO

BY G. LEGMAN

BEING BOOK ONE OF G. LEGMAN'S

AUTOBIOGRAPHY OF INNOCENCE

FAITHFULLY TRANSCRIBED BY
JUDITH EVANS LEGMAN

PUBLISHED BY CREATESPACE
2016

PART TWO

TABLE OF CONTENTS

CHAPTER 8

GIRL CRAZY

COMING back home from New York in disgrace wasn't as bad as I expected it to be. It was summer and people were busy having fun. Nobody had noticed I was gone. It's often that way. What I cared for most about now was reading large non-fiction books. Without consciously trying to scout anybody out sexually, though that's certainly what I was doing, by the next spring there were also a couple of nice girls at school that I'd talk with occasionally in the halls — always terribly serious, where the other guys always knew how to kid — and would sometimes walk them home from school. But of course it never went very far, because there was never anywhere on the way home where you could even stop and kiss. Anyhow, they were all too dumb, really, to talk to. So I began squiring some of the lady teachers home too, especially the young & pretty ones, like our thin brunette French teacher with eyeglasses, Miss Talbot, who had even taken a trip *to Paris* and was therefore evidently hot stuff. And the jolly little plump blonde algebra-and-geometry teacher with the charming name of Mrs. Betty Bee, which she signed appropriately to her notes on test papers as B^2.

The French teacher, Miss Talbot, wasn't exactly willing to be my mentor, but she let me carry her books & papers home to the Y.W.C.A. downtown where she lived with all the other proper young unmarried women. She was extremely self-conscious sexually, as even I could see, and became very embarrassed when I launched into telling her some of my simple love troubles, which I craftily invented. When I mentioned that I didn't like walking high school girls home because they always wanted to stop and kiss under the trees — an awful lie — Miss Talbot turned cherry red and as tense as a bowstring.

"Maybe you ought to, er, talk to your, er, rabbi about that?" she ventured, obviously terribly uneasy listening to things of that kind, and from a boy. Clearly she didn't feel competent to offer any further advice on subjects like that, and was certainly not rising to the bait *if* I was expressing any unspoken preference. For her. I told her Rabbi Arzt was great, and an absolutely brilliant speaker, but that he didn't know a darn thing about love, only about books. I was beyond that now, I said in a manly tone.

"Well, I only know about books too," Miss Talbot said, her cheeks burning. I could see she was hiding something, just as I was. Could it be the same thing, I wondered? Of course it was.

We talked hastily about Paris, instead, which she assured me was just as wonderful as everyone said, and like living in a dream. But everyone in Paris spoke so rapidly, and in slang half the time. Conscious that she wasn't being much help to me on a human level, and that I was asking for help, Miss Talbot followed up her story about Paris by offering to tell me a real French slang phrase, for my dictionary of slang that I had bragged about collecting, if I promised not to use it in class. It was — embarrassed pause — *faire la bombe!*

I whipped out my little notebook, which I knew would impress her, and jotted it down, even though it was a real disappointment to me. With that buildup I had hoped she'd tell me something improper. "What does it mean?" I asked. "Make the bomb."

"It means, well, 'make whoopee'." Miss Talbot blushed bright red. "You know — with *drinking*, and everything."

"Like going to a wild party?" More blushes from Miss Talbot. And I thought: Wow! Gay Paree!! Did that mean our thin little French teacher with her eyeglasses off, running around the room bareass naked, and slick-haired French sheiks with hardons like gorillas chasing after her? Wow! My eyes must have bugged out too far, something they have a habit of doing, and Miss Talbot was overwhelmed with her own verbal daring, or hidden confession, and did not want to answer my indiscreet question. She just quivered, in what I took for blushing assent, over her eyeglasses, grabbed her books and dashed into the Y.W.C.A. French slang is powerful stuff, all right. But when I finally got to France, it was all out of date. Nobody says *faire la bombe* any more.

That French class was always a glory and crucifixion for me anyhow, owing to the girl I sat next to, named Sidonie Honiger. Sidonie was born in Alsace and could speak French perfectly, but she was too dumb, or maybe too confused about English to be able to write the answers to the simplest test and always had to demand my help, which was strictly

8

against the rules. We were taught that we were there to compete, not to co-operate. That's education for you.

Sidonie was a superb animal, a year older than everyone else in class and dripping with sexual readiness which she made no attempt to hide. She had particularly long, beautifully formed legs — all the way up, I was pretty sure — and a mass of rich reddish-brown hair fluffing all around her face like a big sexy squirrel's tail. She walked like a prancing palfrey when she came into the classroom, arching her rump backwards and with her high juicy breasts jiggling out in front as though they got in her way. It brought a lump to my throat, watching, and sometimes in my pants. In short, I ate Sidonie alive with my eyes, and she knew it and accepted it as her due. When I had wet dreams, which I often did, it was always about Sidonie floating open and naked and willing before me, as though borne up by the sea, with all those long legs and arms and hair of hers waving slowly in the water, and reaching out toward me like beckoning tentacles. That was the way I wanted to die.

Actually, her face was of the too-cute type I never much liked, with beestung lips of oxbow pattern on the style of Brigitte Bardot, and an ineffable expression of mixed erotic willingness and unforgivable dumbness and inarticulateness that drove

9

me wild. But I felt it would be no use at all scouting Sidonie for dates, as her clothes and necklaces — which she was always eating at — implied clearly that her family had loads more money than mine, with a car that she could drive and everything. Also, not understanding very much about female character then, I held off in a way because she was the regular girlfriend of an older fellow I knew pretty well, named Jimmy Kennedy, at St. Thomas's College, a crowded Jesuit preparatory school downtown.

I used to see Kennedy every weekend, usually Friday nights at our friend Cy Endfield's house, and Kennedy would regale me with wild stories of laying Sidonie the night before, all the way from vertical with her ass against the radiator in the bathroom at a party, to upside-down with her head hanging out the window to watch the American Legion parade. These stories didn't seem to interest Endfield, who would practice magic tricks endlessly meanwhile, but I would listen absolutely spellbound, punctuating Kennedy's stories with envious groans and appreciative curses. I knew he was a lying bastard, of course, but just looking moonily at Sidonie and her moistly bulging underlip, in the next seat to me in French class, I also knew that every word was true.

That bathroom story practically finished me off. It had happened only very recently, like a night or two before, and Kennedy sat there lank and grinning in one of Endfield's over-stuffed parlor armchairs — they had two parlors — and ruthlessly gave me every heartless detail. They were both slightly high on liquor, of course, he explained, or they wouldn't have been making love in the bathroom at all. But there wasn't anywhere else to go, because the beds in the bedroom were all covered with people's coats & hats. So he had slipped into the bathroom with her, but was too gallant to suggest making love to her sitting on the toilet.

"I should hope so!" I growled.

So there was nothing for it but to work it as a knee-trembler up against the radiator, which was only warm, Kennedy thought, but which was so hot after a few minutes that Sidonie squirmed around even more wildly than usual. And when he pulled his prick out when he felt himself coming, it squirted all over her silk party dress. He didn't even know he had done it because she wouldn't stop sucking his tongue.

Naturally it was impossible for her to go back into the party like that, so she pulled the door half open and called a girlfriend of hers into the bathroom with them, to ask for her help. The friend helped Sidonie strip her dress off over her head and wash out

11

the stain in the sink. Kennedy sat watching them and grinning, as he explained, at the edge of the bathtub, smoking cigarettes and calling out to anyone who knocked at the door that he'd be out in a minute, while the two girls waved and squeezed the dress over the radiator to try to dry it out, with Sidonie bouncing around in brown satin teddies and a brassiere. No petticoat. Neither of the girls paid the slightest further attention to Kennedy while they struggled with the dress.

Kennedy told his story with a sort of happy, shit-eating grin the whole way, his bony Irish face wreathed in the pleasure of remembering. I asked him jealously if he was conscious of having been treated like a beehive drone by the two queen-bees, and said he was lucky he hadn't just been sloughed off to a happy death after having performed his mere male penetration trick. All the answer I got was a triumphant grin, while Endfield got on my nerves even further with his incessant practicing rolling a silver half-dollar over his knuckles.

The only thing I *really* wanted to know, Kennedy wasn't capable of telling me: was the hair on Sidonie's pussy the same magnificent tawny red-brown as the hair of her head? The dumb bastard didn't know — hadn't looked! He had been too busy fucking her standing up to think of noticing. I could have killed him. He had been trying to pull her brassiere up over her tits, to get at them with one hand, he explained. He'd look next time and tell me, he promised. Thanks! And Sidonie appeared in my dreams for weeks afterwards, with one lovely breast up out of her bra, and the other still in, and me burying my face in her monstrously shaggy and marvelously odorous snatch. And terrible ashamed meanwhile of my imaginary adultery with my best friend's girl; and even more ashamed that I didn't have the cold courage just to kill him and make off with Sidonie.

The next time I saw my red-brown temptress in French class I didn't hesitate to say to her in an undertone, "You're driving me crazy. I've been dreaming about you all weekend — stark naked!" I was so far gone by now, having thought about nothing but Sidonie's naked cunt and breasts all weekend, that I didn't hesitate to underline my remarks about dreaming of her naked with making a simultaneous open-mouthed or rather, fangbared biting gesture toward her mouth and imagined naked breasts.

"Who? You or me?" she replied calmly, which was certainly one up for her. I felt like telling her that Jimmy Kennedy had given me a play-by-play description of their adventure in the bathroom — and half a dozen others — but it wasn't necessary. She knew very well that we were friends. Kennedy couldn't have been her first boyfriend either; that was sure. I wondered what age she had started at, back in Alsace. Had she been the Jeanie with the Red-Brown Hair, in a packing-case under somebody's front porch in Strasbourg? Meaning, I guess, was there a chance for a turn for me?

No. I never went out with Sidonie, nor even touched her except once — though she herself touched everyone — but I was enslaved to her and we both knew it. Nevertheless, I felt she was my friend's girlfriend, and didn't even dream of trying to steal her. Well, in fact, I did dream about it, but I didn't do it nor even try. Not even for one marvelous hot sex-date — as though anybody could really ever be satisfied with just one! — at which I would have fucked myself absolutely senseless, and Sidonie too, I betcha. No, not even for that.

I wasn't aware then that a lot of men aren't so noble as Damon & Pythias about male friendship. Nor how easy it is to get beautiful women to be unfaithful. Men too. I should have known the military proverb then about conquered cities: *"Great cities are like beautiful women — easy to conquer, hard to hold."* Or the even more profound one about translations: profound because it

14

makes a hidden stab at the reason, instead of satisfying itself with just describing the phenomenon in elegant paradox. *"Translations are like women: if they're beautiful they're not faithful, and if they're faithful they're not beautiful."* I guess that's not a paradox but a chiasmus. Why quibble?

Just to make things worse for me, orasexually oriented as I always was, Kennedy also had the unkindness to give me full details on another occasion of Sidonie's imported French art with her mouth, and how when he came she swallowed every drop, and then looked up at him, on her knees, and *licked her lips*. That detail really finished me off. Every time I saw Sidonie chewing on her slender gold necklace in class after that, with her eyes glazed in what I was sure was erotic reminiscence, my own eyes would glaze over wildly too. And just looking at her twisting her pouting mouth around her pencil-tip and poking it in & out unconsciously — ?? — as she struggled with some disgustingly simple question on a French quiz, made me frantic to rip open my fly buttons then & there and ram my prick about a mile down her throat. She knew it too — she knew it!

Dumb as I foolishly imagined her to be, Sidonie invariably picked up all the vibrations of my wildness about her, and would cast a calculating, almost professional glance sideways at the not-infrequent hardon in my pants hidden under the wooden school chair-desk as I stared hungrily at her. This was always most frequent on the days I thought I divined a delicate thread of tangy odor emanating from her, a sort of tawny animal presence meaning that she was having her period. Girls were always told that this drives men off and to wash every trace ruthlessly away, but it always made me the horniest and most avid. Sidonie would generally reward my visible phallic homage to her under the desk with a lazy, sensuous smile like a cat that's just polished off the canary. If only she had! I thought of myself as very smart and of beautiful Sidonie as dumb, but in fact I was completely obnubilated by the least tilt of her straight leg and quivering thigh, not to mention the domains that there adjacent lie, as remarked upon by Big Bill Shakespeare.

On one occasion Sidonie brought all the answers to the French test with her — doubtless the subjunctives of improbable verbs that no one would ever use in a lifetime like *plût* and *assassinassiez*, and all the rest of that impossible crap we were always being tested on. She had the slip of paper with the answers tucked under her garter. This involved hiking up the skirt of her dress halfway along the creamiest white thigh imaginable, but as she couldn't figure head or tail

16

out of her own notes, she had herself practically undressed under cover of the desk before she gave up. I flunked that test.

I not only couldn't take my eyes off her creamy thighs, which I knew were teaching me more than being tested on the French language ever could, but I somehow had decided that the brown silk dress with the tight skirt that she was wearing must have been just the dress she was wearing when Jimmy Kennedy made love to her at that party up against the bathroom radiator. I don't know how I thought I knew, but I was positive of it, and my tongue was out half a yard, wanting to rip the skirt the rest of the way up her legs and get at her with my tongue and teeth. As I say, I flunked that test.

Sidonie was having trouble with it too, having bollixed up her hidden notes completely. "Be a sport! What's the answer?" she finally hissed at me, reaching out the fingers of one hand toward me with a delicate flutter of supplication and promise at her fingertips, as though she was going to reach over and squeeze my fly. I wrote out the answer in capital letters on a bit of paper and slipped it to her surreptitiously, trusting that the myopic Miss Talbot wouldn't catch us. When we got up after the test, I took the occasion of Sidonie bending over to pick up her stack of books, and the covering motions of my own body, to slide one hand up under her skirt and all the way up to her crotch. She not only didn't resist or seem surprised, but lifted her bottom toward me delicately so I could get my hand in deeper under the loose edge of her chemise or teddies or whatever it was. We had only a second that way, but it was heaven.

After that, Sidonie did occasionally touch my fly in class, when we figured Miss Talbot wouldn't see. But she caught us at it once, coming down the aisle on my off side, and though she didn't say anything she stared into my eyes with indignation and shock, her cheeks flaming red. After that Miss Talbot would never let me walk her home again to the Y.W.C.A. I don't think it was jealousy; I think she was afraid of having anything more to do with me.

Actually, I wasn't trying to make any of the teachers, which would have been ridiculous, though the gossip was that one of the older language teachers whose father was a big important wheel in local politics did put out for all the boys on the football team. But simultaneously some of the kids also whispered that she was a Lesbian, so it was hard to know what to believe. I had one odd experience with her soon after that made me pretty sure she was a lez. Years later I met a girl in New York who had been at Central High, who told me what the real story was. Miss X, the teacher, used to invite both one of the athletes *and* his girl friend — the girl I knew — to her big old house evenings, give them drinks and leave them alone together so they could make love. Then she would purposely catch them at it, stand around for a while pretending to disapprove, and then join in, mostly in a Lesbian way. She had worked it that way with other couples too, the girl told me.

"Why did you let her interfere like that?" I asked.

"Well, I was sort of afraid of her," she admitted. "It was her house. Besides, if you want to know, it was wonderful having two of them make love to me at once." But she never went back after Miss X finally wanted her to lay face down on top of the athlete while he fucked her, so she could spank her at the same time. "That's when I knew she was a nut," the girl said.

That was how most of us kids felt about sex, when we talked about it, which was often. We wanted sex and yearned for it, and mostly weren't getting it. But no nutty stuff — that was *out* — and we had enormous contempt for the few local effeminate homo-sexuals we could distinguish flitting along Adams Avenue. And we hated and feared the unexpected

19

adults who would occasionally proposition us in the street on one cockamammy pretext or another, to try to exploit us sexually.

Meanwhile, they were very insidious and clever, and it wasn't always easy to recognize their phony-baloney story immediately as a fake until that final moment when they started unbuttoning, and taking out their prick — or yours. Of course, when a well-dressed man followed you or tried to talk to you in the street late at night or very early in the morning, there was no question about it and you knew what to do. You ran, before they could grab you. We had all heard about the Loeb & Leopold case just a few years before, when two rich young perverts murdered a younger boy "for thrills," and cut up his body and put it in a trunk. None of us wanted to be next. It was strange too, how many of the kids told stories of having been molested at one time or another, and how few told our parents. I know *I* never told, and yet men had often bothered me coming home in the evening ever since I was a little kid in Hebrew school. But we never told our parents. Maybe some of the girls did, but the boys knew that if we told our parents they'd be even more strict about letting us out nights. It was a real problem.

Some of the kids said that Scranton had more sex-loonies than anywhere else because they came there on account of the tolerated whorehouses, but I argued that wasn't so and that the whorehouses should be draining most of them off our backs. Which shows how little I understood then about either perverts or police protection and corruption. And I told the others that Scranton's perverts were nothing at all compared to New York, where they prowled the streets and parks and especially the bridges every night. That was why I had come back to go to highschool in Scranton, I said. That wasn't quite true, but it wasn't a lie either. Anyhow, we never told our parents, so they wouldn't keep us home nights.

THE WAY our town was laid out there were mostly large square blocks in the residential sections big enough for ten or a dozen two-story-and-attic houses along each edge, and each house with a small lawn in front and a large yard in back, covering two or three times as much land as the house did. To keep the backyards from butting up against each other, there was a narrow delivery alley about three yards wide, big enough for a wagon or later an automobile to go through, running north and south through each square block. The avenues, going north and south, were named after rivers and presidents of the United States and other notables — all men — and the streets running east and west were named after odd trees and shrubs: Myrtle, Gibson, Pine, Vine, Olive, Mulberry, Linden, and like that. The alleys ran from one tree-named street down to the next, and the houses on those streets necessarily had much smaller back-yards, if any, than the bigger properties on the avenues. We lived up in the eastern hill section of town, on Harrison Avenue, at number 737, which meant the seventh block up from Roaring Brook at the bottom of the hill where the numbering began. That was the house I was born in.

The alleys had no names, or if they did no one knew what they were. On the city map they were all elegantly given as This Court and That Court. I think the one behind our back-yard was named Schultz Court, but I'm not sure. No one ever called them anything but the alley. Theoretically there were no houses on them, but actually there were often a couple of houses in the alleys, here and there, mostly remodeled stables from the century before, now used as garages with poor families living above them. Even after all the streets of the town were paved in the early 1920s, the alleys stayed just dirt roads for another ten years, till they were paved too. Downtown, in the business section, there were paved alleys entirely lined with small low houses, at least on one side, like Dupont Court. These were definitely low-class and no family of any social pretentions lived in an alley. One of my girlfriends did, and was very ashamed of it.

The one alley in town that everybody knew about, even schoolkids, was one of those downtown lined on both sides with low wooden houses. When you said *The Alley*, in Scranton, that was the alley you meant. It was only one block long, running along between Wyoming and Penn Avenues, I think, from the street that faced Central High School down to the next street, that faced the main police station and the Chamber of Commerce and the Y.M.C.A. It was just one block away from all of these — centrally located. All the houses in The Alley were whorehouses, which were perfectly legal in Scranton then, and in Allentown nearby, until about World War II.

Grammar-school kids, of whom I had been one, and all-the-more us highschool kids — the boys only, that is — used to consider it a high old prank, and daring as hell, to hurry through The Alley, which we called plainly The Whoor Alley, staring at the heavyset Polish and Hunky and Irish women who would sit at the windows of the wooden whorehouses, tapping with their rings on the window-glass to attract customers. They all seemed very old to us kids, about like our mothers. Sometimes you could see their breasts, untrammeled and swaying under their thin underwear bodices or shirtwaists.

In spring and summer, when their windows were open, the women would snap at us: "Get outa here, you kids! What are you doing here? Scram!" When it was bigger highschool boys who scurried or boldly sauntered through The Alley, the women's questions became more technical: "You old enough to shave, kid? No? Then get the fuckin' hell outa here!!" Fuzz on your cheeks was supposed to be the test of manhood at the door, where the woman would run her hand over your cheek. No fuzz, and you couldn't get in, even if you were smoking a cigarette. "No shave, no fuck!" they'd say uninterestedly.

The older fellows who were juniors or seniors at Central High told us all about it. The price of a woman was two dollars, which made a two dollar bill bad luck. Upstairs money. The woman laid down and spread her legs, and you jumped right on. You got ten minutes, or as long as it took you to shoot off. If you took too long they charged you more. When the mines were running and there were plenty of customers, each woman had to take on fifty men or more every day, and got ten cents out of the two dollars. The madam who owned the place got all the rest.

Even so, the women could make twenty or thirty dollars a week that way, which was over twice as much as a man could make in the mines. Each house had a "nigger woman" too, who did the cleaning. If you only had one dollar you had to fuck her on a mattress in the coal-shed, the fellows said. It would change your luck. All the other women had beds. If you only had fifty cents, one of them would jerk you off sitting on the bed without undressing. But they were rough about it, and their rings sometimes hurt you. Besides, you could do that yourself, so why save up money to go wasting it that way?

The low wooden houses and the heavyset women and the whole Alley were all kind of scary, anyhow, with a faint ever-present odor that filtered out of the houses, of potassium permanganate fluid. The women kept it in an open container by the bed in every room to wash out their cunts with after each customer, so they wouldn't get diseases. Those diseases were horrible and they destroyed your mind and your nose fell off. But the antiseptic that the women used worked. It was a deadly poison, we told each other, much stronger than the cresol fluids that were advertised in all the papers for married women to use

25

for "hygiene" — meaning birth control, of course. And even the cresol was so strong that farmers used it for cleaning out chicken-coops. All that stuff made the inside of the women's cunts as rough as a board.

If you were smart you stuck to the girls you knew in school, if they would only do it. They were as soft as honey inside when you got your finger in. You could whack off for a week just thinking about it. And there was always Jeanie-With-the-Dark-Brown-Hole, who took on all the boys for nothing on the straw in a packing case under her porch, next to the Nickelette on Prescott Avenue. But I would never touch Jeanie: those dead, fishy eyes she had made me feel funny. Later I was glad, because Jeanie got the clap eventually, when she was about fourteen, and gave it to all the fellows that went under the porch with her, including two Boy Scouts.

Every once in a while we'd hear about one of the women in the houses in The Alley who'd go crazy after years "in the life," and would commit suicide by drinking the antiseptic fluid and die immediately in terrible agony. That permanganate was an absolute poison. But they had to use it between customers so they wouldn't get the clap & the syph and then give them to the next customer. There was a lot of that stuff going around, including some other diseases with

26

names and symptoms us fellows weren't sure of, but the whores got it all from the customers and then the customers got it back from the whores. It was a Vicious Circle, that's for sure.

The cops were all good customers at the houses in the Alley, and knew everything that happened there. Cops didn't have to pay. They knew where all the bodies were buried, and the madams had to pay them regular hush-money each week. Sometimes old men, especially rich ones who ate too much and wore tight collars would die when they shot off while they were with a woman. Then they had to have the dead bodies sneaked out secretly, of course. The most dangerous was when one of the women blew you — you know, sucked you off. It took more of your strength out of you that way, especially the women who liked to drink your gism. They might even keep it in a little glass by the bed, and fill it up with mouthfuls from different customers, and then when the glass would be full they'd just toss it off the way you'd drink a beer.

Women like that could really drain your manhood, but it felt absolutely marvelous, and it was worth it. But only once in a while. Anyhow, the fairies knew how to do it much better than any whore ever could, because the fairies sucked pricks because they loved to do it — they'd even give you money for

27

letting them do it! — but the women only did it professionally, for money. You had to pay them. If you couldn't get a hardon, because you were nervous, they'd suck you a while first: that was called fifty-fifty, or half & half. It always worked.

In among absorbing this folklore, half of which I too believed firmly, I was meanwhile looking very intensely for a confidante or for some older person to advise me. I never really discovered anyone among the teachers whom I imagined were the first ones to turn to. I really did try. But I found the teachers did not want to talk about sex anymore than Rabbi Arzt did, when I tried bracing him first. Nope, no sex. Not even in private. And stymied as I was with Sidonie, sex was essentially my biggest problem. Mostly I had to be satisfied with talking to the teachers I walked with after school about serious extra-curricular things — the books I was reading, my plans to work my way through college, and like that.

One of the men teachers Mr. Cunliffe, whose subject was mathematics, was particularly nice to me. Though fairly young, he was getting bald on top and hated to take off his hat when he didn't have to. When I would see him after school climbing into his little car, which was always parked by the Christian Science temple across the street, he would stop and balance a notebook on the open car window and sketch out complicated mathematical paradoxes for me to try and solve, something he never gave us in class. Too frivolous. The ones I remember best were that *1 equals 2* — proved algebraically — and an elegant geometrical "proof" that *a right angle equals an obtuse angle,* and that therefore *all angles in the world are equal!* That was a honey, but you couldn't construct it with a ruler; it only worked as a rough sketch.

Another young male teacher named Lot Lake, who had a twisted leg and was extremely pleasant, used to talk to me about girls sometimes in an elevated fashion, as he limped along beside me down Washington Avenue after school. How difficult girls were to understand, and how you had to spend so much money on them to keep their interest, and so on. Later I met Lake again one day in New York coming out of the bus station, when he was no longer teaching at Central. I don't know exactly why, but I told him what I had recently found out from one of the girl students about Miss X, the perverted teacher who was involved with highschool kids of both sexes. This was kind of nervy to mention to him, but I did it anyhow. I guess I hoped he'd tell people.

"Oh sure," he said, trying to look casual but turning practically green. "Everybody on the faculty

29

knew Old X-ey was up to something. But we never talked about it. What's the use? You couldn't touch her. Her family was too big in Scranton; her father and the governor were just like that — " Gesture of two entwined fingers.

"My father says Scranton is run entirely on graft," I put in.

"And pull," Lake added sourly. "What town isn't?   Between the mine operators and the whoorhouses, Scranton is a real mess." I was on my way to the library, as I was every day, and he limped along with me another block or two saying how much he wished he could get out of Scranton for good. "I'll bet you're glad you left," he added with a rueful grin. "A person either goes crazy or turns into a numbskull in a rotten little burg like that."

Only one teacher ever talked to me about profound truths: about honor, and true-heartedness, and standing up for what one believed in. That was sweet old Miss Conrad, the Latin teacher, who lived with her father up on Quincey Avenue and had an enormous goiter under her chin. A man at the Mayo Clinic, somewhere in the Midwest, had discovered that goiter was caused by a lack of iodine in the table salt, and you could prevent it; but you couldn't ever really cure the people who had grown goiters when they were

30

little. For them it was a cross they had to carry all their life. But Miss Conrad was so wonderful and sweet, and so tremendously sincere, that you forgot about noticing her goiter after a while.

One day when she saw me passing her house reading a book while I walked, Miss Conrad invited me in and gave me tea with milk to drink — a luxurious beverage I had never tasted before. We sat in her stiff little parlor, with lace antimacassars on the polished wood and tapestry-upholstered chairs, while she looked at the book I was reading. Then she laid it down without comment on the dark upright piano, which I remember had two ornate gilt candle-holders, one at each side of the music rack.

She told me that Virgil and Seneca were the greatest writers who ever lived, and that I would find that the recent novels everybody was reading like Thornton Wilder's *Bridge of San Luis Rey* and Charles Morgan's *The Fountain* were very thin by comparison. "They cannot live," she said; "they're tawdry stuff."

She was right. Have they lived? Not fifty years; not five years. Then she presented me with a framed copy of Rudyard Kipling's inspirational poem *"If"* which she took right down off the wall and dusted with her napkin before handing it to me.

31

"This is the best advice any young man can ever have," Miss Conrad told me solemnly. "Read it again and again until you know it by heart. And then *do* it."

Another day when she invited me in again for tea & milk, I showed her the new book I was reading this time, which was Hervey Allen's big historical novel *Anthony Adverse*. I assured her it wasn't just picaresque fiction but very well written, and full of moral lessons that he was slipping to the reader all the time, hidden in the story. "Like Æsop," I said. Then I tried to tell Miss Conrad about my love problems, in a nice way, but she said she didn't think I was really suffering because I admitted I wasn't in love with Sidonie. Of course I wasn't, but it burned just the same.

"I think it's just the sap rising," she said matter-of-factly. "You can feel that way about a lot of girls. But when you'll feel the way you can only feel about *one* girl — you'll know it."

Miss Conrad did admit that love is a big problem, no matter which way you take it, and that she herself had never solved it. That she had hoped to be married & have a family, but her young man was killed in the War. He was an officer, and had been caught in machine-gun fire leading an attack with his men. So now she taught school instead of being married, and all the students were her family, she said. She also took care of her old father, because her mother was dead and her father still kept the family haberdashery store downtown facing one corner of the Court House Square, so they'd have money to live on. We agreed that it was very wrong for people to invent things like machine-guns, and kill innocent people with them, just to make their own countries a little bigger. "Human beings act like wild animals sometimes," she said. "You have to be prepared for that." Then we went back to talking about love, which she did not consider was the same thing as sex.

"Don't be surprised," Miss Conrad warned me, "if love makes you suffer. There's as much suffering in it as there is happiness. But they go together, and you can't have one without the other. No one can cheat destiny."

I didn't answer and just drank my tea, and poked the small plate of too-sugary cookies she had served. I wanted to argue, cry out, refuse; but her quiet certainty and resignation impressed me. I thought of sex & love as a tremendous pleasure, not a martyrdom the way she did.

"It's like a roller-coaster," Miss Conrad went on. "Don't ever forget that. Not just love, but everything. If you want to go up very high, you have to take the chance of falling very far down afterward." She pursed her lips. "Very far."

She followed this up with a long quotation in Italian, which she said was from Dante, about the greatest sadness being the memory of great happiness, but you still mustn't refuse either; and then another in Latin, to prove it, from Lucretius' *On the Nature of Things*. I didn't understand it very well, but went home and wrote it all down anyway in my already bulging Quotation Book. It seemed strange to me that of all my teachers the only one who seemed to know or care about anything really important and *modern* was Miss Conrad, who was only supposed to know about a dead language like Latin. Wherever she learned it, one thing that's sure is that the roller-coaster of alternate ecstasy and agony is the truest thing I ever heard anyone say about love. And that there's no way to cheat. She knew.

THINKING it over, it also seems strange that all I ever learned from my teachers that I can remember is what they told me outside of school. I suppose this isn't really true, but that's the way it seems. In which case, what was school for, after all? Luckily I wasn't slated to go to school much longer, but I still imagined

34

I'd be ploughing through colleges and universities for another eight or ten years, and then end up as an important psychologist. I would specialize in love problems — I knew that already. Economics was beginning to interest me very much too, but there was no career in that, everybody said. Only the lowest kind of people became ward-heelers and went into politics. "Yes," my father said, "and the *tragedy* is that politics demands the *highest* type. Otherwise it all ends up as graft."

There was this Psychology Club in Scranton that met one night a week in the Chamber of Commerce auditorium, and I went a couple of times. But it was all older people, and they spent so much of the time electing each other and voting for things that nobody ever talked about psychology. It had been known as the *Philosophy* Club until early that year, but they were retooling now to the modern world, they explained. I thought that was extremely funny, and never went back. Anyhow, you could learn a lot more about psychology from Rabbi Arzt's sermons, or rather lectures, especially Friday nights when most of the congregation came straight from a big Shabbos dinner on a full stomach and fell asleep at once. Then he would talk about modern things instead of religion to his sleeping audience, without anybody knowing or caring except me.

I used to sit there bolt upright and hang on his every word & gesture. He'd always start very quietly. "There's an interesting experiment being done recently at Yale," he'd begin, or something like that. And then he'd be off about monkeys competing with each other for food and mates, and whatnot. It was fascinating. At the end he'd always have to hook it up somehow to religion, of course, and would raise his voice at that point so as to wake up all the sleepers, including my father, who'd be slumped sideways in the seat next to me. But that didn't matter. We all realized my father wouldn't ever be anything but a railroad rate-clerk. It was me who had to learn things, especially about religion, and make something of my life. And become a leader in Israël. Well, maybe I wouldn't become a leader in Israël. I'd be leader in America instead. There's lots more things in the world than just being Jewish, and more people than just the Jews. In fact, the Jews are one of the smallest minorities. That's why it was so important to be outstanding *if* you were Jewish — otherwise you didn't stand a chance. I'd be a big psychologist instead of a rabbi. Why not? Unknown to me then, more than one ex-rabbinical student was already retooling to psychoanalysis and psychiatry — all the biggest.

At the same time as these intellectual explorations, I was still going around every other Saturday or so, and sometimes every Saturday after a quick jump to the public library, to see my best girl friend Berta Parrott. I would spend most of the afternoon romancing her in the upstairs sewing room, in the back of their house, followed by a solid hour or two, as night would fall, of pretty serious hugging & kissing. But that was all. I never actually tried to seduce Berta, never put my hand under her sweater or dress, and never even touched any part of her body in any out-&-out way with my hands except her face. I admit I'd be squeezing her breasts discreetly with the *sides* of my arms while we'd be hugging. Pretty tame stuff. I don't know why. Mostly I figured she wouldn't allow any more. I guess I knew her too well from Hebrew school. There wasn't much thrill. Probably not for Berta either. I don't know.

Girls seemed to be able to stand for a lot more kissing and even hugging, without wanting anything more, than any boy could ever bear to be limited to. I yearned for a wild but nice girl with whom I could have real red-hot orgies again, just the two of us, the way I'd had with Merry and Sherry in our cellar. And

37

that one unforgettable time with all three of us in the big double bed where we invented the sixty-nine and higher configurations. Or at least I'd be willing to settle — with Berta too, if she'd only give me a signal that *she* was willing too — for the lovely, complicated rub-and-show games I'd had with a couple of other girls since then in our chicken-coop playhouse in the garden, and in the dust-laden wooden tower of the stonemill at Stipp's Quarry, on the way to & from swimming at the lake. And even a couple of other times with a girl whose name I'd rather not mention, and we found an abandoned frame house on the way to the park, down near Roaring Brook and hidden by the trees, where we could actually chase each other around naked. She was surely as hot as a little red engine, and let me put it in her too. It was heavenly!

The trouble was, there was really never any private place you could take a girl to, except that empty house, which hadn't a stick of furniture in it. And then somebody must've seen us going in or coming out, because the next time we went there it was all boarded up solid. And the girl was afraid somebody knew who she was now, and she wouldn't do anything with me any more. That's how it went. And now, when there was a place, like with Berta, and we were all alone in the house together all afternoon every Saturday if we wanted, things never went far enough to suit me, because I always sensed that the girl was holding back. I never liked to force anybody, because if you did, could you really call it making love? In those days I never knew anything about *making hate* with one's sexual organs, the way I've learned since. Dangerous games: *Winner take nothing*. Do you hear me?

I imagine *if I'd* squeezed a little on Berta's restraint, she'd have done a lot of sex things with me. Maybe it was because I was so young. I've learned to be a little more insistent since. But if the girl wasn't willing I was never willing either. I don't like it when it has to be a hassle. Still don't. The girls then were all much wilder before they turned twelve, and began to be afraid of having a baby, the way their crazy mothers kept warning them frantically. Even now, with birth control, plenty of crazy mothers are still making girls afraid. And not just of having a baby, but of ever making love at all. Or loving any man.

Berta and I never spoke after we'd start our session of hugging & kissing. No tender nothings like in the movies, no vows, no promises, no wild yearning speeches or elaborate compliments and plans for the future, and never ever the word *love*. We just kissed & hugged absolutely endlessly, like mere physical beings, lost in our separate fantasies and plastered together for

39

hours mouth-to-mouth like turned-on tooth-brushing machines. We lay there kissing in the advancing semi-dark and silence as though dazed. Anyone who might have seen us would have thought we were dead, like Romeo & Juliet laid out in the tomb. Meanwhile, to be sure, our tongues were touching and twining and even whirling around like slippery, slithery, crazed little octopuses, exploring each other's mouths as far as our tongues and lips would reach. We were accomplished spit-swappers too.

We always stretched out together, fully dressed & in our right minds as they say, on an old leather chaise-longue by a closed door leading down the back staircase. Then, when the big ticking clock on the table nearby warned that her parents might be coming home soon — I really hated that clock — one last kiss standing up, and I'd tell Berta goodbye and that I'd probably be seeing her again the next Saturday.

And down the backstairs I'd go; out the downstairs kitchen door and along the garden path, to exit by the back alley as I had come. By request, I never met Berta's parents, and her older sister only once for a moment, when she hadn't got away in time when I arrived. Berta didn't like me to come to the house by the front door, along the avenue. Only when I finally threatened that I wouldn't come to see her at

40

all if I had to keep sneaking in the back way and sneaking out again, did she eventually relent and agree to smuggle me rapidly in off the front porch when I arrived on Saturday afternoons and rang the bell like a gentleman.

I kind of hated Berta for that backdoor trot she required of me, on the excuse of nosy neighbors and all that. Especially when you considered that we weren't really doing *anything*, not even some of the stuff you could see in the movies, like where the man would slide both hands down and hold the girl around the ass sometimes when they were dancing. Anyhow, Berta and her sister were really the nosey neighbors themselves, because Berta told me once with fascinated horror how the two of them would sometimes watch from behind the front window curtains when the married woman next door, young and *zaftig* Mrs. Rutkin who didn't have any children after being married seven years, would sometimes have gentleman visitors — and not always the same one, either! — when her husband was out.

"So what?!" I asked indignantly. And I told Berta that what could you expect if her husband couldn't give her a baby, and that after all a person's body was theirs to do as they liked. "It don't belong to the government," I told her sardonically, "except when there's a war going on. Or *if* you commit some crime."

As far as Mrs. Rutkin went, I was wholly vindicated not too long afterward when Mr. Rutkin complained to the rabbi about his wife's adulteries, and demanded a real Consultation of the Law, with the Talmud open on the table in front of the Rabbi, and all. And when Mr. Rutkin admitted, under a certain amount of pressure, that he hadn't made love to Mrs. Rutkin for over three years — ever since her first adultery that he knew about, and had raised a holy stink about it to her — well, to everybody's surprise the rabbi said that Mrs. Rutkin was right. And he jumped up and fetched Mr. Rutkin a crack over the side of his head with the big leather volume of the Talmud, and shrieked at him: *"You are driving this unhappy woman into sin!!"*

I didn't really feel too differently about Berta. But I kept on seeing her Saturdays for well over a year anyhow, mostly because I didn't have any other girlfriend then who would actually lay down on anything with me, even if only for kissing. Or who had anywhere where we *could* lay down. Also, if I have to tell everything, I might as well admit that I was mentally working on the entire science of kissing during those long sessions with Berta on the couch together. After all, it was a science. And our passions were just cool enough so I could study what I was doing to her, and she to me, while we were doing it.

Kissing & hugging were very complicated, when you began thinking about it and observing what was actually happening. First there were all the delicate logistic maneuvers of bodily and facial approach, not to mention getting over the girl's shyness — or your own — about frankly laying down on anything, or moving one's face and body frankly forward into the hug & kiss. There was also the problem of needing a shave, which hadn't actually come up for me yet, not very seriously, but I liked to think so. And the *breathing* while you kissed — that was very difficult — and how you had to match it together & separately, so you squeezed the girl's breasts with your chest at every breath. And the pressure of the lips, and the wonderful complicated use of the tongue by both parties, which was really the best part.

And then there was that ultimate, intimate passing back & forth of each other's warm saliva, or sort of forcing the other person to swallow it by filling up their mouth with it, as the true Dissolved Pearl of mutual affection. It was like being in another world when you felt the girl swallow down your very essence that way, and both of you knew perfectly well that what you really wished you were pouring into her, and by another opening, was big powerful squirts of your manly semen. God Almighty! I couldn't understand how the kids in school could call anything so marvelous "spit-swapping." Talk about inelegant! And then all the whole rest of the fascinating oscillatory art.

I had planned to write a mock-serious treatise on it one day, all laid out like a tractate of the Talmud, with sections and subsections. But I never did. I found out that there was a cheap pamphlet — really cruddy, a square little *schlock* item for a dime on pulp paper — published by Moe Ottenheimer, the same firm in Baltimore that did all the *Irish Joke Books* and *Ford Flivver Joke Books*. This had the nerve to call itself *The New Art of Kissing*, but was written in absurd, old-fashioned, over-elegant style, and with models of love-letters for illiterate farmhands to plagiarize in the back of the booklet. That killed my desire to write my own even more elegant *The Osculatory Art*. I suppose I wanted to be first — like reaching the North Pole first — an ambition I still clung to when I later did write my first book. As to kissing, it was useless, since there was already a grave Latin tractate on the subject by one Martinus Kemp in the seventeenth century, though I didn't know that then. And two even better anonymous big books in French more recently, both entitled *Le Baiser*.

Would you believe it, that sneaky wretch of a Berta Parrott, with her fuzzy brown hair, she eventually went and told our former Hebrew school teacher, Mr. Wolf, all about our Saturday afternoon sessions on the couch together! She didn't even admit it was only kissing, and must've led him to believe, by I-don't-know-what kind of meeching half-statements and shy insinuations, that I had actually seduced her or at least "compromised" her. I don't really know what that's supposed to mean, but I did know that it all added up to fucking, and we sure as hell hadn't done that — and I wish we had. I'll bet she did too.

Mr. Wolf was still the same slender, nervous young Russian idealist — though now not quite so young — always sucking on a cigarette out in the assembly hall before the class began, who had tried to teach us kids respect for sex, shouting at us that we were *"laughing at our mothers!"* when we giggled nervously over the child that "cometh out from between its mother's feet" in the awful Curse and Prophecy of Cannibalism during the siege of Jerusalem in the 29th chapter of *Deuteronomy*. Mr. Wolf caught up with me one afternoon now, hurrying along Monroe Avenue toward the synagogue with fury in his eye, and

45

wanted to know what I had done to Berta Parrott and how I had dared to do it.

"Why, that isn't true!" I informed him indignantly. "I never did anything but kiss her. All the kids play kissing-games at parties. There's nothing wrong with that!"

"That's not what she told me!" he seethed, absolutely livid with anger and his hands trembling.

"Well, she just told a lie, then — a big fat lie. You can bring her to Temple Israel, is what you can do, and just let her say on the Bible what I did. And then she can drink out of a slipper and *swear* to it!" That was all part of the Great Curse of the Levirate — even more awful than the other one, and also in *Deuteronomy.* They must have been having discipline troubles with the Israelites about then. I guess I was confusing this with the trial of the adulteress and a few other things, but Mr. Wolf knew what I meant.

Poor Mr. Wolf, there he was, still rushing out of the room between classes in Hebrew school to gulp down hungrily his grey clouds of cigarette smoke, and always as nervous as a cat having kittens on a paper of pins. Someone told me later that Mr. Wolf was planning to marry Berta himself, and that was why he was furious with me. Maybe he did marry her, for all I know. But getting married just to cure cigarette-jag

46

nervousness — or maybe the reverse: smoking cigarettes compulsively for lack of sexual satisfaction — isn't much of a romantic approach, it seemed to me. I hate "Hygienic" sex: like in whorehouses. What guy, or what girl wants to be a substitute for a package of Camels? I continued serenely seeing Berta.

Not to be imagined, of course, that I was wasting all my time mushing around with repressed girls. Absolutely not. It had unfortunately become one of the smaller parts of my activity, dammit, since it never went far enough. It'd be me smoking cigarettes next! My physical sex-life was down now to almost nothing more than those dreamlike Saturday afternoons studying the Osculatory Art of kissing & hugging with Berta on her couch. And it was hardly enough to keep my erotic motor turning. Maybe that's why I began writing then — to get off my excess libido. I don't know. Sometimes I'd masturbate in the bathtub too, with soapsuds for lubricant, still fantasying up memories of sixtynining like hoop snakes in a circle with Merry and Sherry, who now sometimes had the faces of exotic movie stars like Myrna Loy and Anna May Wong. Masturbation — what a waste! Just like the *Boy Scout Manual* said, about "conservation." I hated it and was humiliated by it, but did it for lack of a girlfriend I truly wanted. Hygienic sex — fah!

47

Sometimes I even imagined I could taste the pungent, acrid savor of Merry's youthful cunt on my lips when I was masturbating, and I'd give my prick a couple of last wild whacks to bring myself off, licking my lips wildly with my eyes tight shut and my mouth wide open and gasping, silently imploring whatever gods there might be to send me the kind of girl I so much needed: hot and shameless and beautiful and *intelligent*.

When I could, in bed or even in the warm, empty bathtub, I'd use the weight of my hips to throw my legs far up & over my head at the last few strokes — I found it impossible to reach far enough bending downwards — and aim my penis so as to catch the semen in my mouth and swallow it down again. The taste was bitter, but creamy and nice, and like nothing else in the world. Swallowing it back down into my system would give the gism another chance to sort of come around again, if I found an *intelligent* girl meanwhile. *Intelligent* meant, in the last analysis, that she'd take her darn panties off without any fuss, and make love with me every which way there was, and not just all that turgid kissing!

I may have been wrong about Berta's intelligence, though, because she was on the Honors List with me when we graduated, and got one of the

48

highest marks in the whole class of three hundred students. There was something wrong there anyhow, because Sidonie Honiger made the Honors List too. Maybe she had somebody helping her on her tests in every class, like me in French. I know that's ungallant to say, because Sidonie knew more about what really counts than any other girl in school. But they didn't give Honors for it then. Maybe they will one day.

IN THE END, there was only one way to find an intelligent girl. There were just too many of the other kind, and lots of them were pretty too, which I always appreciated very much. So did they. Young girls are very gone on identifying with male beauty: *the boy they'd like to be if they were a boy*. But I didn't realize that then, nor that half my success with girls was due to my being very handsome and soulful-looking when I was young. Really angelic. And lots of the girls in highschool already had lovely budding breasts. Some of them were stacked like milch-cows. You could see all the girls' breasts, really, bulging or nestling under their tight bodices or loose sweaters. Naturally you had to use a certain amount of imagination, because they all wore brassieres. Their mothers, and even the school teachers, made them wear 'em *if* they had anything bigger than cupcakes. Letting your breasts bobble when you walked was considered "fast." Or even when you ran, though some of the girls secretly did that on purpose to give the boys a thrill.

No. If you really wanted an intelligent girl — and I did — there was only one way. And that was to lallygag around with all of them a certain amount till you had them sized up. I already knew some of the girls from public school, like Jeannie Miller and Audrey, the one that took that hypocritical medal competition with me. And although I'd had juvenile crushes on some of them, I knew now that they were too cold or distant or typically Christian for me. So the only thing to do was to talk to *all* the girls in school and everywhere else until you found an intelligent one.

My own best audience was always the girls of my own age that I walked home from school with. There were quite a lot of them. I had to change often because most of the girls were shocked by the things I said. I was always very direct about trying to work the conversation with them into a sexual groove. I thought of that as Psychology, but they understood it immediately as Sex. At the same time I was quite unaware that my soulful good looks and Byronic air were very attractive to romantic young girls, not to mention the glib and continuous way I reeled out my soundtrack, hypnotically I hoped. And I took their company for granted, imagining from their expressions of admiration and shock — Oh, you're *terrible!* — that everything I said to them about sex was a revelation.

Except to Sidonie Honiger, of course, but I very seldom spoke about sex to her, for fear of bursting immediately into passionate flames. She was still my friend Jimmy's best girlfriend, and according to my naive code that meant *Hands Off!* Sidonie was quite willing to run both Jimmy and me in tandem — in fact she gave me a few straight hints, mentioning that she was free every other night, and so on. But *I* wasn't willing. I also felt it as a point of pride: I wanted all of her magnificent ass, or none at all. So it had to be none. Oddly enough, it seemed to me, for a girl that sexy, Sidonie never came right out with things the way I always did. She knew you understood. And her straying hands spoke for her. It took me a long time to learn that's the way girls were brought up.

For my part, I was a specialist then in saying positively awful things to the girls I walked home with, as we ambled along after school. The more shocking the better. It was always consciously half lecture and half seduction, though only verbal, and always from a

51

high *moral and psychological* point of view. I never recognized myself for the hypocrite I was, and thought that I was bringing a message of intellectual liberation to these hidebound little virgins. Perhaps I was. If there had been anywhere to take them — like behind a fence or billboard — I would have been glad to stop talking and slip them the real article.

But unfortunately there was never anywhere to go but the movies, and I didn't have enough money to do that very often. Also, you couldn't do anything but kiss and do a little discreet feeling-up in the movies. The old Major Theater on Canal Street in New York, where the girl usherettes with the split pants in the back used to sit down backwards on the customers' laps, as I had seen it done in the half-dark — how many years before was it? — now seemed only a Never-Neverland dream.

No, everything was strictly verbal with the highschool girls, and vertical, no matter what we both might have wanted, as we went slowly treading the square gray slate sidewalks under the shade trees. Never actual erotic overtures — or almost never — but pointedly frank remarks, and elevated but radical observations about love and pregnancy and women and men and trial marriage; also about sex-freaks and rape, and wild tales of the dangers of life in the big city,

52

New York, where I swanked that I once had lived and gone to boarding school. The girls would mostly listen very seriously, or sometimes giggle and remonstrate about my frankness.

"You're *awful!*" they would gasp. This was the highest appreciation they dared to offer, and I accepted it as such. Especially since there they were next day, awful as I was, walking home from school with me again.

Everything I said, though, was couched in the most proper of Latinisms, that I had carefully searched out for in the dictionary, like "vagina" and "intercourse." Never in the downright plain English of "Cunt" and "Fuck," in which boys talked, but that I had enough sense to realize would just scare most girls away. The girls were readily willing to listen to *anything*, as long as you used high-falutin' words. My elegant phraseology, which I would sometimes invent, like "venerealize" and "orgasmiate," worse than any Negro preacher, put everything on a high scientific or philosophical basis of serious discussion which the girls either didn't need to, or didn't know how to reject. Actually, and beyond my unavowed horniness, I *was* very serious and romantic, and thought of sex as a sacrament that was now replacing religion for me, and was greater than any religion, and I did not hesitate to say so.

There was also the tone of my voice, which I tried to make deep and throbbing in such conversations, to disguise my high, clear tenor which I didn't think was manly enough. I must've got the throb just right eventually. One girl told me it made goose-pimples go up & down her back, the way I talked. Or maybe she meant the things I said. Sometimes girls just went into tinkling gales of embarrassed laughter, no matter what I said or how I said it, if the subject was in any way related to love & sex. I knew that meant they were ready to move on from words to action, but I seldom followed it up, anyhow not in our sedate walks down the streets. I thought of myself as disliking feather-headed girls like that. I wanted a serious, sober response to the highly important subjects I knew I was discussing. I had never heard of oral rape and verbal sadism. I did it all by ear.

Once I went so far as to show a nice little brunette girl named Ellen that I had a hardon walking & talking to her, and I outlined it for her through my pants with my hands. She looked as though she was going to faint, and could hardly speak. Then her

54

fingers quivered out, as we paused under the shadow of a big lilac bush. There was no one else in sight.

"Can I touch it?" she quavered. I let her touch it.

"Ooh! You're *awful!*" She kept touching it.

"Why am I awful?" I whispered. "It's absolutely natural, isn't it? Dogs & cats have it that way all the time. They can even lick themselves."

But there I had gone too far and Ellen dashed on ahead without me. I couldn't chase her with my hardon. The next day after school she said she would only walk home with me if I was *polite*. I promised to be polite, and on the walk home politely asked her if she'd like to go to the movies with me that Saturday afternoon. Berta's kisses and kissing-couch could wait. Ellen would certainly be willing to touch my prick again in the dark at the movies, I knew; and she was, and she did. We clung to each other like limpets, side by side, carefully tucked away at the end of one of the aisles, where the lady-usher could see us least and never passed, and we explored as much of each other's anatomy as we could get to reach sitting.

We couldn't have kissed without being seen, even if we had wanted to, but that wasn't what we wanted. And we felt each other up in the dark as seriously as we dared go, my hand up under Ellen's dress and inside the leg of her bloomers, and her hand inside my fly which I had frankly unbuttoned in the dark. I took my hand out of her panties a few times to lick my fingers, to make her wetter and nicer inside, and the acrid salt taste of her pussy on my fingertips was driving me crazy. I began squirming in the tight, motionless grip of her hand, and finally shot into my underwear shorts, half crawling over Ellen to kiss her mouth when I felt the semen coming out of me. We just hung on tight then till the end of the film.

Ellen and I went to the movies together a few more times and then we broke up — I don't remember why. Probably because she wouldn't agree to any of my wild schemes for us to meet alone in some available place together, such as her father's garage behind their house, where we could go much further. She was scared. And we couldn't just keep going to the movies on Saturdays because my allowance, which was now 25¢ a week, simply couldn't cover it if I wanted to buy even one or two five-or-ten-cent books during the week. Going "dutch" with a girl, and expecting her to pay her own ticket, was almost unheard-of then, except among some of the older fellows & girls who were saving up to go to college. Most of us guys considered the mere idea unmanly. The man paid. My pride wouldn't have allowed me to do anything else.

Curiously, in spite of my success in putting my stiff prick into Ellen's hand by way of exciting her interest, it was several years before I used that gambit again with any girl, when I was helping-out taking care of a bookstore in New York. The first time I didn't even do it to try to seduce the girl, who was just a customer. More like to quiet her down. She was an intensely bitchy, castratory young woman, but I felt I ought to be concerned about her problems and simply cut into her continuous hostile talk by starting kissing her, and then when I got a harden opening my fly quietly and plainly putting my prick in her hand. To my surprise she responded at once, and it did calm her nerves. Like loaning her my prick. Laying her was nevertheless kind of difficult later. No surprise for her there, and she had her customary prepared resistance ready.

Now, when I was in highschool, sexy talk was my form of the same thing: phallic display. Safer too. I've run into lots of men since, especially Italians and several Greeks who swore by it as an unfailing method of seduction. I myself never had more than 50% success with it, if I have to tell the truth. Casanova certainly considered it one of his trump cards. Also Maupassant — who, like Casanova, claimed he could produce an erection *at will!* And the two happy sex-lunatics who were Frank Harris and Aleister Crowley. Not to omit our own American erotomaniac, W. Ward Smith, as he describes in his fabulous autobiographical *Letter* to his son, of which a large hunk was eventually published as a sort of American competitor to *My Secret Life*, in 1976.

The whole idea or psychological substructure of this raw sexual approach, of sliding one's erect penis into the hand of a woman one hardly knows and has never yet gone to bed with, could almost be called a surviving remnant of Levantine phallic worship. A worship naturally addressed to women, not men, as with Cleopatra's Needle. It may also not be irrelevant that historians claim that Cleopatra celebrated her advent in Rome, as Goddess of Isis, by sucking off one hundred and ten — there's historical precision for you — stalwart Roman legionnaires.

A modern American heroine attempted to duplicate this historic feat at a sex-palace in New York called Plato's Retreat. According to Josh Alan Friedman's extraordinary *Tales of Times Square:* "They called it the 'Spermathon,' and by evening's end the score of media reps and towelled studs were euphorically certain they'd witnessed a true-blue episode of sexual history . . . Tara Alexandar, the heroine of the night, successfully balled, sucked, and jerked off eighty-two strange men and her husband for a gang-bang total of eighty-three." The Spermathon was recorded on television tape for the "Midnight Blue" program of *Screw,* a weekly sex-newspaper published in New York.

Aside from the historical aspect, one observes that men are really shamed by this type of wholesale sexual ability that essentially *all* women possess but that few care to make use of, except whores of the cheap lower-class fuck-joints of Naples. Perhaps inspired to compete with Mrs. Alexandar, the owner of Plato's Retreat, again according to Mr. Friedman, "won a $6,600 bet by managing with the assistance of four women, fifteen meticulously witnessed and certified ejaculations within twenty-four hours." Pitiful showing, isn't it? Even from the crude monetary viewpoint, there is no competition here with women. At $6,600 for fifteen ejaculations — notice it doesn't say orgasms — that's only $440 a shot. Plenty of high-class call girls make $500 a trick; and society wives net infinitely more than that, if you consider their lifetime take from a rich husband, and his estate later.

All in all, I'd say a great deal remains to be learned about phallic worship as it still survives today, and phallic display to women as a method of seduction. I don't insist on claiming that the trick — if one must

59

call it that — necessarily works; nor can anyone deny that it often does work. Under the right circumstances it worked for me.

But it seemed to me then, when I was hardly into my teens, to be just the way homosexuals acted in public toilets, waggling their own half-stiff penises around and slavering in adoration over anyone else's they might see, in mad lust over the penis; and so I let it drop. Men had often made homosexual overtures to me, since before I was even in my teens, especially in New York. And there seemed to be almost as many now, skulking about downtown in Scranton near the highschool and courthouse, and whispering offers and invitations in my ears, and in the ears of plenty of the other fellows too. Some of the fellows were also homosexual themselves, and would let down their back hair about it on almost any private occasion, to the degree that they were conscious of what they wanted. Several of them wanted me.

No matter how enterprising I may have acted with girls, I was always offended and somewhat frightened on being propositioned myself by a boy or man, as though merely having it happen to me, and having been forced to listen, made me less than male myself and unmanned me. I could also never shake off a certain uneasy disgust on each such occasion, at what seemed to me such obvious abnormality, in the same way that most people feel eerie and endangered in the presence of cripples in wheelchairs, amputees, and snakes. I did finally get over the feeling, of which I disapproved; or at least I learned to hide it, but never very well. I was never able to think of homosexuals & lesbians as anything but emotionally sick and abnormal. I know this opinion is unfashionable now, but I still do.

To get back to girls, the only girl I *never* walked home from school with was my best girlfriend Berta Parrott, even though we were in the same class together, in which she would generally also get the best marks, just as she did in Hebrew school. If she was ashamed to see me standing on her front porch ringing her doorbell Saturday afternoons, the way she said perfectly frankly, I figured she wouldn't want to be seen sauntering up the streets & avenues with me, in full view, coming home from school. And if she was jealous of the other girls I did walk with, and ostentatiously squired about in that way, Berta never dared to say so and I didn't give a damn. She never understood that I hated her in spite of all our kissing sessions because she wouldn't let me do anything but kiss. She never realized how deeply she had hurt my pride. And I never forgave her. Besides we weren't

61

really lovers; we were only marking time with each other, waiting for the real thing.

I also did not draw any religious color-line, though I found out very soon that other people did. Not all the girls I tried to interest in me at school were Jewish. Two were visibly Christian and blonde. There was one slender blonde girl named Doris Bliss that I would walk all the way home up to Hyde Park, a section of town miles away. Her father was our family optometrist, and so her family didn't ever seem very surprised when I would arrive squiring her home, to say a formal goodbye at the steps of her father's shop.

Doris always got the highest marks of any of the girls in class, when it wasn't Berta who did. In addition she used to turn in school notebooks and homework in a fantastically careful and beautiful copperplate handwriting, replete with AA-to-ZZ outline indentations, red double and triple underlining, caption-titles to each page, and all. She was desperate to please the teachers, and also to please me, though my unabashed conversation as we walked home together to Hyde Park used to bring her often to the point of shaking and quivering with tension. I would relax the pressure a little then, not much, mostly out of pity for her nervousness. But it was clear that she was courting my conversation, no matter how improper, and was tremendously eager to learn whatever I wanted to tell her about sex. Perhaps that was why she was so nervous: for fear I'd stop.

In honor of her lovely Blissful name, I explained, I presented Doris with a manuscript copy in my own hand of the fine poem "To Youth," by John V. A. Weaver, which I secretly plagiarized from one of my sister Ruth's books. I didn't actually tell Doris I had written it, but that was the impression I purposely left. If necessary, I would also have lied about it cheerfully. It of course meant awfully much more to her that way, since she believed it was written with her in mind. I had also boldly retitled the poem "Orgasm," which left little else to be said after I explained to Doris what an orgasm was and the relationship with Bliss. The notion that I was doing wrong in stealing another man's poem, and titivating it up with an overstated title he would surely have objected to, was far from my mind. To me the poem was an instrument, like a purposely throbbing voice. Weaver was someone unknown to me — just one of my myrmidons. All's fair in love & war.

It also didn't occur to me that with a poem like that, presumably written for and dedicated to her by a personable young fellow, a sensitive young girl might well consider herself affianced to him body & soul. Or in the beautiful phrase people used, hardly recognizing its beauty, of a girl who gave herself without marriage to her young man, that they were "married in the sight of God." As I say, it didn't even occur to me that in utterly seducing Doris mentally that way, without ever once touching her physically — since she meant almost nothing to me and was just one more girl I was trying to impress — that I was playing fast & loose with her emotions, and setting her up without knowing it for a broken heart.

In fact, it might have been worse. If things had been different I might certainly have written Doris an original poem of my own, which surely wouldn't have been as fine as John V. A. Weaver's but would have had her name and mine inextricably woven into it. But early that autumn one of the fellows I vaguely knew in school, named Alex Grossinger, was sporting around a copy of just such a love-poem that I had sweated out in sonnet style for Myrtle, a girl I went swimming with all the summer before, with the hidden acrostic spelled out in the first letters of each line: "I LOVE MYRTLE PARK." A damn lie, I admit, but acceptable poetic license, and neither Myrtle nor I had taken it any more seriously than that. We were really just practicing.

Nevertheless, I was so furious at finding my even purported love-poem being bandied about among the other guys, who also didn't hesitate to kid me about it, that I promised myself I would never write any more original poems for girls, and I never did. To me, a love-poem to a girl was a sort of private aphrodisiac. For her, not me. I didn't want publicity; I wanted results. Myrtle was now going around with someone else, I knew. So was I, admittedly, but I felt that showing her new swain my *ersatz* love-poem was the absolute limit. It's different when it happens to you. I suppose Myrtle was just showing off, but the fellows were certainly laughing at me. And I could have faced that out — love was a noble sentiment, I knew, having often read about it, even though *they* thought of it as foolish weakness — but how could I forgive the betrayal of letting a later boyfriend have a copy? So Doris Bliss would have to be satisfied this time with a plagiarized "Orgasm."

Doris was always extremely pale, which her blondness heightened even more, and she confided to me that the doctor was treating her for anemia. That was then considered a fatal disease — "weak blood" — even if you took iron pills, as Doris was doing. I told her brutally that she should be careful not to die a virgin. "Sweet sixteen & never been kissed — properly!" I teased.

65

"Are you sure I'm a virgin now?" Doris asked, lips trembling.

"Of *course* you are." And I went on to tell her about the ancient Roman custom of which I had read, perhaps in Gibbon's *Decline & Fall,* that if it was necessary to execute a virgin, maybe one of the Vestal Virgins for treason or something like that, the public executioner would rape her publicly before putting her to death.

"Oh, how awful!" Doris breathed. There was an unaccustomed spot of red high up on each of her cheekbones. I knew she could just see it happening: the girl thrown to the ground, naked & all.

"Not really," I told her matter-of-factly. "I don't think they were trying to make it worse for her. Maybe it made it better. Who'd want to die without knowing what things are all about?"

Years later, on a visit home, my mother told me that one of the Bliss girls had been phoning repeatedly when she learned I would be in town for a day or two. I called back. It was Doris's younger sister. She told me Doris was dead, and asked me please to come and see her because she had something she was supposed to tell me that she couldn't say over the phone. We sat in their parlor — it was a Sunday and no one else was home — and she told me how Doris had died.

66

As her pernicious anemia got worse, in spite of treatment, and Doris realized she had only a little while left, she took all her modest school savings out of the bank and wanted to send away to buy a microscope, so she could study "the secrets of nature" sitting up in bed. Her father, being an optometrist, explained that he could save her money by getting it at a discount through his supply house, and he sent away the order for Doris with her money. When the package arrived and was unwrapped, it turned out not to be a microscope but a telescope. And Dr. Bliss explained calmly that he had changed the order because it came to the same thing, after all, and the telescope would make a fine decoration for the shop window when Doris "wouldn't be using it." Meaning when she would be dead. Doris understood, and died. Like Gogol, after he burned his manuscripts. All the fight had gone out of her, her sister told me, when that telescope was unwrapped.

I listened to her sister's story silent and thunderstruck. It was just what my own father had done to me, with my scholarship money, but worse in a way. At least I hadn't died. I had nothing to say.

"There's something else," her sister added. "Doris made me promise to see you after she'd be gone, because she wanted you to know. She was in love with you the whole time. She was crazy about you. And you never knew."

"I see."

"And she wanted me to tell you," her sister fumbled, "how awful it was to be — to be dying a virgin."

"No, no!" I cried suddenly. *'Not* a virgin! She has me now, and I have her. Forever!"

We stared at each other in tableau. "We made love on a higher, mental level," I told her. I don't know how I could say things that ornate and untrue, but I did. Maybe it was true. Then I asked Doris' sister if I could kiss her — "as a sort of goodbye to Doris." Without waiting for an answer I folded her avuncularly in my arms. Naturally one doesn't ask girls for permission to kiss them, but this was special. She kissed me back more passionately than poor, anemic Doris ever could have. The idea occurred to me, since we were alone in the house, that the sister now surely didn't want to die a virgin either, and I might try to run our phantom kiss up into a whole marriage "in the sight of God" from across the grave. But it seemed too ghoulish. Too much in the style of Casanova or Henry Miller.

I left at once while I was still feeling noble. Otherwise I knew I might spoil everything by rumpling up her sister's dress. That abrupt farewell may not have been what she truly wanted — sisters sexually jealous of each other are the commonest thing in the world: brothers too — but it's what I did. Or rather didn't. Sometimes you give a person a much more magical experience and memory by leaving things more or less incomplete at the genital level. Not often though — not if the person is normal. As to the others, I've had that trouble more than once, owing to my overweening vanity. Imagining I have the Golden Penis that will cure any woman's frigidity.

No. I still say that sometimes you do a person a real favor by *not* making love with them, woman or man as the case may be. That way you don't have to force them up against their own deficiencies, or yours. I know only too well the thrill of horror and pity and dismay, when you realize after moving on for several hours toward an obvious seduction, that the woman is neurotically frigid; or she has the guts to say so in plain words in advance. What's the use refusing to believe her, and forcing the issue? Is it really for her good or for your own? Just phallic vanity — tell the truth. And often it turns out you're wrong. *The challenge of a woman's frigidity is civilized man's highest duty and despair.* And duty often calls. Especially now, when their mothers' newfound strength is turning millions of

69

these intimidated Elektras into loveless imitation-men and plain lesbians. But sometimes you have to take No for an answer. Farewell, Doris — my sister, my bride.

OUR upstairs tenant, now that the house was quite transformed into an upstairs & downstairs apartment, kept changing rapidly when the Depression came. People would move in and then not be able to afford the rent and move out again after three or four months. It got to be a real madhouse, putting classified ads in the *Scranton Times* and getting a whirlwind of telephone inquiries, since the rent we asked was purposely not too high: "HILL SECTION, 5-room apartment, all comforts . . ."

That money was essential to our family economy because it paid the muggidge every three months. People around us were losing their houses right & left as the Depression ground on — right until the war came, in fact, and then everybody had money again: blood money, I told everyone. We ate on whatever my father earned, and when he had to give up his butcher shop in Dunmore, after he cut his hand badly when the knife slipped on a beef-shank he was cutting, we just ate less. My father's admitted

70

malversation of the scholarship money for my rabbinical studies left him in a dangerously self-destructive mood. This took a long while to pass. Even after his florid pretenses at mock-suicide left off, his unconscious stabs at self-punishment were, as they usually are, far more destructive. He became accident prone, particularly with the big knives he used to cut up the beef carcasses at his butcher-shop in Dunmore, and cut himself seriously more than once. My mother understood perfectly what was happening: he never did, or said he didn't. Nevertheless, after the second serious stabbing of himself — the knife slipped on the big greasy shank bone he was stripping, he explained both times — he gave up the butcher shop.

He tried opening a little grocery store, down across the Harrison Avenue bridge, and then when the cockroaches that the former owner hadn't told us about drove my father out of there, he had a very good job for a while as manager of the supermarket that opened just beyond the foot of the bridge. It was the first supermarket anybody had ever seen, in the style of the open Italian and French markets in Europe, but with almost nobody to wait on the trade, and was a big success. Such a big success that some big company bought it out and started a whole chain of them eventually across the country, called Safeway I think;

71

and then the A. & P. stores fired all their clerks except the cashiers and the box-handlers and became supermarkets too. And of course the big company had its own general manager that they moved in, and my father was fired with a month's notice and pay.

But he hustled around and ran like crazy and got another job in the D. L. & W. railroad offices right away. My father told us at the dinner table that getting a job wasn't as hard as people said it was; no, not even then in the middle of the Depression, when there really were no jobs and people were getting fired everywhere like in the new supermarkets. The secret was, he explained to us, that "You have to work as hard trying to *find* the job as you're willing to work when you find it — the same number of hours each day — and every day!" The few times in my life I ever was willing to take a steady job in a store or office, I noticed that this system did actually work. In fact, you had to work harder and run faster getting the job, than you ever worked when you got it.

My sister Ruth was just getting out of highschool then, and she too got a job right away with a meat-wholesaler as a bookkeeper-stenographer, which was what she'd studied at Tech. My father used the system for her, this time, because it was him that got her the job with a man he knew. Matilda got her part-time job the hard way, in the Subway Shoestore downtown. But that was really a stinker, because not only did she have to smell the customers' feet all day long, she said, and she never saw the light of day, but the steam-vapor from the furnaces just next door to the stockroom gave all the girls who worked there a headache all day long.

My father's own new job in the railroad office was kind of peculiar. They didn't pay him anything. My mother was all up in arms when she heard about this, and we all figured it was just one more of my father's wonderful loser operations. But this time he was right. They told him his training and experience as a bookkeeper didn't really fit him for the job, which was rate-clerk, but that if he'd take the job for two months without pay, while he learned the work and showed he could do it, the job would be his permanently. And that was what he did. The kick-ass money from the supermarket job replaced any wages the first month, and we just tightened our belts on Friday nights with just fish and no chicken for a couple of months after that, which was when Matilda went out and got her part-time job too. After my brief experience as a breaker-boy in the mines, where the boy right next to me got killed and plenty of others had their balls hit by the slate-chunks and would have

73

swollen-up scrotums for life, my mother put her foot down and wouldn't allow me to take that job again now, as my father was hinting.

"How about Daisy?" she asked bitterly. Daisy was eleven then. "Maybe we could get her a job in the silk-mill too, up by the kindergarten?" So Daisy and I were the two drones. We continued to go to school.

My father kept us informed about the progress of his two months' apprenticeship every Saturday night when he'd be blessing the end of the Sabbath with the glass of brandy and candle and spices, and dousing the candle in the spilled glass of brandy to make it burn on the oilcloth on the kitchen table. While we would be dabbing our fingers gingerly in the low blue flames "for luck all next week," my father would explain how hard it had been, and how heroic it was of him, to just sit there at his desk that day when the paymaster came down the aisles of desks with the pay envelopes, calling out the men's names desk by desk, and silently passing by my father's desk every time.

But my father had to stick it, as he explained gravely and pointedly, especially to me, because "Life demands sacrifices of you sometimes." He was right. It also bothered him very much that he now had to work on Saturdays, even if only a half day, as he had in the supermarket. Because now he couldn't go to the

74

synagogue any more, except Friday nights, and was certainly committing a sin. But God would just have to forgive him, he said ruefully, because a Jew could break any Jewish law if it would save a life; and he had to earn money so we could eat and live. I understood. God would have to make sacrifices too.

Our upstairs tenant now, and the one that stayed longest, was Mr. Kazan, the tenor in the synagogue choir, and his family. Mr. Kazan said he was an Armenian but my mother said he was really a Russian. He was young, about thirty-five, and had a very prominent nose and very special way of shaking his head in a tiny, intense motion from side to side when he held the high notes. But he had a splendid clear voice that you could hear downstairs like a bell when the windows were open, and a fine range that astounded me.

I was trying to teach myself how to play the piano then, because I was jealous of both of my older sisters having had lessons and then just giving it up. I loved singing too, and would sit in the parlor pounding out *"La Donna è mobile"* from Verdi's *Rigoletto* on the piano, and trying to sing the words but having to fake all the high notes because I refused to sing in falsetto. The very first time Mr. Kazan heard me slaughtering this, a Sunday afternoon when he was home and practicing too, he dashed down the stairs and dragged me back upstairs with him and sat me down beside him on his piano bench while he vamped out the powerful *oom-pah-pah oom-pah-pah* opening, and then swung into the same aria the way it *should* be sung. When he got to the high one, the second time around — where he holds it intensely before smashing down for the end — I knew that my own career as a singer was over. But I stayed to admire someone who could do it.

Leo Kazan knew all the great, ringing operatic arias and songs for tenor, and was only too happy to sing them all for me, swonking it out in masterful style to his own Schubertian barrelhouse piano accompaniment, and without the presence of our synagogue cantor, Mr. Horn, to cramp his style. He appreciated my enthusiasm, because I love loving things and can never hide it. I've been cheated out of a fortune that way by wily book dealers, who know I'm the world's worst chump because I admit it when I think something is wonderful, and get carried away and forget to bargain about the price. Of course, that also gives me the right to say things are rotten, when I think so, and that makes me the world's biggest bastard too.

To my surprise, Mr. Kazan admitted frankly and even proudly that he learned how to sing the songs properly and patterned his style on phonograph records by the greatest operatic artists, of whom that was the Golden Age, with tremendous singers like Feodor Chaliapin and Conchita Supervia alive and singing at their prime. It turns out that learning from phonograph records is the rule for practically all performers nowadays, though few of them admit it as candidly as Mr. Kazan. That's why every new recording of Beethoven's *Emperor Concerto* or Dvorak's *Cello Concerto,* by some unknown freshwater kid from Podunk or Slobodka, always sounds exactly like the greatest interpretations of these pieces half a century before by Artur Schnabel or Pablo Casals.

Don't knock it. It's a lot better than having to listen to what might be the original Podunk or Slobodka interpretations, as you can easily hear yourself when they stick in their own personal cadenzas at the end, and so RUIN the new records every time! I'm not too proud of it, but will admit that I-myself-personally recently made a bonfire of the latest Dutch recording of the Beethoven *Violin Concerto,* just to get off the violence created in me by the first-movement cadenza which nearly gave me a fatal heart-attack when I first heard it, and knocked me to the floor shouting and gesticulating, it was so bloody awful!! I then asked the company in Holland for my money back but they refused to give it to me. What this merciless individualist of the fiddle — who happens to have been a marvelous performer — did with the last-movement cadenza, I guess I'll never know. They're lucky they're not being sued for manslaughter by my widow. That'd teach 'em to use the Fritz Kreisler cadenzas like everybody else.

Mr. Kazan had a recording upstairs of a very fine Welsh tenor rendering the stentorian *"Sound an Alarm!"* from Handel's *Judas Maccabeus,* and he sang it right along with the record. It was like hearing the Hosts of Heaven swinging open the gates, and all the angels come charging down with trumpets! I was more than thrilled; I was electrified. Which shows what a master like Handel can do with a simple *do-me-sol-do!* right up the scale. The same tenor sang all the rarest Welsh beauties too, especially *The Ash Grove* and *The Pure White Dove.* But nothing could move me as much as the powerful *"Di quella pira"* from Verdi's *Il Trovatore* — not the corny anvil-chorus — which Kazan would sing in English as "Trem-ble ye ty-y-rants!!" And I would break down every time at the rising trumpets of the reprise, in sudden tears of happiness and inspiration.

When the choir baritone would come to practice with Mr. Kazan, I would get them to do operatic duets when they were through with their

78

synagogue rehearsal. The arias that meant most to me were the great oath, *"Solenn' in quest' hora"* from Verdi's *La Forza del Destino* — of which the mere title thrilled me too — where the tenor voice suddenly soars up & away; and the slow, sensuous, and frankly symbolic *"Mon coeur s'ouvre a ta voix"* from Saint-Saens' *Samson & Delilah,* in which Kazan would agree to sing the part of Delilah in tenor transcription so all three of us could hear the throbbing, infinitely sexual beauty of the two voices combining in syzygy.

DOWNSTAIRS the main enlargement of our phonograph repertory was due to my older sister Ruth, who also bought almost all the books that ever came into the house until I caught up with her. When old Uncle Phillips died we inherited a bunch of operatic records which Tante Phillips had said should be left to me, because I'd always sit and listen to them when we visited her. We also received with them their big Victor Talking-Machine, which immediately replaced our little table model with the horn inside. The big one was of brown wood, with bow-legs at the bottom and louvered slats covering the deep square hole in front where the music came out. You had to wind it up with a crank, just like the old one, before each record.

I can still remember them: they were the best. In those days there wasn't much of a selection — it was the best or nothing! There was *"Caro nome,"* and *"Una voce poco fa"* from *The Barber of Seville*, sung in a powerful, thin voice like a locomotive whistle up a canary's ass by Amelita Galli-Curci. And of course Caruso singing — the wild, mad tarantella of *"La Danza"* was the one we had — and Figaro's *"Largo al factotum,"* though I don't remember who sang it. And Chaliapin in *"La Calunnia"* and *"Ecco il Mondo"* from Boito's *Mefistofele*, in surely the most virile basso voice the world ever heard. And everybody all together in the Quartet from *Rigoletto* and the tremendous Sextet from *Lucia di Lammermoor*, which were all my glory and delight.

Ruth's own records were very different. She had been exceedingly impressed by a jolly little book called *Seductio ad Absurdum* written about then by Emily Hahn, a woman who later led a desperately awful life of drug addiction and moral and literal enslavement, all of which she duly reports in her excruciating autobiography. Yet she was careful at the same time to expunge *Seductio ad Absurdum* from the list of her publications facing her title-pages, as though this were

80

some unforgivable folly of her youth. In fact, it was a series of perfectly delicious skits on the various *lines* all the young men were using then — maybe still are? — in trying to seduce the liberated college girls and others, in the short-skirted, bobbed-haired, and hipflask-toting, bootleg-whiskey-drinking, raccoon-coatbearing, rumbleseat-joyriding Revolt of Modern Youth, charlestoning to white imitation-jazz through the money-mad Twenties into the cynically disillusioned Thirties.

Miss Hahn's short turns & encores were cast in the form of brief dramatic dialogues, with action, and each one was preceded by a list of necessary props: *One Sofa, soft; One Floor Lamp, dim; One Waterfall, gurgling;* and so forth. The indoor scenes would also sometimes call for the phonograph, naming the most useful records the Compleat Lothario would need for seduction purposes. My sister Ruth methodically went out and bought each & every one of the records in this informal discography, clearly intending to get seduced or die trying. Even if she unequivocally had to set up the seduction situation herself, musical background and all, without waiting for the clumsy young men to study Miss Hahn's charming book.

I was studying it, though — oh boy, how I studied it! *'Would you care to come up to my bachelor*

81

apartment and see my (naughty) etchings?" Girl answers: *"Liquor is quicker."* — *"Do you like Kipling?"* Girl answers: *"I don't know; I've never Kippled"* — *"Let's talk about life — and how to prevent it!"* That one was very bold. And the old favorite: *"Let's have another drink! — this stuff is right off the boat."* Likewise for use in automobiles: *"Lissen, baby, if you're not here after what I'm after, you're gonna be here after I'm gone!"* Only a real cad would pull that hereafter game, known more frankly as *"Fuck or walk!"* And the same, applied to the delicately softcore orgies of mass seduction: — College Girls: *"Hello, fellows! We can't stay long — we're out after hours."* College boys: *"We're out after ours too!"*

All these ancient pirouettes and *répliques* are not in Emily Hahn's book, but they were the ones I was studying. Also clipping out of humor magazines, and writing down carefully to file for future use. But the truth is, I never used a single one of them, and especially not *"Have another drink!"* which at first I didn't consider sporting. But what did you do when the girl offered *you* a drink? Who's seducing who?

Nobody can deny, though, that I thought of music, then and all my life, as just the right background to help any seduction along. Don't you? Emily Hahn and my sister both agreed with me, and so — if small things might be compared with great — did William

82

Shakespeare, that hoary old seducer, who doesn't hesitate to have his Duke begin *Twelfth Night* with the order to his musicians: *"If music be the food of love, play on!"* The gem of Ruth's new collection of erotic background music was far & away Claude Debussy's *Prélude à l'Après-Midi d'un Faune,* which had just the right dreamy, languorous, river-like flowing farawayness for making a certain kind of lazy love to, as any fool could plainly see.

We knew nothing about the sex scandal created at the premiere of this "Afternoon of a Faun" as a ballet, hardly twenty years before, when danced by Nijinsky in a brown-splotched leotard while making suggestive hand-motions in profile supposed to represent a Pan-like erection. But we didn't need to know — the music said it all.

Ruth also had an orchestral version of Wagner's "Love Death" from *Tristan* & *Isolde,* which she bought without Miss Hahn's suggestion, just for its title. This gave an even clearer musical depiction of sexual intercourse, but of a less sinuous and vegetarian kind than Debussy's, and with a tremendous musically-achieved orgasm at the end, including — very specifically symbolized by the proper instruments — the final clutching spasms in all the sphincters. Don't

83

be shocked: Wagner is only referring to nice clean death. Death has its sphincters too.

Ruth and I shared everything in our private cultural education, but she clearly thought of man-style music as more vigorous than the mood music she was buying for her own purposes. She may even have been right. The plain facts told by all the sex-life surveys for decades now, and in all countries, say that sexual intercourse as performed by white males is done preponderantly with the man on his knees & elbows over the woman lying on her back, and *takes an average of two minutes* from intromission to ejaculation! So play that on your marriage-manual bazooka, chump!

The proper music to that is neither Debussy nor Wagner, but Schubert's *"Marche Militaire,"* or maybe "The Parade of the Wooden Soldiers." *Whip it in, whip it out & Wipe it! — Wham! bam! Thank you, mam! Call this number anytime, and ask for Sam.* Ruth may have been doing the wrong thing, without knowing it, in the records she bought specially for me at my every birthday: Von Suppe's "Poet & Peasant Overture," with his "Light Cavalry Overture" on the other side — *Wham! bam! You hear me, Sam?* — and on my most recent birthday Rossini's "William Tell Overture," of which everybody knows the part with the horses at the

84

end: Titty-rump, titty-rump, titty-rump-rump-RUMP!! Need I say more?

As Ruth shared all her collection of books with me, without a single hesitation, expurgation or taboo — except that I couldn't eat the corners off the pages any more — I naturally read *Seductio ad Absurdum* too. I was fourteen by then, and although I was far beyond, in practice, anything that Emily Hahn was willing to make explicit before dropping the fast curtain on each of her heartbreaking little comedy scenes, I certainly learned a lot from the masculine sales-talks she so mockingly exposed. Without knowing it, I probably picked up a hint of the feminine point of view too, about the clumsy way men have of luffing into Subject A, and how in the Spring a young man's fancy lightly turns to thoughts of what young women have been thinking about all winter. Not to put too fine a point to it, I think Ruth and I both thought of Miss Hahn's comedy-skits as floorplans.

I'd already decided, therefore, that the very next time I heard the strains of Debussy's "Afternoon of a Faun" winding dreamily into the kitchen, from out of our darkened parlor along about eleven p.m., I would get there before my father could — he was strong on busting in on the girls and their dates and making a scene — and I would sneak in silently to see what I could see. As I really didn't need any pointers, I suppose that what I truly wanted was to peep on my sister's amours as a sort of private visual erotica, to take the place of the physical sexual pleasure I knew I lacked. Maybe that was what my father wanted too.

But it never happened. Ruth never played "The Afternoon of a Faun" at night, not once. Instead, she'd play it lonesomely for herself Sunday afternoons about dusk, usually curled up on the parlor sofa and looking yearningly out the window at the darkening sky in the east. One Sunday I decided to mock her open sentimentality, of which I did not recognize the heavy physical undercurrent, and I marched in on her while the record was playing. She looked up and cast a little welcoming smile at me, motioning me to sit in the other armchair or at her side on the sofa, and listen to the music with her as I usually did. This time, instead, I struck an attitude in the middle of the room with one foot on the piano bench and one forefinger uplifted, and announced in my blattiest life-of-the-party voice: "We will now hear 'The Lounge-Lizard's Wiggle,' played by Claude Balls and his Hot Jazzers' Jock-Strop Band!"

Ruth looked at me, terribly hurt, her mouth suddenly thin. "You shouldn't do that," she said finally. "You love that music just as much as I do.

And when you love something, you shouldn't try to drag it down and pee on it!"

Tears began dripping out from under her suddenly winking eyelashes. I ran to her, kissed her on the cheek, hugging her tight, and telling her that I was awfully sorry! We sat together in the dusk then, shoulder to shoulder on the sofa, listening the sensuous music out. That day turned a page for me.

Don't let me pretend that I did a lot of thinking about it. I didn't. It was more like an amount of confused, chaotic feelings for an hour or two, or maybe a day, the way in dreams there are places and people and buildings and crowded or empty streets you don't quite grasp, or large bodies of water or snow or icy fields or deserts that sweep by while you're trying to traverse them in some diagonally opposite direction. And then suddenly, oceanically, there you are — but where? And yet, you've arrived. Something in me had *changed*, the most tangible effect being that I didn't want to be funny . . . humorous . . . anymore. I did not want to make people laugh, to be Hilarious Harry the Hero of Humor, who knows a joke for every occasion and can't be prevented from telling it.

How to say it? I was no longer *personally* interested in the bum jokes and in the crummy sex-slang and puns and jollities I'd been gathering for two years now, or more. And hadn't been able to find anything better to do with them than to hurt and mock the sister I loved, and who wanted only to love me too and train me to be a *man*. Oh, I wouldn't throw away my joke collections and clippings and my laboriously handwritten notebooks; no. More like I would study them, or make up jokes of my own to see what made them tick. I would be a man. But I, personally, would be a *funny* man no more.

Another thing was spying on people. Now maybe reading sexy books, or whacking off over Aholah and Aholibah in the bathroom or dreaming off over Myrna Loy naked was like watching other people fucking, in a way, and I wouldn't deny it. But you weren't really busting in on anybody. You were there, all right, but *they* weren't really there — or maybe they wouldn't care, or they were dead a thousand years — so you weren't really hurting them. But actually sneaking behind doors or into darkened dining-rooms under the table — yeah, and what about making holes in the bathroom walls to watch that pretty Spanish girl getting naked? What about *that?* Well, it wasn't manly. It was yellow. Just yellow. Afraid to do it yourself, but you're watching *them* do it. Not for me. No more. Not for P. Marion Sims of Seattle!

Manly was what I had been doing before, with all my girlfriends up to Merry and Sherry — and whither had they flown? What was the matter with me now, anyhow? Jerking off wasn't manly, was it? Would Prince Otto have snuck into the toilet to play with his prick, flipping over the pages to find *Ezekiel* chapter 23? Now I ask you! Would he have taken that hot-pants Duchess there? Never! And it wasn't manly either, when that was *all* you did with girls — in the movies, or walking home or wherever: that and kissing! — or them watching you do it, or you watching them, and everybody peeing in their pants, scared to put it in. Come *on!* No more of that for me. I wanted a girlfriend now, and to *hell* with the Widow Palm and her five snaky daughters, from Thumbkin to Pinkie! I wanted a girlfriend now. A real girlfriend, if you know what I mean. I wanted to be a man.

Upstairs, the Kazans had a very sweet and jolly young housemaid who came in twice a week to do the heavy cleaning and laundry. Her name was Anna and she was Polish, as most of the housemaids in Pennsylvania were. Rich people in New Jersey had Negroes, and called them "wenches," but they were strange. Anna was really nice, always with her hair in a braid and her top-shirt off and bare arms when she did the laundry in the tubs upstairs, with just her petticoat on and a big apron and floppy slippers. The only thing I didn't like, was when she was doing the laundry she always smelled pretty much of chlorox, the way the laundry did, and it got in my nose and eyes. But she could wash it off?!

So, as I was always in & out of the Kazan's apartment to listen to Mr. Kazan singing, and help him find the records for the phonograph in the big pile stuck in the bottom of their talking machine, I took to hanging around a bit in the kitchen there when only Anna was home doing the laundry. And, it being spring, I asked her one day if she'd like to go to the movies with me that night. I forget what they were showing at the Nickelette, but it was something good.

Anna had been laughing and kidding with me the whole time up to then, and slapping my arms with a wrung-out wet end of a sheet when I occasionally got too fresh. But when I actually asked her to go out with me, she got sort of saucer-eyed and serious. And you wouldn't *believe* what she told me! I had to really drag it out of her too. She didn't want to hurt my feelings, because she really liked me.

She told me that all the Polish girls who worked for Jewish people like we were, and the Kazans too, of course — well, they were told, *by the priest*, when they went to confess Saturday nights so they could take Holy Communion on Sunday, that in the springtime they must *never, never* go out with the boys in the families they worked for, or with the man of the house either. Because the Jewish Passover was coming now, which was always very close to Easter, and the Jews would be eating matzohs — the big, flat, tasteless square breads they ate for a week. And to make the matzohs they had to kill a Catholic girl — that's right, kill a Catholic girl — and take some of her blood, and *mix* it with the flour to make the matzoh-breads out of. It was all there in the Bible, she said. And that's where I stopped her.

"Are you crazy, Anna?" I asked her indignantly. "Who ever told you a load of horse-kacky like that? There's no such thing in the Bible at all! Why, I've been studying the Bible *for years!* Jews are especially forbidden ever to eat *anything* that has even one drop of blood in it!"

Anna just shook her head with a sheepish little smile and turned back to her laundry with her chlorox smell. Cajoling her didn't work. I walked over and looked out the window a while, and then came back to try to argue with her some more.

"Anna?" I asked, "Do you *really* believe I'd kill you?"

"Maybe not you," she mumbled. "But somebody . . . The . . . the Rabbi."

"Why you especially?"

"Because I'm a maiden!" She really blurted that out.

"A maiden?"

"You know — like the Blessed Virgin. They . . . take . . . the blood . . . from *there.*"

Well, that stopped me. I knew about the Blood Accusation already — and always in springtime, at Passover. My father had told us all about it, and the Mendel Bayliss case, and how the Pope in Rome finally had to intervene. And especially the pogroms they'd started with accusations like that, in Russia and the Ukraine, and Rumania — that had been the worst pogrom of all. But the Christians' crazy idea was always that Jews *eat* the little boy, wasn't it? Like in that old song about "Hugh of Lincoln" that made them have a pogrom in England too. Never a girl, anyhow! And all that about the blood? Wasn't that why I had to hold the door open at the Passover service: so any damfool sneaking around could look in and see that we certainly were not drinking blood. But if it was supposed to be mixed into the matzohs — well! Talk about the Huns and the Belgian babies' cut-off hands!

And what was all that about it being in the Bible? There was nothing *anywhere* in the Bible about eating any blood. Or drinking it either. Strictly forbidden! It did say in *Exodus*, where they prepare the Paschal Lamb in chapter 12, that the blood of the lamb should be put for a token on the doorjambs of the Jewish houses, so the Angel of Death would pass-over in the final plague of Egypt, the Smiting of the Firstborn Sons. The *goyim* certainly did a lot more talking about that Blood of the Lamb than the Jews ever did. And furthermore, they *drank* it every Sunday in church, or said they did, but it was really wine. So now who's drinking blood?! Did you ever hear such horseshit in your life? And that insane stuff about taking a Catholic maiden's blood "... from *there!?*"

"Anna!" I appealed to her. "You *know* I really like you, don't you? You *know* I wouldn't let them do a thing like that to you!"

She wrung out a big hank of clothes with her hands, looking at me intently, biting her lips. "I *forgive* you," she said earnestly. "I know you like me . . . but you'd *have* to do it . . . on account of your religion."

CHAPTER 9

WHEN THE SLEEPER WAKES

THE TRUTH is, girls simply weren't the biggest thing in my life just then. After my intense erotic apprenticeship with Merry and Sherry, and two or three other girls before & since, it didn't seem possible that I could fall back so completely to a latency period, where the mild partialisms of hugging & kissing and sexy talk could satisfy me, even with a certain amount of solitary masturbation in private to reduce the pressure. But there was something much more important now that kept me up to fever pitch for several very important years. With my leftover Talmudic interests now trailing away, I was deep in radical economics and Socialism, on which I spent hours reading anything I could get hold of and talking frenetically to everyone I knew.

94

Very soon I got to my older sister Ruth with it, and even my father, forcing them both to read Bellamy's Utopian romance, *Looking Backward,* which had absolutely bowled me over. It had the same effect on my innocent father, and for a while he too was going around spouting Bellamy's single-wage ideas to anyone who would listen. By the time he got into Bellamy's follow-up volume, *Equality,* with its meticulous denunciation of the inequalities of mad-dog capitalism, my father began to see what the drift really was and started back-paddling very fast. My mother also confided to me that someone he had been trying to "Bellamize" at his office at the Lackawanna Railroad had warned him he'd probably be fired if he kept sounding off with his Socialist stuff, and that closed the subject for my father forever. But not soon enough. Within a few months he was indeed fired. My fault and I admit it. Ruth never really gave a damn about economics at all, and was just trying to be loyal to the intellectual burrowings and burgeonings of her over-smart kid brother, whose unquenchable gift of the gab was already the family's despair. Especially after Daddy lost his job and had to go around with a tiny scale from door-to-door buying up old widows' wedding rings to melt down for old gold.

There were also a few mildly radical friends and associates of my own age who gave me aid & comfort. Not to put too fine a point to it, my two best friends Manny Grossman, Mel Cantor, and I, were the mainstays and almost the total membership of the kid Communist faction in our school. You said "Socialism" when you talked to grownups, so as not to scare them. But we knew that what we believed in was Communism, and the Noble Experiment in Human Equality and Marxist Principles that had come with the Bolshevik Revolution in Russia sixteen years before — the week I was born.

Naturally, it made things all the more predestined for me, that the Revolution had broken out in Russia the very week I was born, in November 1917. They called it the "October Revolution," but only because the Russian calendar hadn't yet caught up with the Gregorian as it did a year later, when Russian New Year's Day was halfway through January. This auspicious revolutionary coincidence with my birth date — as though I personally was Lenin's brother — always meant a lot more to me than the cynically abrogated Balfour Declaration, also on my birthday, ever had. Especially when the Bolsheviks discovered in the Czarist secret archives, just one month later, and published the fact, that not only the British had double-crossed Chaim Weizman and the Jewish Zionists by simultaneously and secretly making all the same lying promises to the Arabs through Lawrence of Arabia, but that they had buggered Lawrence too, and in fact *triple*-crossed everybody more than a month before, in the ultra secret Sykes-Picot treaty with the French, arranging to give Palestine neither to the Jews *nor* to the Arabs but to divide up both Palestine and Lebanon with France. And did so too, with the blessing of a mandate from the newly-formed League of Nations. "Dirty Bolsheviks, or 'Perfidious Albion'?" I asked my father once. — "Take your pick."

Manny, Mel and I had come to our new Marxist beliefs entirely separately; that was the curious part. They were both much hotter Communists than me, too, and also saw the error of their ways much faster a few years later when it got to be unfashionable. Actually Communism was palpable in the air in America, those years. The whole world was at the worst part of the Depression, right after the stock market crash of 1929 that had practically dismantled the economy in both America and Europe. Everybody was running scared. In a way it was the same as the scared anti-communism in the air *these* years. Not an intellectual but wholly emotional gut-thing.

97

I came to my Socialist convictions slowly, without suffering or starving or ever having missed practically a single meal, and certainly before I had ever worked seriously for any wage. I first realized I was a hardrock, dyed-in-the-wool, heart-&-soul Marxian Socialist through reading Edward Bellamy's *Looking Backward,* about the inevitable Sleeper who wakes a hundred years from now in an ideal world in which capitalism has been done away with. I had never read Jerome K. Jerome's hilarious parody of *Looking Backward,* written in bile, as "The MAJORITY!" and if I had it would have touched me not at all. I was beyond argument and totally convinced.

By then I had also branched out to reading a raft of Communist party pamphlets by Lenin and Marx, in particular *The Communist Manifesto,* which even its worst enemies will admit is written in white-hot prose of electrifying effect. This and the other less brilliant pamphlets of the same faith I found, of all places, in my fat friend Ivor Colfax's house, in spite of the fact that the Colfaxes were visibly well-to-do and even had a grand piano that Ivor played, instead of the usual sturdy upright like the rest of us. Ivor was a funny guy and unpleasant in many ways, but a sterling musician. I didn't really like him. I read all his pamphlets but was never able to talk to him about

98

anything but music. It was the same with the Ratajski brothers, Joe and Ray, who both played piano and violin and taught me everything they could about music. But their widowed mother had a statue of the Polish dictator Pilsudski in the parlor, and brought up her sons in total hatred of everything Russian.

Manny Grossman's father was a machine-shop steward and a prime mover in the local Communist party, so Manny could hardly avoid being involved. That's not quite true, though, because his older brother Arnold who had gone to Princeton — it was his own idea: he hated what his family stood for — was now a corporation lawyer and a complete square. As Arnold later became my first and almost only cuckold, I admit I'm prejudiced against him. But Manny and I were as thick as inkle-weavers for a while there, and always deep in heated discussions of Russian Revolutionary tactics and history. Manny was seriously planning to go to New York as soon as he got out of school, and get a job as a journalist on one of the party magazines operating out of Union Square, which he later did. As to Mel Cantor, I'm not so sure. It's possible it was me that influenced him in that direction. His family was completely non-political, like mine. Later he changed his mind and turncoated fastest of all.

But even before I took to hanging around at the Grossmans' and Colfaxes', and feeding greedily on all their gloriously inflammatory pamphlet literature, I used to meet once a week with a couple of other very sincere young Socialist kids — at my suggestion we called ourselves The Bellamists and had all read *Looking Backward* — on the glassed-in porch at Joey Wallach's house down on Linden Street. There his father who was a tailor from the Old Country used to sit cross-legged on a big padded kitchen table and hand-sew men's evening dress suits. Old Mr. Wallach did not identify at all with the rich customers he was sewing the fancy suits for, but he nevertheless took a very dim view indeed of the Revolution, and used to razz us, in a nice way but unmercifully, while we planned and proposed the coming American revolution, the end of capitalism, and the liberation of the Downtrodden Working Class.

Mr. Wallach told us flatly, not once but several times, that we didn't know what we were talking about, and that he had personally lived through *two* revolutions in Russia, in 1905 and again in 1917, after Czarist Russia was defeated in two wars in a row, first with Japan and then with Germany. He said revolutions were just made by a bunch of no-good bums who didn't want to work, and were only good

100

for getting a lot of other decent fellows killed and women raped. Worse than the wars were, he told us, because it all happened right there in the cities and not somewhere on a battlefield or in the middle of the ocean. And afterwards, there would be gangs of homeless orphaned kids, just our age, roaming around everywhere like little wolves, and starving to death and stealing everything, and finally getting themselves killed too.

"And for what, God Almighty?" he admonished us. "What for?! For *nothing*! Just for a big word that doesn't mean anything: Revolution. Hoo-hah! And then they took everybody's land away."

I really hated Mr. Wallach, who also wore a sort of circular cake-shaped skullcap all the time because he was so bald — half Russian fur cap and half Jewish *yarmulke* — and had a sort of scraggy little beard. He looked altogether like an anti-Semitic caricature of that standard bogey, the bearded, bomb-throwing Anarchist: the sort of person that gave Revolution a bad name just looking at him. Meanwhile, it was him that was the staunch anti-revolutionary, pooh-poohing all our radical ideas and projects from his perch on the table, like the hookah-smoking caterpillar in *Alice in Wonderland*. He also had a particularly irritating way of interrupting and asking us, as the acid test of any plan

101

or news-event under discussion, *"Is it good for the Jews?"* This seemed to be all that mattered to him. God's Chosen People, that was *it*. Everybody else could go to hell. And the fact was, he wasn't even religious and never went to a synagogue, and neither did Joey or anybody in the family.

One day when he pulled this favorite line of his I had enough, and told him flat out, "You know, Mr. Wallach, the Jews aren't the only people in the world. In fact, there's less Jews than anybody else."

"You said it!" he agreed. "So what d'you expect? With all these Hamans and Hitlers and pogroms, I'm surprised there's any Jews left at *all*. Just get it straight through your head, sonny: I'm a Jew and you're a Jew, and nobody is ever going to let us be anything else. So you better start looking out for the Jews, and let the working class look out for themself. How long have you been a workingman anyhow?"

He must have seen me flush in embarrassment at that thrust, and tried to let me down easy. Also his own son and the other Bellamists, all just raw kids in the same boat with me. "Listen," he added broadly, "believe me: it's all a pile of baloney. Revolution-*shmevolution!* The Russians and the Ookranians are the biggest Jew-killers of them all, and *always* have been"

102

Well I knew I had him there. "Maybe in the past, Mr. Wallach," I informed him triumphantly, "but not anymore. One of the very first laws promulgated under the Revolution in 1918 was that there's the *death* penalty for trying to foment pogroms anywhere in Soviet Russia. And there hasn't been a *single* pogrom since then, after centuries of them under the Czars. And they're getting rid of prostitution and drug addiction the same way, with the death penalty for pimps and drug peddlers. That *stops* 'em!"

"Is that so, sonny?" said Mr. Wallach, looking at me twistedly with infinite sadness in his watery eyes and in the very craning forward of his scrawny neck and fur cap. "Well, I'm sorry to have to tell you, but it ain't true. What about when the Ookranians and the Cossacks were slaughtering Jews by the ten thousands right after the war, not even a dozen years ago? Did anybody shoot all those Ookranians? Stop trying *to fool* yourself."

"How could they?" I countered indignantly. "The Cossacks were all bunched together and being protected by the British and French armies — and the American A.E.F. too, don't let's forget — all attacking Russia from Archangel and protecting Generals Deniken and Kolchak and the White Army. *That's* who the Jew-killers were!"

"Oy, vay!" Mr. Wallach corrected me, "are *you* at the wrong end of Russia! In the Ookraine it was Petlyura. And what about that Polack son-of-a-bitch, Pilsudski, helping him?"

I was mortified by my ignorance but pressed on regardless. "*Yes!* So if anybody was responsible for the Cossack pogroms it was the Allies; really the British. And that's the *truth!*"

But sly little wry-necked old Mr. Wallach had imperceptibly turned the tables on me without my seeing it. And now he had me taking his own position: that what really mattered most was the Jews and protecting them from pogroms. It annoyed me to be manipulated in that way, by means of loyalties to my people that I would certainly not deny. When the loyalty that really counts, I told them ringingly, was our loyalty to *all* the people of the world, not just the Jews. To the exploited workers and colonial populations everywhere — more than half the population of the world. Of Humanity! The enemy wasn't any special nation, I pleaded, not remembering that I had just thrown the British out of my amnesty. The real enemy, the only enemy, was the Dirty Capitalist Class, grinding the Innocent Workers into the dust!

"Hoo-hah!" Mr. Wallach chortled. He held up his needle sideways like a magnifying glass, and sighted at me sardonically through the needle's eye. "You just wait, sonny, till one those Dirty Capitalists offers you a good job making speeches for *them*. You'll snap at it like all the others."

I glared at him without answering, but I was thinking, "In a pig's ass I'll snap at it!" After that I didn't go back again to the Bellamists' meetings on Joey Wallach's porch on Fridays. It was true enough: Judaism didn't make it simple or convenient to be a revolutionary, no matter what people who knew nothing about it thought. But I was sure I could find some compromise between the two, at least for my own self. Meanwhile I was still trailing off on my proposed translation of the Babylonian *Talmud*. I didn't have too much time for it, because I was spending at least an hour every night copying out in longhand in a special Quotation Notebook all the most striking passages of wisdom and oratory from the important books I was now reading, concentrating on the hard-headed denunciatory pamphlets by Lenin and Marx that Ivor Colfax was lending me from the stack in his room. Especially *"Left" Communism, an Infantile Disorder*.

I tried a chapter of *Das Kapital* once, but recognized instantly that the sledding was too tough for me and took the rest on faith. I didn't have to be

105

convinced that capitalism was no good; I wanted to destroy it. I had by now read *The Communist Manifesto* three or four times, and found its rhetoric just as thrilling as Lincoln's Gettysburg Address or William Lloyd Garrison's salutary to *The Liberator*, which I would sometimes stalk into my mother's bedroom when there was no one else home and declaim to myself in powerful tones in front of the full-length mirror of her dressing table: *"I am in earnest — I will not equivocate — I will not excuse — I will not retreat a single inch — AND I WILL BE HEARD!"* My ideal was Lenin, who had said: "Our century's job is no longer to explain the world, but to *CHANGE* it!"

Don't listen to the shit they tell you now. Everybody was flirting with Communism then. Even the very rich. But of course, they weren't sincere. We were sincere. They were just scared. The country was still at the bottom of the Depression, and things were even worse in Germany and Europe. The millionaires were just worried about which way the cat would jump. One millionaire publisher in New York named Bennett Cerf was reprinting the *Manifesto* and other "Basic Writings" of Karl Marx; two others ventured timidly as far as reprinting Bellamy's Utopian dreams.

But don't forget: the even bigger millionaires were hedging all their bets on Hitler too — at first.

106

The English especially were positive Hitler was going to win, and were kissing his ass blue, and secretly begging him to knock off Russia for them, where the Archangel Expedition had failed a decade before. And were openly arranging to put Hitler in a position to do it, and sacrificing all the rest of mainland Europe to him for that purpose, under high-sounding lying words about "peace in our time" by Neville Chamberlain and his moth-eaten umbrella. And after him Winston Churchill, whose career never really consisted of anything else.

Yes, the millionaires took a hand too, when they realized that if everyone was unemployed everything would collapse, and that their true social position was Riding On The Workers' Backs; that their proud increment of wealth was based *wholly* on the millions of workers' work, just as Marx & Lenin had observed. Franklin D. Roosevelt was elected president then, mainly to get rid of Herbert Hoover who was blamed for it all, and Roosevelt's New Deal was doing a lot of fake optimistic hoorahing, to the effect that "We have nothing to fear but fear itself," et cetera. We all knew that the New Deal was obviously worlds away from any real Socialistic plan, but even so the millionaires hated it and they hated Roosevelt too. He was a millionaire himself, prep-school educated at

Groton, and supposed to be the great-grandson of a Yankee slave trader, Captain Amasa Delano, the one that Melville's brooding *Benito Cereno* is about. How much higher pedigree in the WASP hegemony can you get than that? But Roosevelt was a *traitor* to his class, as the millionaires saw it, just for his namby-pamby New Deal reforms.

The American public *adored* Roosevelt and his Harvahd accent over the radio: he was Big Daddy Warbucks leaning down from atop the moneybags to give us all a hand. Even the millionaires understood, really, and so did everyone else, that the New Deal was nothing like a revolution, and was simply intended as priming the pump for monopoly capitalism. Till the expected next war would start, and the big munitions and airplane orders would start pouring in from the combatants — abroad, one hoped — and solve unemployment. People pretended America was "isolationist," and wanted nothing to do with decadent Europe and its "foreign" wars. No — only to make the total profit out of them. Just as it had in 1914, when exports to Europe *quintupled* just in the first six months of World War I.

The wars were geared to come every twenty years. *Had* to, if they were to keep capitalism going and avoid Depressions. You could only waste so much money on "preparedness," and then they had to start blowing the stuff up so they could start all over again. The wars were spaced twenty years apart, we knew, because twenty years was just long enough to push up another generation of cannon-fodder, after having coldly murdered the one before. And that new batch coming up was *us*. The next war was already badly overdue, if it was to bail capitalism out, and us kids were shitting green. We realized with absolute clarity that we were slated to die soon in puddles of our own guts, to keep the world banking and imperialist system solvent and the greedy old coupon-clippers eating high on the hog. Nobody would be fooled this time by slogans. It would just be a simple process of provost-officers dragging us away, with side-arms at the ready in case we tried to go over the hill.

Withal, we were just a bunch of naive highschool students. We felt we should do our damndest to try to prevent the coming war, if only to save our own skins. Capitalism wanted to save its skin too, and the only way for it to do so was war. War would therefore come. In fact, everyone was beginning to realize that the war had started already, with Japan grabbing Manchuria, and very soon Mussolini attacking Abyssinia, and Hitler marching into the Ruhr and annexing Austria and

109

Czechoslovakia. And especially the full-dress rehearsal for war in Spain, where Hitler and Mussolini were sending whole divisions of men & machines to test them out by massacring the Spanish Loyalists to support Generalissimo Franco and his right-wing putsch.

By then most of us had woken up, of course, and had become solidly anti-fascist. *"Premature* anti-fascist" would be the label later, when it was a matter of blackballing us off jobs. We were all fiercely anti-Nazi and pro-Loyalist. But at first all we were thinking of was to save our youthful hides, and to hell with what happened to capitalism! And we spoke angrily to each other — and to our elders when they would listen — about the Merchants of Death, of whom we had heard, who were all degenerate, money-crazed billionaire Europeans like Krupp in Germany and Schneider Creusot in France, and the mysterious Sir Basil Zaharoff in England.

The idea that our very own U.S. Steel and Dupont de Nemours might be aching to become even bigger Merchants of Death was carefully kept dark, till later. As also the treacherous notion that there might even be high-level *understandings* between the airplane-and-cannon manufacturers on both sides of every war. That the Allies had *forgotten* to dismantle the Krupp

110

factories at Essen at the end of World War I, and would also *overlook* to dismantle or destroy them in World War II, though the long-range bombers would fly far beyond and annihilate Dresden. The Big Money and its Dollar-a-Year Big Boys — hoo-hah! — were thinking ahead. Far ahead. War was the only way to save its hide for capitalism. War therefore came. There wasn't anything that us kids could do to stop it. Our job was to die in it. Still is. The next war to save capitalism is still coming — fast. Only the slogans have changed, and the presumable "enemy." Big Money talks.

Some of the older fellows I knew were also knowledgeable just then about the coming Revolution. Cy Endfield, who though Jewish, was now in the local Jesuit college in Scranton with Jimmy Kennedy and a couple of other Irish Jesuit trainees, was really great on airy discussions of politics and economics. Kennedy and I would meet over at Endfield's house every Friday night, and we'd stay talking till very late in the Endfields' luxurious parlors, of which they had two because Cy's father was a rich furrier. Kennedy would never talk about anything but cunt. That was all he seemed to live for, and everything else just made him laugh. Uproariously. But his erotic successes were marvelous, in particular with my wetdream goddess,

Sidonie Honiger, to hear him tell it. And the son-of-a-bitch, I do believe he was telling the truth.

The trouble with Endfield was that his real interest wasn't in Revolution at all, and certainly not in girls, but in stage magic, mostly card tricks and legerdemain. It really nauseated me to hear him orating in his cold, supercilious way about "the cultural needs and goals" of the intellectual elite he was sure he belonged to by right, while simultaneously spending most of the evening practicing rolling a silver half-dollar expertly across the back & front of his knuckles. Or attempting to spring a whole deck of playing cards from one hand to the other, held a yard away, in what amateur magicians like him referred to as "The Waterfall." Then, his fat ass up in the air, he continued to orate while picking the cards up off the floor.

I tried for a while to keep up with Endfield's arts of prestidigitation with coins and cards, since he was so clearly implying silently that tricks like these made him superior to mere *hoi polloi* dabblers in intellect like me and Jim Kennedy. But I never succeeded. The one thing I ever really learned from Cy Endfield in that line was a beautiful paper-folding trick, far beyond the paper airplanes and darts I had played around with as a kid in grade school. This was called "The Lotus," with paper petals unfolding before your eyes in a lovely final motion of both wrists bowing outwards, and it fired my imagination. Cy said he learned this in one of "Professor" Hoffmann's old books on stage magic, though I could never find it there. I did improve the Lotus slightly, by devising extra folded pleats and petals that opened out at all sides instead of just at the top & bottom. The pleats made the central bell bulge so much at the edges that I called my revised lotus "The Persimmon."

This was the beginning for me of a passionate hobby that was to last most of the rest of my life, and that took me to some very unexpected places. And I used to sit and fold my paper folding inventions those Friday nights, while Endfield and I argued endlessly till nearly morning about his intellectual development — never mine — and the progress of the working class toward revolutionary awareness, in which it was obvious that Endfield was self-appointed to lead them. Whatever I said was always wrong, Endfield would explain in his precise, meeching, supercilious and insulting fashion. But I didn't mind. I knew that he was really ice-cold inside and I was red-hot. I wouldn't have traded places with him for all the fur hats in Astrakhan.

Those were happy Friday evenings, they were, with me the closest I ever got to becoming the combined Assistant Commissar of Peoples' Education, and Honored Artist of the Republic in paperfolding. It was clear to me that Endfield's heart wasn't really in anything but magic, and in admiring himself verbally, like a plump Buddha of clay licking its own navel. I remember once accusing him of not even being able to masturbate without staring at himself in a mirror, which made Jimmy Kennedy laugh, uproariously as usual. Endfield replied disdainfully that he never masturbated at all, which Kennedy hooted at and refused to believe, but I did.

In the end I got heartily sick of Cy Endfield, though he still wanted me as his straight-man and intellectual stropping-post. I realized that he talked splendidly about Socialism simply because he adored talking and loved to hold the center of the stage, and especially to sling around inordinately big words and orotund phrases. Without being homosexual himself, he was really a sort of overstuffed bag of socialistic wind like the fat narcissistic cupid he resembled most, Oscar Wilde.

There can't be a better example of this than the one & only book this intellectual titan ever signed. It had nothing to do with the Revolution: *Cy Endfield's Entertaining Card Magic,* a booklet published in Bidelford, Devon, probably around 1955. As it seemed

114

necessary to have this in plain English, rather than in his own special gobbledygook, Endfield was allowed only this one paragraph of Introduction, dedicated to his ghost-writer, but it's enough:

"To the Reader,

I wrote a long foreword — a very long foreword — to this three part work more or less taking advantage of appearance in print to become verbosely autobiographical, pedantically philosophical, and heavily handed authoritative on all controversial matters in the domain of card manipulation. My most esteemed chronicler, Lewis Ganson, feels that it is more in the nature of a summing up, and thus belongs properly to the third part of this, my magical tripartite. I defer to him, for has he not dignified my ramblings and dabblings into this art by giving them the substance of readability, and use these few words to thank eagerly first Lewis himself..."

That's just the sort of stuff I had to listen to, all right, and week after week. The longer form of the magic book here alluded to, naturally got bumped after being politely shoved ahead to the never-never land of Part Three, and never appeared at all. I suppose the awful syntax is the worst part, but Endfield's helpless lolloping in too large a vocabulary is also here perfectly adumbrated, not to say limned. Later, he did become a perfectly creditable movie-director, as will be seen — concentrating on violence — but what a vocabulary-slusher when it came to either talking or writing!

In fact, he was nearly as good at it as me, but I had the advantage of secretly being in the process of reading through the biggest dictionary I could find, alphabetically, for a half hour every night but Fridays, and keeping a notebook of all the marvelous but uselessly recondite words I found there, like *allotrichous* and *lissotrichous,* for curly and straight hair — but how often does that come up in conversation? Any more than half an hour of reading that small type hurt my eyes too much anyhow. No, Cy Endfield's real future was in the artificial world of magic and the theatre, just as he planned. He was already hamming it up in college productions of the usual guaranteed harmless talky-talk plays, Sheridan's *The Rivals* and George Bernard Shaw's *The Devil's Disciple,* in which the

116

American Revolution of 1776 was the most recent revolution referred to, and was played strictly for comedy background. That was his speed.

Us deeper and darker Reds — Manny and Mel and I — had decided that the spot where we could hit the Imperialist System hardest was in the matter of preparations for World War II that were visible to all the world, and that young people like us were very worried about everywhere. The main problem was that the principal of our highschool, Mr. Jones, a hardworking, red-faced Welshman from Hyde Park, had got his job in education as a reward for services to his country as a "defense" chemist during World War I. We knew what that meant, for sure, but exactly why that was supposed to have fitted him for educating adolescents was something of a mystery. At least we were pretty sure that any anti-war sentiments publicly expressed would end up getting us all thrown out of school. Manny and Mel therefore outvoted me, and agreed to exclude any anti-war material from the little four-page mimeographed parody of the school's insipid literary magazine, *Impressions,* that we were secretly preparing to issue. Under the name of *Suppressions,* to be sure. We three were the entire staff, and didn't really expect to continue beyond our first one-shot issue.

117

I was absolutely furious at the realization that Manny and Mel were willing to fight on any front except the anti-war crusade that we all agreed was the most important. And I was ready to walk out, but held back by the secret suspicion that perhaps that was what they really wanted, so they could take over *Suppressions* without me, even though it had all been my own idea. Hadn't I already lost the Bellamists' discussion club that way? Besides, I was the only one of us that was ever really submitting manuscripts to the highschool magazine and getting suppressed. The faculty adviser on *Impressions,* a plump dowdy little ultra-modern English teacher, Miss Hunt, had told me frankly that she felt I would do more harm than good to their rag with the sort of intransigent prose contributions I offered. She thought the "fairy world of fantasy" much superior, she told me. We could all learn a great deal from that.

"Why can't you do something like that wonderful piece Teddy Weiss wrote, proving that Columbus was Jewish?" she suggested, when I didn't seem to be nibbling the bait of the fairy world.

"I didn't see that. What issue was it in?"

"Oh, we didn't run it in *Impressions.* The faculty thought it was so good, Teddy is going to read it aloud to the whole school at the next auditorium. You could do something like that, surely?"

That was Theodore Herzl Weiss, all right, already studying to be a lawyer. Sure I could do something like that, I agreed, but would they print it? I'd give them some figures on how many thousands of Jews were burnt alive by the Inquisition in Spain since 1492, till Napoleon stopped the *auto-da-fés* three hundred years later — the year Abraham Lincoln was born. No, that wouldn't do at all, Miss Hunt assured me primly. It was too negative. Depressing.

"Yes," I said, "especially for Jews. What if Hitler decides to do the same thing in Germany?" She pressed her lips together in a firm line.

"We do not discuss politics in *Impressions*," she said.

Miss Hunt accepted, however, and they actually printed in *Impressions* one incredibly stupid and badly-scanned poem I had whumped up, and shamelessly entitled *"L'Après-Midi d'un Faune,"* after Debussy's music. I was not then aware of the existence of the poem of the same name by Mallarmé that had inspired Debussy. My own poem was so bad that it belonged in a cage, not in print. As I remember — and it was printed, so I could find out if I felt like torturing myself — it began bravely with eight artificially accented,

119

finger-counted iambs just in the first line: "Up*on* the *rol*-ling *plea*-sant *lawn* of *a* de-*crep*-it *manse* in *ruin*," the word *ruin* being pronounced as one syllable, "roon," to rhyme of course with *afternoon* (of a faun). I'm also wondering now about that careful tautology of "a decrepit manse in ruin," however pronounced. What other kind of decrepit manses have they got? It then went on, stanza after merciless stanza, all nearly as good, and somehow ending without any visible faun at all unless it was me, but with the poet (me) outrunning Atlanta, winning the golden apples, being feasted, toasted, boasted (inner rhyme), and all. Mallarmé should only be able to write poetry so good.

As I remember, that was all they ever printed of mine. Maybe I shouldn't complain. Everything else I submitted was "too negative," as our staff Pollyanna, Miss Hunt, observed every time. On the quiet, she was meanwhile writing exquisite little handwritten notes to Manny Grossman, warning him against associating with me. I was sure to get him in trouble, she wrote; I had an illogical mind and often contradicted myself. Curtains for me! He was proud of the letter and showed it to me. Manny's star and mine were clearly moving apart.

Well anyhow, I simply went ahead with my job on our magazine *Suppressions,* which consisted of

120

writing the entire little four-pager, except for a brief plea for free lunches for poor students and also a doctor in attendance at the school gymnasium, which was indited by Mel. Fat chance of either! I also typed all the stencils, which were in two columns and filled with unexpected difficulties. As to the free lunches and doctor, we were of course conscious of the total unlikelihood of achieving even such modest goals. But we were told that *we had to have grievances* by our out-of-town party organizer. Manny and I had been sent by his father to go and meet him across town, in a dingy little badly-lighted furnished room somewhere up in Welshtown in Hyde Park.

      The organizer was young and tough and completely without any intellectual airs. He promised to get our mimeographed stencils run off for us at the union office, and was as good as his word. He also supplied us with a matching two hundred copies of a printed magazinelet of general social protest for us to circulate with *Suppressions*. It was a professional envelope-stuffer, obviously done out of town somewhere, and we were glad to have it, though I was confused by the little typographical slogans scattered through its pages about freeing Tom Mooney and Billings and, I believe, the Scottsboro boys, none of whom I had ever heard of. But it made a fine backup to *Suppressions,* which looked so pitifully amateur when I finally first held in my hands the little stack of finished copies, smeary and stinking of stencil ink on yellow mimeograph paper. Especially the badly-drawn boy's face with a gag over his mouth that I had laboriously etched out at the top of the first stencil, while hand-lettering the masthead. It had seemed like the appropriate artwork, considering our title, but looked as though I had drawn it with my foot.

Zero hour for distributing our subversive literature was to be before classes one morning, on the steps leading up from the boys' locker-room to the classrooms. Mel and Manny were to be at other locations where they couldn't observe me, so I prepared my own ultra-secret weapon, or anti-war coup, to add to our printed matter. In one downtown drugstore book department, I bought three copies of an illustrated pacifist pamphlet called *The Horror of It,* composed entirely of ghastly photographs of the mutilated faces and bodies of victims of World War I, in which the basket-case survivors were even more horrible to look at than the sickening battlefield photos of the bloated bodies of the dead. One survivor had no face left; only part of a useless jaw and some hair.

I had cut up two of my three copies into their separate sheets, and was thrusting one frightful photographic page or another into the hands of each of the students passing me on their way up the stairs to class, along with the mimeographed *Suppressions* plus the professional agit-prop pamphlet. I also snuck into the boys' washroom just a few minutes earlier, on arriving that morning, and pasted up on each of the mirrors over the washbasins one or two of the more ghastly close-up photos from *The Horror of It.* When the inevitable Second World War would come, it would not be entirely my fault. I had done what I could to stop it — in the boys' washroom at Central High.

As it turned out, Manny and Mel were perfectly right that any anti-war propaganda could get us into serious trouble. The local newspaper carried a brief item that night concerning our handouts of inflammatory matter, and quoted the school principal, Mr. Jones, to the effect that the agitation had been the work of a mere handful of young trouble-makers in the student body, *known to the authorities.* "There is no Communism in the school itself," he announced. I was then called down to Jonesy's office the following day and told that I was thrown out. Manny and Mel were not . . .

They had, it was true, handed out their copies of *Suppressions* and the printed leaflet at their appointed posts in other parts of the school building. But no one could say — and I imagine they vigorously denied — that they had also been handing out any horror photos of war victims. That had been entirely my own idea and my own fault, and I admitted as much to Jonesy, who inquired very closely as to that point. He also proudly mentioned his war service to the country as a chemist.

"Did you make poison gas?" I asked, as bold as brass.

"No," he said slowly. "I didn't work on anything like that."

I supposed that meant he had *only* worked on explosives, but didn't want to follow it up. I had already been nervy enough. Besides, it was a delicate point. My father had told me, long before, that the real reason the British government gave Weizmann the phony Balfour Declaration in 1917 — and therefore Israel to the Jewish people, as we then imagined — was because he was a chemist and they needed his invention of oxy-acetone to make T.N.T. If Jonesy was guilty, wasn't Weizmann equally guilty too? And by extension, then, me and every other Jew? We surely were, I told myself, and that was why I wanted the shooting & killing stopped *now*.

In any case, since the other two boys weren't to be punished with me, Jonesy explained, I would only be suspended — I wasn't expelled. Big difference! And I was told to come back after two weeks, presumably to be spent in meditation of my sin in not wanting kids to be gorily murdered or else be horribly mutilated in the new patriotic chemists' patriotic chemical and mechanical World War that everybody was waiting for. Napalm, anthrax poisoning, atomic bombs, and booby-trapped castration and a few other nightmare dainties such as only *scientists* can conjure up.

I avoided Manny Grossman and Mel Cantor for the entire two weeks of my expulsion. I suspected they had ratted on me somehow, in their own interviews with Mr. Jones, but I didn't want to hear about it. It was bad enough suspecting it. Nothing was ever said by anyone, students or faculty, about any of our other expressed grievances and bravely militant goals, mimeographed or printed. *Suppressions* was a total dud. Only the anti-war horror photos had made any splash. Everybody was talking about them. Lesson Number One: One picture is worth a million words.

I didn't tell my parents anything about being thrown out. Why cause a big explosion around the family, as I knew it would? I pretended to be leaving for school every morning with the usual lunch sandwich in my bookbag, and came back at the usual time late every afternoon. Actually I spent the whole time in the park nearby, at the Everhart Museum, working peacefully on my English translation of *Baba-Metziah* in the Babylonian *Talmud*, the one & only tractate I could even stumble through, since it was the only one I had begun to study at the Yeshiva in New York. I would translate all the harder ones later.

And there I would sit with all my notebooks and my Jastrow *Dictionary of the Talmud and Targumin* spread out in front of me on one of the study tables, in a roomful of cases of stuffed birds and sections of treetrunks containing birds' nests that occupied one whole museum wing. I was pretty sure that no truant officers would ever go into an art and natural history museum looking for kids skipping school, nor did they. When one of the museum attendants got around to asking me on about the third day what I was doing there, I explained politely that I was doing research for a special issue of our highschool magazine to be devoted to "Audubon and the Birds of Eastern Appalachia." No one ever bothered me after that. How the hairsplitting legal niceties of *Baba-Metziah* about lost prayer-shawls would help prevent the impending war and its horrors I never asked myself. I'm still not sure.

The one thing that *was* sure was that something inside me had long since been programmed to become a rabbi and a "leader in Israel." So no matter how I might have to retool it — for example to psychoanalysis later, like all the other Hungarian rabbis in America — I was *still* going to be a rabbi and translate the Talmud, especially the tractate *Niddah* about menstruation, and help prevent war, and defend women from cruel and unsympathetic men. Or both.

By the time the two weeks of my exile were over, I didn't want to go back to school at all. I certainly wasn't learning anything useful there except French, and I was already getting the habit of freedom and of writing and research in a quiet library. It was great! My new plan was to stick it out at the Everhart Museum till Christmas vacation and midterm, and then hitchhike out west to become a Communist party organizer among the horses and cowboys — like Jack London, if I remembered rightly. Or maybe I could be a Wobbly organizer for the International Workers of the World, if they were still around. Or get to be a Hollywood writer, the way Endfield's friend Izzy, in California, had told him and the Benkaim boys was a lead-pipe cinch. I might regret not going to college, of course, but I was sure I'd learn a lot more out west.

When I hadn't shown up again in school by the third week, Jonesy sent my family a letter stating that I had only been suspended, and would be *expelled* if I didn't go back to classes at once. Fortunately the letter arrived on a Saturday morning, when I was home, and I was able to snag it on noticing the return address, before my mother saw it. I realized the jig was up. Jonesy would start phoning next if I didn't go back to school, and that would make my mother very ashamed and unhappy. So the next week I went back. I'd hitchhike west the next time around. Besides, the one thing I really did miss, those quiet days at the museum in among the pickled treetrunks and birds' nests, was ogling Sidonie's bobbling titties and her lithe, long legs under the desk, in French class. I went back.

CHAPTER 10

TIA

FIRST LOVE took me completely by surprise. I had wrongly imagined I was in love half a dozen times more or less since kindergarten. When it came, it was my turn to become suddenly all vulnerable. It hit me very hard and suddenly — out of the blue — on a day when I least expected it. The hook went in very deep. I knew it then and I know it now. It hasn't really ever come out yet. Teresa French was the first girl I ever loved, and we were broken apart by our parents almost at the beginning. I was just turning fifteen then, and I never got over it. It took me nearly thirty years, during which I went through I don't know how many dozens of girls and women, before I fell in love again with any other woman with the same violence and total commitment. And I was married for twenty of those years to somebody else. That's a long time to go through the motions, without love. Thirty years — a big chunk of my lifetime, and all my youth. Here is how it happened.

My friend Mel Cantor liked to talk about his girlfriends to me, maybe to everybody. I always listened with fascination, just as I did to Jimmy Kennedy telling me about Sidonie, though on principle I would never tell anybody anything about mine. Mel always had several girls going at once, which I guess was supposed to make me jealous but didn't because so did I, and I didn't like any of my own girlfriends very much. Also, the fact that Mel kept changing from one to the other made me think he wasn't very satisfied with any of his girlfriends either. He had been telling me, among other brags, about a very pretty girl he'd met early that summer and then dropped her. He didn't say why. Her name was Esther French, he told me, and she was kind of cute if you liked dark, Chinesey-looking girls. Everybody called her Teresa, or Tia for short. We went on then about other subjects. He never said any more about her.

One day that autumn, after I was back in school again sitting in the big cafeteria upstairs eating my usual homemade omelet sandwich out of a paper bag, I suddenly noticed this extremely striking-looking girl at a table some distance away. She was quite small and dark, with an exquisite heart-shaped face, accented by a widow's peak of black hair coming down a fraction of the way on her forehead, the rest being pulled tightly back. She had enormous eyes and pouting lips, and had altogether an Oriental look about her, exactly like the movie actress Myrna Loy. Or maybe Sylvia Sidney, partly. As if in a dream, I immediately stood up, walked halfway across the cafeteria to her table, paying no attention to the other girls she was sitting with, and said these banal but fateful words:

"Do you, or did you ever know a boy named Mel Cantor?" Just like the Martin Dies and McCarthy Anti-American Committee.

"Yes," said the girl, "I do." Just like the sacrament of marriage: "I do."

I stood over her table a moment longer, not knowing what else to say. I wasn't really talking at all; I was looking at her. She was wearing a rather full-bodied garnet colored woollen dress, I remember very well, with a long narrow opening at the neck going from side to side. The dress covered her bust completely, but I was thinking that I could divine the exact shape of her breasts beneath it as clearly as if the dress were made of glass, and she was opening her bosom to me like a golden book. I sat down at the table with her, silently, and stared at her so long and intensely that we were both embarrassed, and I could hear the other girls at the table beginning to chatter and giggle with each other a little. Finally I began talking to her with great animation. I have no idea what I said, or what she answered. I know I never asked her name. She had to be the beautiful, Chinesey girl Mel had told me about. There couldn't be two.

There's a famous pre-Raphaelite painting — it's probably by Millais or Holman Hunt — [editor's note: It is Henry Holiday's *Dante and Beatrice* in the Walker Art Gallery in Liverpool] that shows Dante on first seeing Beatrice by the bridge over the Arno. He stands there eagle-beaked and enveloped in himself, as befits a classic poet, while striding along toward him come a bevy of lovely young women, the one floating among them in the center in a Botticelli pose of purity and a white or blue dress being Beatrice, of course. That's not the one.

To me, Tia French was the *other* girl, the one Dante presumably had no eyes for, but I did — the artist too — molded into a shamelessly tight red dress, and obviously representing sinful passion at the very least, as opposed to whatever Beatrice represents. To tell the truth, the girl in the red dress was Sidonie Honiger. Tia's dress wasn't a bit tight that day. In fact,

132

it covered her like a tent or a maternity gown, and I saw nothing of her but her olive face, straight raven hair, and deep dark eyes. All the rest I had to divine, and did. People say it doesn't exist, but there it was: *Love at first sight.*

Every day after that, I'd be waiting for Tia after school to walk her home. Of course. At first on the ramp of the public library across the street, where the barbarian literary gang I hung out with would always go to discuss books & things for an hour or so each afternoon: me and Manny Grossman and sometimes Mel, and sharp-nosed Jane Butzner, the dentist's daughter, who was as smart as a whip, and Bob Sewall who had graduated already but didn't want to leave, inseparable from his silent pal, John "Gee Whiz" Brown, and Bidderman who wrote string quartets while everybody else talked, and that girl Alma who used to hang on my every word, and a couple of other girls too, and that pest Charlie Besnard who just hung around and didn't really belong to the gang: he was a noisy pain in the pratt and didn't even go to Central — just made snotty remarks so we'd think he was clever. Or we'd all go inside and sit there for an hour or more, each afternoon when it was cold or rainy, shoving each other around and discussing literature and politics in loud whispers, in spite of the delighted lady-librarians' shushings.

But books suddenly didn't interest me any more, and neither did any of the gang or the things they talked about. In an unspoken way I was even jealous of them talking to my Tia. And I took to waiting for her instead half a block away from school, at the first corner she'd pass going home, at Adams Avenue. This was an unlucky choice. Our rendezvous there every day was now observed by all the non-literary kids whose hangout was the overcrowded little candy store just at that corner. But Tia and I walked by them sightless, totally involved in each other and in endless talk of which I remember almost nothing, except that we never talked politics. I had no desire to radicalize Tia on the politico-economic level. It was sufficient for me that she was perfectly liberated mentally, at the age of fifteen, on the subject of sex. There too, I had not influenced her in any way. Tia and I both believed that sex was absolutely normal and right, and the main thing bothering us was that we weren't having any, because we had nowhere to go where we could be alone together.

As it turned out, we lived only a few blocks away from each other, but Tia's tall, bulky, beetling-browed older brother was always home from school by

134

the time we got there. So there was no chance of any heavy petting or more on the sofa in the family parlor, as we might have hoped for since her parents had a small radio store downtown and never got home till seven or eight. I never met Tia's totally middle-class parents until she gave a young people's party, one weekend evening about a month after we met.

This was so she could introduce me formally to her family, among all the other young fellow-me-lads invited, without saying right out I was the boy who was so madly in love with her. Which could be read right off my face without difficulty. But she must have said something in advance — or maybe her brother snitched about our daily mushing it up in the hallway on saying goodbye each afternoon. Because to my surprise her mother gave me a quick lecture in the next room, in a nice way, to the effect that Esther was after all a very intelligent girl and planned to go on to a highclass college education later, and her studying and homework were therefore terribly important, and that *no one* was to keep her out late after school. Meaning me.

This also effectively put the kibosh on any project of Tia and me going to the local movie some evening, and petting violently in the side-seats in the dark during the show, as I had with Ellen. So the only

135

moment of intimacy we ever really found was saying goodbye every afternoon in the tiny downstairs hallway of her apartment house, squeezing our bodies together hungrily as we hugged & kissed.

This wasn't anything like my former, elegantly repressed kissing sessions with Berta Parrott on Saturday afternoons, now quite forgotten. This was as close to the real thing as we could get — standing up, after all — and we socked it in hard, through our clothes, squirming together in the cold little square hall. Tia of course made no objection at all when I manhandled her soft breasts while we would be kissing goodbye, and I'd put my hand down the neck of her dress and yank up her bra to touch her bare breasts. I'd also pull up her skirt in front or in back under cover of her coat, to slide one hand into her panties and luxuriate in the silken wetness of her pussy-hair and slit. She loved it all just as much as I did, and obviously expected it, and we both knew well that we panted for more. But we had nowhere to go! Nowhere to go! Nowhere to go!

One afternoon, waiting for Tia by the candy store at Adams Avenue, I ran into bad luck. The members of the school football team were not allowed to congregate at the candy store, as they were all on strict diets. The coach, Bob Fitzke, also taught us

136

hygiene and dietetics, and was quite a hand at vitamins and all that, with long acrostics lettered on the blackboards in his classroom, all in colored chalk, giving the names of the foods that provided the dietary most and best: "Coach Bob Fitzke Says Eat Right For Health," which translated as meaning that Carrots, Beets, Fish, Spinach, Rutabaga, and so on, would make your hair curly and tail bushy — which nobody can deny. So the poor intimidated football team couldn't even get close to the temptations of the crowded little candy store, with its chocolate delights, nut-filled Hershey Bars, and sugary Juicy Fruit chewing gum.

And this day they milled around instead on the opposite corner, across from Megargee's Paper Factory, by a low stone wall on which they sat and sprawled in classic Yale varsity style. The star of their group, around whom they all gravitated adoringly, was a broken-nosed heavyset goon by the name of Carleton Aldren, the quarterback and captain of the team. He was also the main anti-Semite among the students, and specialist in insulting "jewboy sheeny kikes," as he called us. As star player, Aldren had a shooting-permit for anything he did. I should have known better, now that I was nailed to the wall as the class Communist, ever to have ventured on the football team's side of the street. But my mind was full of Tia, who was delayed in arriving that day. I didn't even notice them until it was too late.

Suddenly somebody was snarling at me. "What are *you* hanging around for, *sheeny*-boy?" Aldren was rasping. I looked up, startled, but had no intention of answering that kind of crack. No doubt they mistook my presence at the corner of Adams for some kind of intramural spying for the hated rival, Technical High, up the street: colors red and white — Booh!! — instead of yellow and blue — Rah!!

"He's just waiting for that French girl," one of his massive interference-runners explained conciliatingly. Nobody wanted trouble but Aldren. My walking Tia home every day was evidently an open secret to everyone in the school except him.

Aldren's broken nose twisted up in a gargoyle sneer. "A good name for a kike cock-sucker," he spat contemptuously, half turning back to his players.

I came off the sidewalk toward him without even realizing what I was doing, all my arms flailing. He was waiting for me, and dropped me flat on the ground like a sack of potatoes with one heavy punch to my midriff. He had hardly moved; just shot out one arm like a piston to floor me at arm's length, on my back, while his underlings grinned their admiration.

From the ground, unable to catch my breath and feeling I was about to vomit, I kicked up at Aldren by reflex and accidentally hit him right in the balls with my heel. He staggered, gave a horrible cry, and fell moaning against some of the other players, who caught him with tender arms and frightened faces, their voices begging, "Y'all right, Carley? Y'all right?"

Two of them leapt at me and began pummelling me around the head where I lay on the ground, but their attention was drawn off by the others laying Aldren down on the low stone wall at the corner, and I half-limped, half-scuttled away with my face all bloody. Everything was all over before Tia arrived, if she did arrive. I turned left at Jefferson, the first street I came to, and rushed home by a way we never used together. I didn't want Tia to see me all bloody, nor ever to tell her what happened. Nor what he had said.

My mother cleaned up my face for me when I got home, and put sticking plasters on the two worst cuts at my temple. I told her shortly I had been in a fight, which was visible, but wouldn't say anything more. I couldn't eat supper, nor sleep. My stomach was in a rock-hard knot of tension and self-hatred, at having been beaten to the ground like that with a single punch. The only feeling I had about having kicked my anti-Semite in the balls was a fierce exulting. I hoped he'd die of it, but feared he wouldn't.

The next morning early, Coach Bob Fitzke grabbed me by the arm as I came up the steps from the boys' locker-room, and pulled me into a corner of the hallway.

"You hurt my quarterback, Carleton Aldren, didn't you?" he accused me.

I knew I could never tell a grown-up Boy Scout like Fitzke what his quarterback had said. "He made a crack about my religion," I muttered.

"That's no reason. You could have done the same."

Oh sure I could've, I thought. Maybe I should've told those Polacks, "To Hell with the Pope!" Or, "Jesus Christ was just a Jew-bastard too!" And I wouldn't have had a court-plaster on my head that morning. I'd be dead. The whole team would've jumped me. They did anyhow. No sense mentioning Aldren had knocked me to the ground and was obviously a Goliath twice my size. I had swung the first punch, and according to Fitzke's rules I knew I was the assailant. I looked into the coach's eyes, very steady.

"And he said something real dirty about my girl," I added.

140

"Carle has a filthy tongue," Fitzke admitted, in his clean, high, right-thinking voice. "But he's Central's best player."

I said nothing more; just kept staring at him. If anybody actually thought I was going to beg Aldren's pardon, they could think again. What was I supposed to do, kiss his foot?

"If we lose the game, Thanksgiving, you'd better get out of town," Fitzke told me. "Start now. I'm giving you an errand to run, to Olyphant. Go out the center door. Something tells me the other team members are laying for you."

I laid low for the next couple of days till Thanksgiving, phoning Tia late every afternoon when she'd be getting home from school. I told her nothing of what had happened, and made it sound as though I'd been suspended again because of *Suppressions*. I didn't go to school at all; just went back to Everhart Museum with my notebook and the big floppy quarto of *Baba Metziah* every morning. But I couldn't focus on the translation, and would leave almost at once to go and shuffle through the tame little winding mine-shaft on display behind the museum, or sit in my special stone hideout by Nay-Aug Falls, at the tiny, twisting wooden bridge down near the bottom of the gorge. It was a dangerous spot without any railing,

141

high over the water at the foot of the falls. But Tia and I had sat there once or twice to show our bravery when we went walking together weekends. It was just at the bottom of Lovers' Lane. That was where I wanted to be.

Who cared about reading the *Talmud* in English anyhow, I asked myself? Just a lot of ridiculous *pilpul* — pullyhawlying and argufying by a bunch of bearded old hair-splitters in Sura and Pumbeditha two thousand years ago. How could that help liberate the world and prevent war? Well, *How?* I watched the striped chipmunks flirting their tails up & down the slanting young birch trees in the woods, and gave them part of the egg sandwiches my mother kept preparing for my lunches, imagining I was going to school.

Fortunately, that year Central High won the Thanksgiving football game with Tech, if that's who it was. I don't know if quarterback Carle Aldren played or not — I certainly didn't go. The important thing was that they won. I came back to school, very alert and ready to take off like greased lightning at the first alarm, but no one bothered me. Later I learned that Fitzke had told them he would fire right off the team anybody that touched a hair of my head. Including Aldren. Fitzke never spoke to me again but once more, even in hygiene class, having in the meantime

142

learned a few more details of my brief fight with the football hero.

"You didn't fight fair!" he accused me, his crewcut hair all bristling upward toward the WASP Olympus where his head was. "The boys said you *kicked* Aldren that time. And he wasn't wearing his jock." No need of any further details of where I kicked him.

"Yes, coach," I said. "I always kick when I'm on the ground. If I was a greaser I'd have cut him with a knife, too."

I never touched my proposed translation of the *Talmud* again. I found out later that a whole committee was doing it in England, surely infinitely better, but that wasn't why I stopped. I had stopped already that Thanksgiving week when I was beaten to the ground by an anti-Semite and had to go into hiding because I fought back. I was about through with professional Judaism, I felt. Religion was all a lie anyhow. The trouble with Judaism wasn't the horseshit juice squeezed into your eyes and the punches in the gut. It was that after two thousand years of praying and pogroms there was still no organized way of fighting back. I was through with the *Mistakes of Moses*. Lenin was my man now: *"The philosophers of earlier centuries have interpreted the world according to their various lights. The job of*

143

our century is to change it!" Fighting for the Revolution and for peace — and to hell with the visible paradox — was something you could really believe in. Where you could stick your manly phallic crank into the Machine, and *make it turn!* Where it meant something. My choice was made.

AS THE WEATHER got colder, Tia and I couldn't go on polishing the doorbells at her house every afternoon when we said goodbye. Scranton is pretty high up in the mountains and the winters come early. We knew we couldn't find a place really to make love, as we both wanted, but we needed at least somewhere to kiss each other without freezing her sweet little behinder off each time. Using the principle of Poe's *Purloined Letter,* that the best place to hide something is in full view, we took to unashamed necking every day after school up on the unused balcony of the Public Library reading room, in the darkest corner high among the bookstacks, where daylight filtered in rather murkily through the stained glass windows representing fine Grolier bindings.

We would make a token appearance at the discussion table downstairs, where the Gang would be

144

milling about. We'd just say "Hi," and maybe sit a
minute, and I'd argue perfunctorily with the others and
then go off to check out a book or some other
subterfuge. Tia would then leave quietly too, and wait
for me at the top of the stairs by the reference room.
And we would slip unobtrusively into the abandoned
display gallery at one side, with a tired old Breeches
Bible open in a case to the passage where Adam and
Eve in Eden took leaves of the Tree of Knowledge to
make themselves "breeches" — because they were
naked and ashamed: we wouldn't have been! — where
all the other translations say "skirts" or "aprons." One
more glass door to open & close quietly, and we were
out on the balcony, and we'd put two chairs facing
together and sit close with our knees and chests
touching and both my hands up between us cupping
Tia's breasts. And we would kiss & cling with our eyes
shut, star-struck, as though there were no tomorrow.

No one ever came through there. The cases of
musty old volumes embalmed behind glass-and-wire
doors watched us sightlessly: Prescott's *History of the
Conquest of Mexico and Peru* and Schoolcraft's *Indian
Tribes of the United States,* that I planned to say we were
there to consult if anyone should bother us. But no
one ever did. Until one afternoon, when one of the
thin little middle-aged librarians with a pencil stuck in

145

the back-bun of her hair came scurrying like a treacherous Redskin through from the top level of the stacks on some pretext or other, out for our scalps. I think she had already sighted us earlier, and was skulking up there purposely to catch us red-peckered. We hardly even broke apart. I looked up at the thin woman standing primly over us, her lips in a tight line, quivering wildly with tensions and repression:

"This balcony is only for reading purposes," she quavered at us, in what was supposed to be a properly muted librarian's voice.

"We're reading," I said without a qualm, slowly letting my off-arm slide away from between Tia and me.

"So I see." The poor thing was evidently terribly upset. An old virgin, fading on the stem of life. We stared at her. What was there to say?

"Please either read or leave," she told us. "Do you have permission to be up here from Miss Kalbich?" Fat chance. We took our schoolbooks and left, my arm around Tia protectively. At the door I looked back over her shoulder. Our Angel with the Flaming Sword and pencil in her hair was motionlessly watching us, biting her lips as though she was sorry now she had driven us away. I closed the glass door

146

quietly. It didn't matter. Aprons or breeches, we were out.

After that, Tia and I didn't bother anymore with our feint of being part of the literary gang downstairs. Instead, we took to going to the bookshop only a few blocks down on Washington Avenue, past the great mock-gothic Masonic Temple and the Elks Club and the goofy little turreted City Hall left over from the Civil War. Each day after school we would arrive happily, usually hand in hand, at Stück's secondhand bookshop near the courthouse square, where there was a pot-bellied stove and an enormous overhead globe gaslight that lit with a powerful *whoomp*, and it was warm.

It was late in January, with snow falling every few days. Tia's little fur-trimmed galoshes and wool coat and my red mackinaw windbreaker drifted snow into the bookshop each time we tramped in; the broad, worn wooden flooring giving slightly as we stamped off the snow on our boots. We had talked things over carefully. We didn't understand why we should be hounded out of the library and made to feel like criminals for wanting to love and kiss each other. We knew we weren't doing anything wrong. We would have liked to, but there was just no place to do it. Meanwhile, I was very very much in love with Tia, and

147

my heart would sometimes swell up so much I thought it surely would choke me when I'd be waiting on the library ramp and see her coming across the street from the girls' locker room downstairs at school and out the little stone door, her dark Chinesey face heart-shaped under her straight dark hair and the pointed widow's peak above her forehead.

Stück's bookshop wasn't very private, of course, but I was at home there among the dusty piles of books and obscure shelves and cluttered aisles, crowded with all the junky trash and unwanted travel books, undelivered sermons, forgotten novels, and bad poetry anthologies in worse typographical red-&-black frames with crossed corners, mostly left over from the nineteenth century. Naturally, we never paid much attention to the books. No one did. We were there because no one bothered us there. It surely lacked the tight-assed Tudor elegance and dismal stained-glass windows of the balcony at the public library, but no one would chase us out of here for kissing in the book stacks.

Old Mr. Stück had died a short while before and the store was being run now by his son Orvie, a big, powerful, totally non-intellectual guy, about thirty-five, whose main interest in life was fishing. His wife adored him, and the summer before when he had taken

148

me fishing with him a couple of times to thread the bait, his wife had come along too. She couldn't stand putting the worms on the hooks, but she was no prude, and sat in the boat with hands clasped calmly in her lap while Orvie and I would fish at one end and, standing proudly, pee over the gunwales at the other end.

In the bookstore there was also generally a cousin of my mother's named Friedman — my mother had a great assortment of cousins and uncles-by-marriage, who had all come over before her from Austria-Hungary and all named Friedman, Rothman, Phillips, or Krauss. My uncle Joel didn't really work there, but he'd hang around in the bookstore and accept the money from the infrequent customers when Orvie had to go out buying books.

The books didn't sell at all well. Most of the trade was supplying sets of cancelled postage stamps to kid collectors. There were dozens of tiny, bright exotic sample stamps under a pane of glass in the center of the counter under the big gas light: Tanganyika, Costa Rica, Tanna Touva, giraffes, penguins, secretary birds, triangles with airplanes in them, and the rest of that silly crap for kids. Very penny-ante. I had tried collecting and trading stamps with my schoolmates from Temple Israel, for a month or two when I was much younger. Especially with the Feuerstein brothers, who fought all the time, and the taller one, Merle, accidentally hit me in the mouth and blackened my front tooth for life when I tried to separate them. That'll teach me. God loveth a peacemaker — nobody else does. There was one boy who stole all my best stamps by sleight-of-hand while pretending to be examining them, and then denied it when I tried to make him give them back. That disgusted me with the whole nonsensical *schmear;* that and the sample packets you had to send away for, full of duplicates. Everybody stole from those too.

I never really could understand being interested in idiotic junk like stamps, and spending all your pocket-money and all those hours mounting little maculated bits of engraved paper in great heavy expensive scrapbooks by means of tiny glassine hinges. And tongs! It was work for lunatics. Not like collecting books! A long time later I met a man at a hobby fair who collected cast-iron tractor seats. He had over two hundred *duplicates* mounted on the wall to trade. Also bits of barbed wire nailed to pieces of board: hundreds of them, all different models, he said. So maybe stamp collecting isn't as ridiculous, comparatively, as I thought it was then.

My uncle Joel Friedman had for some reason undertaken to inform my ignorance and lick me into

150

shape, unformed bear-cub as I was. He was my only "career orientation adviser" who didn't think I ought to become a rabbi, and encouraged me instead in my collecting and pasting up of jokes cut out of magazines and arranged by subject.

"A rabbi?" he snorted. "What for? You wanna circumcise little kids? Let 'em *wear* it off the way their old man did!"

Uncle Joel was a seasoned vaudeville performer and cornball, a real oldtimer, unmarried and about forty or forty-five at most. He did a masterly low-German comedy dialect act, including whistles and beeps, which he slipped often into his ordinary conversation to keep in practice. He had snagged a great job on the radio two or three years before, as foil to one of the biggest comics, but had fought with him about refusing to marry one of the comic's older daughters as was expected of him, and had been summarily tossed off the program. Now he had to munch poison & gall in the humiliation of hearing his own act badly imitated by someone else on the program every week. Dialect comedians were replaceable, especially on radio where nobody could see you anyhow. So Joel Friedman joked all the time, mostly in dialect. A true Pagliacci.

151

As he explained to me often, the bookstore was temporary. He was waiting incessantly for some deal to mature that would put him back in radio or the Keith-Orpheum vaudeville circuit, or burlesque, or both, much bigger than before. But there were delays. Meanwhile, he sat around in Stück's bookstore, negligently accepting the nickels & dimes of the kid postage-stamp collectors, and reading odd books now & then with a toothpick sticking out the corner of his mouth. He lived with his old mother up on Taylor Hill, and my mother said he had been supporting her all the years since his father died.

When Orvie was in the store, Friedman had his own private throne in a book-lined aisle in back, a partly broken big kitchen-chair with arms, chocked up against an old safe under the little back window. The safe couldn't be locked, and was divided inside into steel compartments containing only a dusty card-index dating back from about 1910, all carefully done in ink in old Mr. Stück's spidery handwriting, on curiously cross-ruled blue cards. There were more subject-dividers in the file boxes than index-cards, which struck me as unreasonable. No one knew what it was for or why they kept it. Uncle Joel used the safe to stash his worn old army trench coat and rubbers in.

152

He was a bit put out by our forays into his inner sanctum behind the stacks in the bookshop. When Tia and I pretended to be browsing, or just sat on piles of books on the floor and listened to his German Baron act, and tales of backstage adventure, barnstorming it across the country in vaudeville, he was grandiose. But twice, when he was called to the front by the overhead doorbell, to wait on some kid wanting to buy stamps while Orvie was out, he came back and found me kissing Tia up against the safe by the little hidden window. He put on a big coughing act the first time, to give us time to break apart, and the second time he stayed pointedly at the front counter till we decided to leave. We accepted the opportunity and slid into the kitchen-chair throne together for some slightly more passionate embraces than usual. The next day, after school, when I came in alone to wait for Tia, the store was empty and he braced me immediately. I wrote down all Joel's lines in my joke-clipping notebook at the time, as though it were a Quotation Book transcript, and it's fairly exact. I believe it's also the first "oral" material I ever transcribed other than straight jokes, folksongs, and slang synonymies for my proposed *Sex Dictionary*.

"Vell, mine friendt," he started, in his best Dutch accent, "dot's some heavy smushing you kids iss doing in de back room, ain't it? Vot do you do ven you're alone, climb on the volls?"

"We're never alone, Uncle Joel," I wailed. "And now I bet you're hinting we can't even come in here out of the cold."

"Yah-sure, kids kin come here, but you godda behave. Vot do you tink dis is, ain't it?"

I didn't say anything.

"Look," he added in plain English, "are you going to get that nice little girl in trouble?"

"We're in trouble already," I said, launching into a recital of our problems with Tia's mother and our doorbell-polishing.

He brushed all that aside. "I mean in *trouble*," he said. "How soon is she going to have the baby?"

I was shocked. "What do you think we are, crazy?"

"Yes!"

"Why we don't even have anywhere to go to sit down, let alone lay down."

"Dun't hand de Baron oll dot boloney," he grimaced, lifting high a warning forefinger. "You kids always find somewhere to go to get yourself in trouble. Read history. Napoleon's old father planted him standing up — in a canoe! Holding a growler of beer in each hand, too."

"And whistling 'The Mayonnaise'," I added, going along. After all, I had my reputation to consider. After three years of clipping & pasting bum jokes from *The Literary Digest* and *Saturday Evening Post*, it was my brag that I knew at least one joke on any subject you can name, and could scoop back mere verbal gags as fast as anyone could bat them at me. At night I wrote down all the best lines to memorize them. You never knew when they'd come in handy.

"Sharlie, pleess!" he cautioned me, "De Baron makes oll de jokes on diss program. Tell the truth, kid," he added suddenly, changing tone completely, "Do you know anything about ANYthing?"

"You mean *What Every Boy Should Know*, by Dr. Sylvanus Stall?"

"To Hell vid dott! You ain't gonna get the clap from a sweet little Jewish honey like that! I mean *Vot Every Boy Better Remember*, by Dr. Joel Friedman. Kid, I got two things to say to you about women, and I've had hundreds if I say so myself. Sit down."

I sat down, and prayed the store would stay empty.

"First, you got to *satisfy* 'em. Then, you got to *protect* 'em. You know how to satisfy 'em?"

"Uhh . . ."

155

"Read history. *You got to satisfy 'em!* If you don't, they'll go to somebody else that will — so fast it'll make your head spin. It ain't hard, except in the pants. You follow? It's just like home-cooking: *First get the pan hot.* — You got it?"

"First get the pan hot."

"Then put in the meat! Y'unnerstand? Positive control — right till the last minute. Positive!" He stared at me belligerently, like an angry traffic cop.

"Positive control! Then put in the meat. What's the second thing, Uncle Joel?"

"The second thing — the *main* thing: You *got* to protect 'em! Read history. *Don't shoot till you see the whites of their eyes!* You got it? That means they're satisfied. Then — SHOOT IN THE AIR!!"

This accompanied by a violent two-arm gesture of an aviator bringing down the red German ace, Baron von Richtofen, with a machine-gun pointed at the ceiling. At this exact moment Tia walks in, letting a swirling burst of snow through the door with her as she enters, the doorbell jangling over our heads. We all stand in tableau, staring at the bell.

"Vell!" says Uncle Joel proudly, "I guess I von tree cigars dott time." He puffs a big welcome on his toothpick to Tia, who looks good enough to eat from head to toe, with snow on her hood and on the little

156

fuzzy rubber galoshes, with their soft fur trim in horse-collar shape just like a girl's pussy.

"Uncle Joel says he wants to be godfather to our first baby," I tell her defiantly.

"Yah," he growls. "Und dun't vorget, you gotta get married — first!"

Tia looked at me; then at Uncle Joel. She throws back the snowy hood, her liquid eyes earnest but smiling, her lips thrust forward quizzically. I yearn to leap on her and kiss her to death, something not yet included in Uncle Joel's numbered steps for satisfying the women in one's life. Tia reaches into her pocket and takes out a square maple-coconut candy bar which she divides between herself and me. She offers him the first piece, but Uncle Joel refuses any with a gesture at his stomach as though to imply that he has stomach trouble. I know he's really refusing because he disapproves of ladies paying for anything themselves. So do I, but Tia's pocket allowance is six times as much as mine, she has learned, so she always buys us dessert. I accept without humiliation. I love her.

"Our parents would never let us get married, Mr. Friedman," Tia says, "I'm only a Junior in high school."

"Iz dot so?" But he drops the Dutch accent fast and speaks to her with tenderness in his voice. For

157

all his big talk about having hundreds of women, I sense that Uncle Joel is just as shy and struck to the heart before a beautiful girl as I am. We start gravitating toward the back of the shop, and he comes along part way with us, evidently to play chaperone. I try to head him off unobtrusively with my body, but Uncle Joel sidesteps me with consummate stage managing and slips by ahead of us to stand beside his throne.

"Listen, little lady," he says to Tia, "the best thing you can do: read history. *Romeo and Juliet*. You know how old she is at the end of Act Three? — when they're all dead — she's fourteen."

"But they wouldn't let them get married, would they?" I put in. "That's why everybody dies."

"Ach! They're married all right," he groans. "They just do crazy things. Don't do crazy things, you kids!"

So why is he telling me about the pan and the meat, I wonder, and shooting in the air? "Uncle Joel," I announce intensely, "this isn't crazy. I love Tia. I really do. The barb is in me — it will never come out."

"You ain't de only vun!" he rasps, and goes back out into the front of the store suddenly as though someone had rung.

158

We went out too. We didn't want to stay. We walked around the courthouse in the snow, which was stopping. We found a music store opposite, where I bought Beethoven's *Moonlight Sonata*. Tia had said she wanted to learn to play it for me. That used up my allowance for the week — twenty-five cents — and wasn't even enough. Tia silently insisted on putting up twenty-five cents too. She carried the music home rolled up under her arm.

The next day of school it was still snowing. It was the day after Lincoln's birthday — February 13th, never can I forget it. The new snow, continually falling, had renewed the fairyland layer of white everywhere except on the main traffic streets where the car-tire chains were slushing up the snow. My Uncle Joel took me back to his safe-cracker's office the moment we turned up, and told me there would be no necking & petting in the back of *his* shop that day.

"Never?" I asked. "Isn't that part of loving somebody?"

"Shaddup!"

Then he relented, reached in his pocket and handed me a quarter, then reached in again and gave me another nickel too.

"Here," he said. "Take that little lady next door and buy her a chocolate ice-cream soda, *like a*

159

chentlemans! You ain't just here to polish her radio-knobs!"

We went next door and had an ice-cream soda, each of us, in the big candy-and-magazine store on the corner. We were the only customers. It was snowing. I told Tia the sodas were Uncle Joel's bounty, not mine, and that he was buying it for her through me. That he talked very tough but was really shy.

"You're exactly the same underneath," she said.

"I'm not shy with *you*."

"Yes you are."

I filed that for future reference. Complaint department, hey? Then we walked home the easiest and slowest way, up Mulberry and Vine, drawing hearts in the piled-up, sticky snow on the walls all the way, and stopping to kiss under the snow-laden branches when we thought no one could see. It was terribly cold, and we couldn't stay outside talking. On impulse I invited Tia to come along to my house — she had never been there — and meet my mother; but no one was home. I showed her all over the house. The cellar was another part of my life entirely, and had nothing to do with love. I didn't show her that. I was ashamed of my narrow little room too, when I opened the door into it. I knew Tia's room was twice as big and nicely furnished. I took her into my mother's bedroom.

160

There was a big orange silk embroidered pillow cater-cornered there at the head of the bed.

"Your hair would look beautiful against the orange," I told Tia, not trying to play the seducer but really thinking of the orange silk and her raven hair together. We sat down on the bedside. Tia pushed off her fur-trimmed galoshes, and I pressed her backwards against the orange pillow, laying her lovely black hair elaborately out in a halo around her head, hair by hair, and smiling into her eyes. She shifted her head to me, her hair making sinuous patterns against the orange silk, and her bosom swelling. I leaned forward to kiss her. Deep.

"Oh! Pardon *me*. Am I disturbing you?" said a loud, mock-polite voice behind us, in my father's most sarcastic tone.

Tia and I sat up hastily, and froze looking at him.

He examined us with his eyes, looking pointedly at Tia's galoshes on the floor. "I'd like to see you both in the parlor," he said, and turned away. He may have added something about "— when you've arranged yourselves."

I don't remember the rest very clearly, except that my father was the soul of charm when we went into the parlor. He sat in the tapestry armchair by the big radio and began by asking Tia her name and what her parents did, and all, but in such dulcet accents that I knew he was playing with us like a cat & mouse. I wanted to scream with suspicion and foreboding, and kept pressing Tia's hand in mine.

"Well," he said finally, in the same mock-polite way, "I'm always glad to meet my son's friends. And I'm very glad I had a headache and came home early today."

I went out with Tia, to walk her home down the hill in the fallen snow.

"He's awfully nice, isn't he?" she said dubiously.

"No, he isn't," I muttered. "He's sly — believe you me! You should never have told him about your store."

"But how could I refuse? How many families named French are there in Scranton? All he'd have to do is look us up in the phonebook."

Which is exactly what he did. Immediately. Before Tia and I were even off the front porch, probably, and stamping down Harrison in the snow to her house, my father had her mother on the phone at their store downtown. And he told her — I only found this out afterward — "*I have just found my son and your daughter in a very compromising position, and I would like*

162

to see you, at once!" He then grabbed the next streetcar back downtown. His headache was cured.

Actually, my father had done much more than that: more than anyone could have imagined, but I didn't know that yet. It was clear that he had immediately gone to see her mother right at their store, before night fell, as Tia told me in hushed tones in the hall at school next morning between two classes. She added that she had been sworn blue in the face never even to talk to me again. An oath made only to be broken, of course.

"But what could he say to your mother?" I boggled. "We weren't doing anything but kissing."

"Well, they think we did."

"All because you had your galoshes off?"

"He must have made it out that he found us practically in the nude."

It seemed so ridiculous. There had been plenty of times, especially in the darkened downstairs hall at Tia's house, when I would be seeing her home after school, when I would certainly get my hands inside her coat to cup her breasts, or even up under her dress and inside her panties. But this time, lying together on my parents' bed, we had been doing nothing at all except soul-kissing, tongue & throat deep, and both my hands had been occupied in her long black hair fanned out on

163

my mother's orange silk pillow. And this was the time that was being used insanely as the pretext for ripping us apart!

After school that day, lurking elaborately with me at the foot of the dark staircase to the upstairs reference room in the Public Library, where students seldom went, Tia soberly told me all the rest. She really would not be able to see me anymore, she said, nor even walk home with me after school every day as before.

"Let's elope," I said, in the sort of violent tone usually reserved for "Let's commit murder!"

"We're not old enough," Tia objected.

Always that phrase — that we were too young. What everybody was always telling us. But we felt all the same things as grownups, didn't we? If you cut us we bled, didn't we? We were old enough for *that!* I listened to Tia explaining the rest, with my face and mouth stretched grotesquely in a scowl, and my eyes violently staring, like a Japanese devil-mask. My inner world was toppling. Not only would they take her out of high school, Tia said, and stick her in a private girls' school somewhere in New Jersey if she was ever seen with me again, but her father had been held back with difficulty by her distraught mother from getting out his hunting shotgun and rushing over to our house to kill

164

me. No question of making me marry her. He was merely going to shoot me dead. All fathers are like that, it appears. Tia was too beautiful for her father not to be jealous. Mine too.

"Jesus Peezes," I said wonderingly, "we might as well have made love all over the walls and ceiling, like Uncle Joel said, if I'm going to get shot just for kissing you."

"That's *just* what we should've," Tia agreed, with a conviction in her voice that surprised me. I would file that for next time. I was sure there would be a next time too. You could always sneak around somehow and fool grown-ups. They were always busy doing something else, and would never listen to you talk anyway about what mattered to you most. So how could they know anything about what you felt? The way grown-ups always liked it, they did the talking and you listened. Or else they looked absently in some other direction, and picked a piece of fluff off your clothes while you were trying to tell them the most important things you felt. Because all you had the right to say or want would only be what they had told you, anyhow. Because they knew. And you were too young. Whatever it was and however old you were, you would always be too young. When you were eighty years old with a long white beard, you'd still be too young. Because they'd be a hundred then, and their beard would be longer.

Part of my life came to an end that day. I'm not over-dramatizing. It was like being in a horrible motor-car accident. You're spinning along on the highway, expecting nothing, watching the scenery go by, being happy, exhilarated, content. And suddenly — no one knows how or why — a wheel flies off!! Maybe the bolts weren't screwed tight enough. Maybe too tight. And there's a great sudden thrumming and banging and knocking of everybody around, with doors ripping open and bodies flying and glass crashing, maybe a barrelroll and an explosion too. And after that you're a cripple for life. All twisted up, in a wheel-chair, pieces of you gone. If you're even alive at all — maybe better if you're not. And all it is, is exactly one minute after the moment when you were so happy and content inside, spinning along the highway, watching the scenery go by. That's how it was for me, and maybe in a way for Tia too, that cold February day.

Tia's mother had apparently calmed her father down with the positive promise, to which Tia had been required to swear, that she would never under any circumstances see or speak to me again. That's what she told me. I wondered vaguely what she had been required to swear on. Her family was the kind of mid-

166

dle-class oafs who didn't have a single book in the house except maybe the telephone book. Just glossy magazines and the Sunday newspapers. Except for my older sister Ruth, my own family was exactly the same, for all my father's cultural pretentions. But at least we did have a family Bible — mine. Tia's older brother Harry had also chimed in, glowering and swearing for his part to punch my nose flat and leave me for dead the next time he saw me. Fortunately he didn't go to the same highschool we did. Tia told me all this in some worriment, but none of it ever did happen. Except that it was almost impossible to meet her openly, or walk her home after that.

They even had housewife spies hanging out the windows watching us. All Mrs. French's bridge-club members who lived along the streets we had to take on the way to or from school, were briefed to watch out their windows in the early morning and late afternoon, and to alert the Frenches by phone if Tia and I were ever observed walking together. It was going to be like the Boxer Rebellion: we were going to need some kind of phony exercises or Underground Railroad to be together, with all sorts of tricks and feints. In fact, I was afraid we'd be back in Muhlenberg kindergarten again, with Tia and me walking to school down parallel streets a block apart, waiting to blow each other

167

hopeful kisses at the street intersections across our snowy mittens. But her father spoiled even that possibility by insisting now on driving Tia to school every morning in his new low-slung Essex roadster. That only lasted a couple of weeks.

By that point I wasn't even angry at Tia's family about their wild threats and demanded oaths, and their trying to wrench us apart with sneaky tricks just like Romeo & Juliet. I could even see they were sincerely trying to do the right thing. The fault was all my father's who had gone tattling on us, the way even the snottiest little kids in grade school wouldn't have done. And God only knew what my treacherous father had reported to Mrs. French that afternoon. Not the truth, surely. Of course there was plenty he could have told her if he wanted to, like that I was a red-assed Communist of deepest dye. But then, that was true. And he'd certainly said or implied that we were actually fucking when he walked in on us. Which unfortunately wasn't true.

As I say, I could never have imagined — no one could have — what he really told her. It was so ridiculously far beyond believability that Tia's petrified family believed it at once. Hitler's "Enormous Lie" principle, that he was using so successfully then to persecute the Jews with, and that my father had

168

spontaneously reinvented by himself to persecute Tia and me. That's what comes of having too beautiful a girlfriend in your teens. And a jealous father. But it took me a while to find out the enormity of my father's lie.

CHAPTER 11

STIPP'S QUARRY

EVERYTHING possible was done after that by Tia's family to keep us apart. Even the network of nosey neighbors along the route to & from school, who were to alert Mrs. French if they saw Tia and me ever daring to walk home together, stayed in operation all through that spring, the whole school term. This was not a fantasy of ours: one of the neighbors who was asked to spy on us was a dressmaking customer of my mother's. My mother said she'd asked her in hushed tones whether she knew "what we had done."

"So what did they do?" my mother demanded belligerently. "He kissed her, that's all. It's in all the movies, isn't it? Six feet high! Some kids their age play Spin-the-Bottle and Postoffice, and they give each other Special Delivery kisses in a dark closet ten minutes long. You heard about that? Maybe you even did it, when you were their age?" My mother had never done it in Rumania, that was sure. I'd had to explain to her all about kissing games, or maybe it was my sisters that explained it.

"Well," the customer told her, "I don't think Sylvia French would get all that upset about a kiss. She said *your husband* told her that he found the two of them together in your bedroom — like. he. Found. them!"

My outraged mother had, of course, heard that part of it sixteen times already from my father, and also knew that he had found us laying together on the bed hugging each other, with Tia on *bottom* and me *on top*. Also that Tia's shoes were off. No further close-up photographic details of our intimacy were available, but they weren't necessary. Our position and her shoes presumably proved everything. There it is: a married man with four children, and he couldn't tell the difference between kissing and fucking. Or maybe he didn't want to. I wanted to say that, but corked it in instead.

"I'm surprised they didn't take her to a doctor to have her examined," my mother told me. "Lots of mothers & fathers would do that."

171

"Would you do that, Ma?" No answer. What if it had been Daisy or Matilda kissing a fellow, I wondered — before Matilda's baby, anyhow. Other people were always getting caught, much more bare-assed too, than Tia and me. And admitting everything, anyhow. What about Ruth and Matilda's girlfriends up in Green Ridge? Where they told my mother right out — I heard them say it — that the older sister Lillian, the fat one, was known as "The Cowgirl, because she milked all the boys." And us, just a kiss!

My mother went on silently with her needlework. Accusingly. I felt myself all in a sweat. I was desperate for a friend.

"Ma," I blurted out, "I swear to *God!* It's not *true!* I just spread out her hair on the orange pillow like a fan, because it looked so beautiful. Like an angel. Then I kissed her." Silence from my mother. "Sure I kissed her! Maybe ten times. But that's all! Then we heard him saying that phony 'Pardon *me,*' in back of us. I could've walked in on you the same way a million times, couldn't I? But I never did."

"We're married, honey," my mother said. I just sniffed. Big difference!

"Does God really look down from Heaven and count wedding-rings?" I asked. It was like pushing an enormous boulder uphill trying to make her

172

understand. "Honest, Ma," I insisted helplessly. "Honest! We were *just kissing!*"

"Why were her shoes off? So you could reach the top of her head better?"

"She had on galoshes! She's a well brought-up girl! She didn't want to wipe her slushy galoshes all over your nice bedspread!"

Now my mother sniffed. "Some well brought-up girls take off their galoshes at the door. But they leave their shoes on anyway."

"Gee, Ma," I said — one last try. "Are you the same lady that was telling me last week that Rumanian joke about how you hug a fat girl? *You hug as far as you can, and then you make a chalk-mark and slide around and hug the rest.* And now you're counting galoshes under the bed, just like him."

"I'm not counting galoshes; I'm counting months. I'm just wondering if I ought to be doing this crocheting. Maybe I'd better start knitting some baby clothes, if I'm going to be a grandmother by Chanukah."

She bit off her thread and stared at me reproachfully, her lips tightly pouted and the ball of thread still upraised. I was ready to cry. I knew my own father had betrayed me, and here was my mother looking at me like I was some kind of crook and

173

making common cause with him against me, Tia and me, both. The fight went out of me.

"Look, Ma, I can't argue with you any more. We didn't do anything! I wish we did. I *love* Tia — I love her very much. I only wish her father and her brother Harry would come and force me to marry her with a shotgun."

"They may come yet," she said dourly, "if you're not telling me the truth."

I was crying. "Mama," I wept, clasping my hands together as though in prayer, and shaking them desperately up & down, "this isn't what Daddy is pretending. I'm *in love* with that girl! I *love* her! Weren't you ever in love?"

"When I got married," my mother said solemnly, "I loved your father so much my heart swelled right up out of my body."

"Well then you know."

But there was no help for it. Tia and I were split apart, and the crack never healed right. Too much suspicion and sneaking around and having to lie about it. In the end it spoiled everything. The only thing left for us was that we'd have enormous, long phone calls together when no one was home. If anyone came in at Tia's end of the wire she would immediately start calling me "Mildred," and we'd hang up at once.

174

Mildred was her closest friend, at whose house on Irving Avenue nearby both girls did their homework together sometimes. And we would meet for brief minutes in the dark beside Mildred's house, before or after or instead of the homework, and hug & kiss like the desperate creatures we were, hanging on each other's lips.

The only time I could actually *see* Tia's face anymore was on the way home from school, when we'd carefully pace each other a block apart on parallel streets with measured steps, and wave our hands hopefully to each other at the street intersections. It was like kindergarten all over again, exactly. Except that there was no way now of alternating this with playing peepee games together! At the end of each school day I'd race across Vine Street and dash up the stairs of the public library to the reference room, where I'd watch out the window for Tia to emerge from the girls' side of the locker rooms at school. Sometimes she'd stand there a while with a lallygag of fellows & girls, and I'd be eaten alive with jealousy and fury watching her speak to other boys, or even — worst of betrayals — laugh with them! Then I'd wait patiently till Tia started toward home, and I would race up along the opposite side of Vine Street to our rendezvous at the corner of a big, green, lawn-enclosed property at

175

the corner of Webster, where we could climb secretly up the back of Taylor Hill together.

Tia's mother apparently had no spies in that rich a neighborhood, and we could sit on the cold stone steps inside the toppling gateway of an abandoned mansion up at the hill top, with a high hedge around it that hid us while we talked and kissed. But Tia's time was counted, and her rotten older brother might notice and squeal on us if she took even so much as half an hour too long getting home. So our kisses were hasty and too few — sparse sprinklings of sacramental wine to feed the absolute torrents of love I felt.

By the time spring arrived, the tension of seeing each other at school without talking or touching became too much to stand. In the cafeteria at noon we would station ourselves at tables not very far apart, and I would drill into Tia with my eyes hard enough to make her pregnant, and with twins, as I'd tell her. Finally that was unendurable to both of us — it appears I have a wandering left eye that turns out when I focus too long or too hard on things, and people think I'm hypnotizing them or planning murder. We simply began sitting together again at lunch, and to hell with her parents' threats!

We would sit intensely close, side by side, our legs touching under the table the whole way down from hip to calf and foot, sharing our sandwiches and always the one sweet, square maple-coconut bar Tia would buy at the cafeteria counter for our dessert — really mine — out of her lavish pocket money. And we would divide it diagonally in half and trade bites out of our mouths with our fingertips, representing deep deep French kisses secretly exchanged in public. That was our communion, and I lived only for those sacred moments squeezed up against Tia's side in the cafeteria — like Tristan & Isolde lying chastely by each other's side — under the wooden cafeteria tabletop that was our bed of love. Mercifully, none of the other students were in the spy ring. No one told.

On the phone with Tia. Enormous, unending conversations, spinning themselves out like the coils of a python and hours long or so it seemed, and filled with yearning and an unspoken anger. We would phone when no one was around to hear us in the late afternoons after arriving home separately and disconsolate from school, nervously watching the clock and spying out our appointed moments. My mother always took two afternoons out of the house each week, one to go shopping downtown for cheap kosher meat and sewing accessories, of which she used up

177

untellable miles of sewing thread and cloth, and crocheting cord, and knitting wool always in dark, practical shades for our utility sweaters.

The other afternoon off, each week, was when she went to her ladies' bridge club, seven out of every eight weeks. That was two tables of bridge, or eight ladies. The eighth week she was home that day, and I'd set up the two folding card-tables for her in the parlor with her hand-embroidered party-cloths tied to the legs over each corner, and shallow bowls of chocolate-covered mints and sucking candies and caramels laid out on the dining-room table for the ladies' refreshment with tea and cookies that my mother would have baked, to be sure. My mother got this candy free from my sisters: half of each boxful when any boys gave my sisters a box of candy. She explained that was her rakeoff on the dresses she was always making for them. That way she spent nothing on her bridge-club except two dollars each time, that went for the winner's table-favor and the booby-prize for the loser. This she paid for out of the money she got for dressmaking and embroidering tablecloths for rich customers. Otherwise my father would've hit the roof if she spent *his* money on candy.

Everyone agreed that my mother was the best bridge-player in town, so it was her duty to be at every bridge-club meeting, at which every rubber ended with enormous discussions of who did what wrong and why, and what they should have bid or played instead. Tia and I could therefore count on her being out of the house on Thursdays, seven weeks in a row. My mother eventually became the Pennsylvania state champion, just in the women's division, and the biggest thrill of her life, she said, was once being the doubles partner of the reigning bridge expert, an expatriate Russian named or perhaps renamed Ely Culbertson, especially when she took the bid with three no-trump and Culbertson laid down dummy while she played the hand victoriously. And everybody was watching!

The secret of her game, she told me, was concentration. *Concentration.* She was continuously counting trumps as they appeared face-up during the play, and that way she knew exactly when to make her move and what suit to play. Concentration and counting trumps were the whole secret. She never could understand why everybody else didn't count trumps too. Needless to say, her little victory as the local bridge-champ drove my father nearly insane with jealousy, as he himself never did anything but lose at cards since the day he first held one in his hands when I was born. What made it even worse was that my mother had never played cards either, until my father

179

taught her to play rummy so he'd have someone to play with when he was broke. The sarcasms he invariably heaped on her eighth week bridge-club party at home, as "a bunch of middle-aged hens shuffling cards instead of doing their housework" and similar niceties, were wonderful to hear, especially falling from the bloodless lips of a guy who'd already mortgaged the family homestead twice, if not three times — the Night of the Broken Milk Bottle — to pay his gambling debts.

It was finally agreed between them that the week my mother had her two tables of middle-aged hens in the house playing bridge of a Thursday afternoon, my father had the matching right to invite his pinochle-playing cronies to sit up all night with him the following Saturday, playing cards around the big dining-room table and stinking up the house with cigar smoke. There was also the important but seldom-mentioned difference that the hens were playing bridge only for table-favors and booby-prizes, worth at most a dollar, but the cocks were playing for cash. As usual, my father always lost. I'd have a chance to observe him playing those nights, when I'd walk through the room coming home usually from the library. He was a noisy player, full of rueful jokes and self-mockery when he lost, and loud threats to the winning players that

180

they'd have to send all the other players on vacation to Miami Beach with their winnings, and so forth.

If Daisy came home while Tia and I were on the phone, on bridge-club or shopping days especially, I would glower at her furiously until she'd dash out of the house again, and leave Tia and me dreaming and murmuring in our sempiternal telephone-bashes. Sometimes, evenings, when her parents went out, she could even call me back, and I'd slide the too-short telephone cord under the dining-room door, sitting on the floor with my back jammed against the kitchen door closed behind me so the rest of the family in the parlor couldn't hear anything I said. We surely never said anything worth overhearing, but I was frantic to keep it intensely private anyhow.

Tia's standard excuse for getting out after dark, of going over to do her homework with Mildred, just never seemed to wear thin. How any suspicious mother could really believe two fifteen-year-old girls were so anxious to do homework evening after evening in high spring is hard to see. But it worked. And Tia would instead streak like a shadow up along Pine Street, while I dashed along Gibson and down the hill in the dark, parallel to her but a block apart so none of her mother's housewife spies would ever see us together. And we would meet in the middle, down on the lonely dusty clay road, just inside a hole in the fence on a stony cutout cliff overhanging Stipp's Quarry. That was our Lovers' Leap, though we weren't yet ready to leap.

If I got to the trysting place ahead of Tia, as I generally did, I'd pluck flowers -- any kind, or even weeds — along the way, to have some paltry bouquet to give her when she'd come tripping up the road around the cow field from Mildred's. We never had more than an hour together there, or at most two hours. And it was uncomfortable lying on the ground at the edge of the cliff over the quarry, and obviously dangerous too, as we might roll off at any minute in our desperate hugging & kissing and thrashing about.

Sometimes a lonesome car would turn slowly down the unpaved part of Colfax Avenue, right outside the fence behind us, and would park nearby. I'd tell Tia they were just lovers like ourselves, looking for a place to neck & pet, and it was true. One night, after a couple had parked there only a brief quarter of an hour, we heard a girl's long, sung-out, shivering cry of ecstasy coming not-too-muffled from the car. I guess they had the window open. Tia and I looked at each other with drawn faces, half in pleasure and identification with the other couple, and half tenseness about ourselves who didn't have the luck, or maybe it

182

was the nerve, to do what they were doing. I loved the sound of the girl's cry at her orgasm. It was so beautiful.

After that we'd use our hour covered by Mildred and the homework story, to wander farther along past the colliery and into the woods at the bend of Roaring Brook as it swept past from Snook's Addition. The old empty frame-house was always locked up now, or my story would probably be very, very different for the next few years. Because I was a lot more devil-may-care inside four walls than it was possible to be out of doors. Girls were that way too, I'd already noticed. But Tia and I couldn't get in. So we'd continue along the riverbank, not far, and slide to the ground together among the bushes along the river's edge where it went gurgling over the roughhewn rocks. And I would push up Tia's dress very roughly and press aside her panty-crotch, fortunately always the loose teddy kind, and play stinkfinger endlessly with her. Yes, that's what I called it angrily inside myself — secretly being as vulgar as I could — because that was about all we ever did.

Sometimes I'd open her dress and suck her breasts first, but not always, and Tia would unbutton my fly meanwhile with fingers as soft and tender as a dream of love, and caress me as delicately as if she was

183

playing the Moonlight Sonata on my throbbing organ. But when we'd know our brief, counted hour was up, we'd rush back along the woodland path and up the hill, for Tia to run on to Mildred's, through the backdoor and home. Some day I'll understand why we didn't ever just simply throw ourselves down on the ground, by the quarry or the river, and make love together all the way, the way we wanted to. And yet we never did. I think we felt we were waiting to be all beautifully naked together and in bed. We certainly talked about that a lot: that we wanted it to be beautiful. Because this was so evidently *real love,* something in our souls; and sex wasn't just something the body wanted this time. I wanted it to be an expression of my love. It would have to be beautiful. Hasty and surreptitious was not good enough.

No frustration or humiliation was spared us. Even this one: we got word well ahead one week that Tia's parents would both have to be in the store all the next Saturday morning when they were running a special sale, and her Cerberus-like watchdog brother with them. Scenting that this might be our chance, we arranged that we'd meet at the quarry half an hour after the family left, and would hike on together up past the swimming lake and tame park, and hit it out over the last high girdle of hills around the town, as far as the

184

mountain reservoir where no one ever went. There we would be alone and safe from prying eyes, and would be able to make love beautifully in some forest glade in broad daylight. "And they were naked and unashamed." Our dearest dream!

While waiting around the house for H-hour on D-day, I prepared a blanket for Tia to lie on when we'd get to our rendezvous in the forest, and rolled it up into what I hoped would be a tight and unobtrusive roll, but which turned out to look like a contraband baby-grand piano when I got it tucked under my arm and started striding out of the house. My mother was standing right there looking at me as I walked out the door, and couldn't have failed to ask herself why I was toting a rolled-up blanket, presumably to go swimming at Lake Lincoln, on a day when it wasn't even sure that there was any water in the lake. If she had asked me any questions I was ready to fly in the air, but she said absolutely nothing, and neither did I.

All our planning and excited anticipation came to nothing however, when Tia shyly told me as we started up the river path, that her period, which she thought had just finished, unexpectedly started again the night before. I didn't answer and just kept striding on with that damn blanket-roll, as big as a house afire in my arms.

185

"So maybe we shouldn't go?" she ventured after a moment.

"Why not?" I snapped. "What do I care? You know the motto of the Marines, don't you? — *Through mud and blood to Glory!*"

Even so mentally-liberated a young woman as Tia found this free translation of the Marines' *Ad astra per aspera* a bit shocking. And she decided, sweetly but firmly, that she did not want to continue on up to the reservoir.

"Well, we'll go just for the hike," I urged.

"I know you," she said with a little smile. "When we get up there, all alone in the woods, I'm not going to be able to stop you."

"What makes you think *you'll* want to stop? Sweetheart," I told her fiercely, "a thing like that just doesn't matter. It doesn't *matter!* It just means that all your working parts work. I'll pluck that damn belt off you *with my teeth!* Fang-baring grimace to match. This shocked Tia even worse.

"Oh, no, darling!" she moaned. "No! We wanted it to be so beautiful the first time."

"It'll be beautiful," I grated. "It'll *be* beautiful! We're not going to turn back now, are we, just because you had a . . . a *recrudescence!*"

My linguistic resources and control were perfect, but Tia refused to be convinced. We turned back, and never got but one more chance, which turned out even worse.

IN MY UNENDING anguish at being virtually separated from the girl I loved so much and with every breath I took, I did what I suppose was a rather strange thing. I went back to walking another girl home after school — the last girl I had been walking with the very day before I first clapped eyes on Tia. This girl, whose name was Nadia Wasylkiw, was probably the sweetest and loveliest girl in the whole school, with a strange, ethereal other-worldliness matching her delicate blonde hair, which she kept braided and twisted up around her head. She was tall, too, with rather heavy hips and a small bosom. In fact she was the exact opposite of Tia in just about every way. At the beginning perhaps I had talked to Nadia about sex rather mildly, as I usually did to everyone. But now, when I started walking her home again to somewhere far in Hyde Park, up beyond the Susquehanna River bridges, I never talked to her about anything except how much I loved Tia and how

187

my heart was breaking at being forcibly separated from her.

Nadia was very sympathetic, and never seemed to tire of listening to my surely very tiresome laments and refrain. She was surprisingly maternal for a girl so young — she couldn't have been more than seventeen, or at most a year or two older than me. And she had a special soft spot for me in her overflowing heart, probably in part because I would always pronounce her name right, as *Nahd-ya*, in the Russian style, where everyone else except her family Americanized her name roughly to Nay-dee-a, which she didn't like much, but never complained. Pronouncing girls' foreign names right was an art I learned young, and it never failed to set me rapidly on some special inner track.

I knew how intensely important it was for other people to pronounce one's name right, ever since I'd gone back to my own Hebrew name of Gershon from George when I came back from the yeshiva in New York. No one but my intimates seemed able to understand that the *e*, as I would explain endlessly, was pronounced "as in *bed* — Gair-shun; not Gurr-shun, like a dog growling." That was my standard gloss and diacritic explanation, but it practically never had any effect until about the tenth time, when people would

188

finally break down and say the damned thing right, if only to shut me up about *Gair* and *Gurr* and that dog growling.

But I still often have to stand for people just meeting me, or never having met me at all and pretending to be old pals, hitting me with that "Gurshun" stuff; and even a certain urban hillbilly college professor and rock-music fancier who would never call me anything but "Gursh." Still, it's better than France, where I found when I got there that I had officially become "Djer-*SAWN!*" The French have a twelfth-century Jewish apostate philosopher, named Joannis Gerson, who's supposed to have been the real author of *The Imitation of Christ* attributed to Thomas à Kempis, and they're not listening to any nonsense about the pronunciation of his name.

It was also an important but unspoken part of my relationship with the sweet and understanding Nadia that there was never anything at all sexual in our own relationship. Before I met Tia I hadn't gotten to that point yet with Nadia, and after Tia it would have been sacrilege even to think about trying to make love to another girl, or so I felt for the first heartbreaking months.

Not everyone realized, of course, that Nadia and I were on so high and vaporous a level of sexual

189

repression with each other. Some of the teachers in the school, who hadn't failed to notice me waiting for Nadia every afternoon the autumn before when school let out, were very disapproving. At first I didn't understand why. Eventually my English teacher, plump, dowdy little Miss Hunt, who was also the adviser for the school literary magazine, *Impressions,* let the cat out of the bag.

She took me aside after class one day and explained that some of the other teachers — not her, of course! — felt that I ought to go around with girls of "Ah, my own religion," and not presumably be seducing tall blonde Catholic girls like Nadia. Who was following on, as it happened, right after Doris Bliss, also wispy, blonde, and Christian, in my nefarious Hebraic clutches. I found many years later, to my surprise, that Professor Alfred Kinsey — yup, him! — also objected to Jews like me going around with nice Christian girls and teaching them godnose what kind of sexy tricks, after which the said girls are liable to refuse to go around with good clean Christian men any more. — Ain't it awful, Mabel?

This particular crime was known just then, as Hitler moved into high gear in Germany, as "Blood-Defiling." I was lucky I didn't live there, because Jews who were caught at it were sent to concentration camps to be tortured vengefully to death. The German girls involved had their heads shaved and were promenaded in their underwear through the streets under armed guard by the Nazi troopers, with a sign around the girl's neck reading: "I HAVE GIVEN MY ARYAN BODY TO A KIKE!"

"Do you know who Nadia Wasylkiw is?" I finally challenged Miss Hunt. "She's Rima, the tree-girl in *Green Mansions*. I am not trying to seduce her! I don't think anybody would. It'd be like trying to seduce a swan!"

"Is that what the poem meant that you called *Orgasm?*"

"I didn't give that to her. That was a different girl." Yes, that had been Doris.

"But aren't there girls of your own, ah, religion — ?"

"Like in Germany, you mean?" I snapped back, getting rigid.

"Please, Gershon," said Miss Hunt, pronouncing it elegantly and wrongly Gur-shahn, "you know perfectly well I myself do not share such prejudices. But you are making enemies."

"Who? — enemies?"

Miss Hunt looked at me reproachfully. "Now what type of construction is that?"

191

"*Who* are my enemies?"

"Enemies. Suffice it to say." And now what type of construction was *that?* And from an English teacher. But I didn't say anything about it, nor try to argue that Nadia and I wouldn't ever even dream of having a physical love-affair. Who'd believe me? And I was getting real sore at my plump little, smug little English teacher who of course didn't *share* such unworthy Nazi prejudices, but was right there to warn me off. At that, I was lucky they hadn't told Nadia I was going to kill her to get the blood of her maidenhead to make matzos out of.

At the changing of the term in midwinter I found out who my secret enemy was. Central High school used the system where the students milled about at a bell rung every hour in the halls, going to the different classrooms carrying their books, while the teachers stayed put. That gave everybody a chance to stretch their legs and take a pee once an hour, while the teachers had their sacred chambers where they kept their effects and held court over their different classes. At the beginning of each term we never knew what teacher we'd have for any subject. Our class-cards just gave the room numbers, and when we'd arrive for the first time, there would be the new teacher — almost never the same one you'd had the term before.

192

This time when I arrived in the new English class, which I could see was not Miss Hunt's room, I was very pleased to find Nadia sitting in one of the seats already. She would be in my class the whole next half-year. Tia was never in any of my classes, as she was a whole year behind me: a junior when I was a senior. The teacher hadn't arrived yet, and I walked over to talk to Nadia and try to find a seat near her. Suddenly she looked up over my shoulder and froze. The new teacher had walked in. I sat down in the closest seat and looked the woman over.

It was a teacher I'd never had before, the one I'll call Miss X. I had seen her around but had never spoken to her, nor she to me, in my life. Some of the kids said she was a Lesbian. Others said she would drive all the boys on the football team home in her car, and would pull up her dress very high to shift gears and show them her legs. They claimed she was laying the whole team — different guys every year. I wondered what Coach Bob Fitzke thought about that, in among the vitamins. Anyhow, everybody hated her; that was sure. She was staring at me now with her eyes intensely wide open, like a fury, not speaking, but I could clearly feel her shrieking and tearing at me inside like a hurricane. I'm a pretty good starer myself, and stared back at Miss X's hennaed hairline for a few seconds, as stiff and proud as a statue, with one arm clenched across my chest and the other flung out and gripping the desktop. And I thought to myself, *"That's her."* No other words.

The whole class was watching our silent duel by now. As I could see I was going to flunk English that term, I stood up, took my books, gave frightened Nadia a brief smile, and walked out and down to the school office without a word. I told the woman at the desk there that a mistake had been made; that I was in the wrong English class. She looked over my card and started explaining that the class was correct, and that there was no picking & choosing allowed to the students.

"I'm not the one that's doing the picking," I said grimly.

When she continued to look helpless, I told her to go on in and see the principal, Mr. Jones, and to tell him some mistake had been made. He could phone Miss X and ask her, I said. The woman gave me an odd look and scurried into Jonesy's inner office. I could hear him dialing his phone. Then the woman came out and scratched out the room number on my card and gave me another one. My new English teacher would be Miss Oldham, a sporty old dame that everybody liked, including me.

194

Miss Oldham was a real doll. She didn't make any fuss about my coming in late, but just waved me to a seat in back. Then she took off her gilt pince-nez and polished it while she looked over the class. She told us there wouldn't be any formal lessons; that we were seniors in our final semester now, and "about to be graduated and go out into the world." Two classes a week we would write themes on subjects of which we'd find a list we could pick from on the blackboard; and the other three days we'd each be expected to give little speeches, or recite something before the class, or anything we wanted. That was to give us self-confidence and the ability to express ourselves when we went out in life. My heart swole with pleasure when I heard that. Now *there* was the way to run a school, I thought! But I'd had to wait twelve years to get there. It also appears that Miss Oldham was the only senior teacher in the whole school system who used that method — God bless her!

ONE EVENING, just a few days to the end of the school term, I couldn't stand it anymore. The trouble over Matilda's shaygetz boyfriend had died down, so I guess the last straw was those white icecream shoes all the fellows were supposed to wear at my graduation, and that I couldn't have. My mother was very sorry, but it was completely impractical and impossible. There was only just enough money in the family for one pair of shoes for me each year, the same as with the girls. She herself never got any new shoes at all. She said she was still wearing the same pair since Coolidge was president, her old black pumps with the strap across them, endlessly resoled by the Italian shoemaker in his little wooden cabin next door to Jaffe's store across from the Nickelette. Not even black-&-white, then, the way I had begged? I knew I could get away with that. Other guys would be wearing black-&-white. No, not even that, my mother said. How would that look in the middle of next winter? Besides, nobody would notice my shoes at the graduation, she added, even if they were green, not black. They'd all be watching their own kids, you could be sure.

I seethed in that stew of white shoes, and other things too. But mostly in not being able to see Tia except rarely. And our long phone calls were now so hard to plan, afternoons, because her darn brother was always home. Couldn't he ever go out and fly a kite, or go off swimming or something? No, never. The weather was getting hot too. And I fretted & fumed. I

196

couldn't read. Couldn't think, couldn't sleep, hated everybody. Nothing mattered, nothing interested me. Tia!!

That evening I decided I would have to bust out of the trap they'd locked me into. I had to. I would have a showdown with Tia's family, and just *force* them to let me see her! I figured that if I rang their doorbell they'd simply slam the door in my face when they saw it was me. So instead, when evening came, I lurked at the bottom of the hill under the trees, a block or two away from their house. I knew her mother would have to walk by there, going along Pine Street, when she got off the streetcar coming home. Tia's father had his new Essex now, dark and low-slung — the Jaguar of that decade — like something in the automobile-of-the-future sketches then in *Esquire* magazine by Alexis de Sakhnoffsky. Her father zoomed around in it proudly and impatiently, Tia told me, without ever waiting for his family. So her mother had to take the streetcar to get home from their store evenings.

She came clicking right along on schedule in the half-dark: it must've been eight o'clock or later, when I'd been waiting for over an hour. I caught up with her as she crossed from the streetcar-stop toward Irving Avenue. When she turned nervously to see who it was, I braced her immediately. She was thinner than I remembered, and younger.

"Mrs. French," I faltered. "It's me — Gershon Legman. Why won't you let me see Esther?" I meant to pitch my voice low and calm, but it came out all crackling like dead branches in the winter wind.

She threw me a frightened look. "You go away and let us alone!" she cried, and tried to hurry on, but I raced along at her side.

"Why can't I see Esther?" I insisted. "I never did anything wrong to her, or to your family, or *anybody.*"

Sylvia French stopped now and faced me. "Your own father says you're mixed up with crooks!" she flung at me intensely. " —*White-slavers!* And he ought to know. Go away and *let us alone!*"

"That's crazy!" I moaned, boggling at the mere idea. "I *love* Tia! I'm wild about her! I can't sleep. I can't eat. I *love* her!"

Mrs. French tried to turn and run on, but I grabbed her desperately by both wrists. She pulled her arms away from me violently.

"You don't know what you're talking about!" she cried. "You don't know what you're talking about!"

198

And she ran on without me. I could hear her heels clicking, like tiny metallic doors closing in the dark. I wanted to run after her but the soul was draining out of me.

MY FATHER was a pathological liar. I know that isn't the way you're supposed to write this sort of autobiography. You're supposed to slip it artistically to the Old Bastard with all the elaborately lethal deftness and underplayed venom of Samuel "Erewhon" Butler's *The Way of All Flesh* — which the author didn't have the guts to publish and it only appeared posthumously twenty years later — and Edmund Gosse's *Father and Son*. I don't know how to be that devious and terse. Let me just say it straight.

My father was a pathological liar. I knew it, my mother and my sisters knew it — everybody knew it. Sometimes I think he knew it himself. This made him a great story-teller, and he had the art and wit to make it all seem particularly true and real by telling carefully selected items from his quite large stock of jokes and old folktales with very precise personal details. It always had happened to him personally, or to someone he knew well. A lot of raconteurs use this system of personalizing and updating their ancient chestnuts. But the difference is that after a few tellings my father then believed firmly that it *had* happened to him. Under other circumstances, this ravaging mythomania might have made him a highly successful writer of the cheaper type of fiction: maybe murder mysteries or scenarios for soap-operas. As it was, it only made him a pest to everyone around him; and, to his family, his wife and his children, a lifelong crucifixion. Of his other endearing little tricks and vices there have already been sufficient testimonies since page 1.

Not realizing consciously, for the first five or six years, that my father's stories were all hokum, I believed every word of them just as sincerely as I believed the Bible, which it took me a few more years to find out was mostly the identical sort of hokum and written by precisely the same kind of mythomaniacs — in those days called priests and scribes, later Talmudists and commentators. Their not very gallant purpose throughout was to so manipulate the food taboos and sexual taboos they themselves instituted that they personally ended up with most of the food, often most of the women too, and kept everyone else's sexual life in a holy mess. There are lots of priestly groups that do exactly this, including all of those in the East, and most prominently the Mormons in the West. This seems to have been my father's goal too. A true crooked patriarch, double-dealing to everyone in his power from the bottom of the psychological deck. Constructive taboo.

One stunning example, only in part about my family. People who think that Jews are cleverer than other people, owing to the Mendelian improvement of the race by the natural selection of two thousand years of persecution and slaughter by their enemies, are sometimes amazed to learn that for thousands of years — in fact since the destruction of Solomon's Temple in Jerusalem and the consequent suppression of animal sacrifices for the benefit of the two-in-ten priestly groups of Cohenites and Levites — orthodox religious Jews have been slaughtering beeves for food, and then refusing to eat any part of the animal farther back from the nose than the ribs.

Every other part — all the best stuff, that is; all the steaks, chops, haunches of beef, and every other morsel really worth eating — these brilliant *Judlach,* so envied by every other nation for their formidable brainpower, originally turned over docilely to the one-fifth minority of their priestly caste, whose only useful activity was collecting this tribute; just as Jews nowadays sell off the whole back half of every slaughtered animal, in one grand kosher chunk, to the ignorant, well-fed Christians or other host nation.

There is, I am told, some complex ritual purification method whereby Jews could retain and eat even the back half of the animal when under siege, famine, or other emergency, but as it involves the practically impossible fairytale task of removing all the arteries and veins in the meat to be eaten so that not a single drop of blood remains, it is practically never done. Shakespeare alludes to this pointedly in *The Merchant of Venice*, where the bloodthirsty Jew, Shylock, is prevented from getting the pound of flesh of his Christian prey by the gentle Portia's wise judgment, that he can have only the pound of flesh but not a hairsbreadth more, nor a single drop of blood — which is presumably what he is really after, like me and the Polish housemaid at Passover.

All this, by the way, on the stupefyingly irrelevant grounds, inculcated into their chumpy Jewish co-religionists millennia ago by the same said wily one-fifth minority of priests, and codified in the book of *Leviticus*, that the patriarch Jacob wrestled with an angel in the 32nd chapter of the book of *Genesis* in the *Bible* — written, that is to say forged, by a far earlier generation of the same priests — and that the angel "touched the hollow of Jacob's thigh," this being a

202

euphemism for his penis, and put his leg (not his penis) out of joint.

The mock logical development, by means of exegetical and hermeneutical argumentation and *pilpul*, whereby this out-of-joint patriarchal hip (or penis) still prevents millions of Jews all over the world from eating T-bone steaks, even assuming they could find or afford them, would form a study for a transactional psychologist, not a historian. Freud made a start at it, in *Totem* & *Taboo*. The implication of remote and not very well repressed urges towards cannibalism, and specifically the eating of one's patriarchs' penis such as Noah and Jacob, is certainly clear.

The Jewish heretic sect formerly known as the Essenes and now as Christians make this even clearer by performing, as their weekly act of worship, a primitive cannibalistic mummery in which they ingest sanctified wafers & wine — which they are also not allowed to swallow with any purposeful movements of deglutition, and which their digestive organs are stated never to deliver to the bowels — under the avowed name of the *blood & body* of their deity, Jehovah's only son. In a genital repression matching the almost total oral repression here, Jehovah has impregnated the mother of this son through her *ear,* in the character of a bird or ghost representing his penis, leaving her *Virgo*

Intacta vaginally.   In the matching Roman & Greek mythologies, the impregnating god, here called Jove, not Jehovah, takes an animal or other material disguise instead, in his human amours.

If I still seem in any way bitter or irritable about this, I am. But not because of the steaks. And not because my father, after having been trained from childhood to be a meat-butcher and spending the first fifteen years of his working life in that profession, somehow managed by some monumental and purposeful mismanagement very typical of him, to have opened his own butcher shop when I was seven years old — a shop in which I never worked, and was only the delivery boy; but a shop which dealt only in non-kosher meat which we were all forbidden to eat by my father's religious principles. The result was when the Depression hit, a few years later, and money and food were very scarce, our family never got one single ounce of food to eat from my father's butcher-shop. I don't care. Don't give a damn. I never liked steaks anyhow, of which I ate my first one at the age of eighteen, after leaving home. I prefer chops, which I admit are the T-bone steaks of sheep and pigs.

No. What got to me about the whole thing was the self-elected priestly organization of sexual prohibitions and mythomania, when my father now

204

geared into high in this area too, after I turned fifteen. That my father was a pitiful prude — not a specifically required or desired Jewish trait — I had always known, and so did my sisters. My mother had no real complaint on this score, because he remained sexually potent with her, as she told me the last time I saw her, right up to the age of ninety-four. I hope I do as well.

My sisters suffered a great deal more than I did, on the crude physical level too, from my father's simultaneous prudery and his fanatical incestuous interest in their bodies under the polite disguise, which fooled him completely but nobody else, of watching out for their "morality." As in his great nighttime scenes where he would pull up my sisters' skirts when they were going out on dates, or preferably when they were coming back accompanied by the hated rival swain, on the grounds that he wanted to see whether they had any whirling-spray syringes or other birth control devices hidden in their bloomers, by which he visibly meant in their cunts.

Few of the young men who assisted at these midnight scenes of delicate paternal moral solicitude, as unwilling brother-husbands to my shrieking sisters being quasi-raped by their father in this way, ever came back. I doubt if that was my father's main purpose here — which was obviously just to get at their cunts

205

under some cockamammy excuse — but it was an extra or secondary neurotic advantage, as they say. My trouble was that I didn't realize this type of lunatic patriarchal sexual privilege or control could & would be applied to me very soon too, but it was.

My sister Ruth, who I thought had all the brains among the girls in our family, was for some reason so naïve or so unconsciously prone to these incestuous psychodramas being enacted in her own petticoats and panties, that she really believed my father was clumsily attempting to protect her morality in their quasi-erotic rape scenes. Matilda and I tried to argue with her, but Ruth insisted on believing that his motives were strictly as he stated, and his outlandish moral-police activities exactly what he construed them to be. Even my mother had her doubts. But there was no shaking Ruth, and I think I was right in suspecting that underneath she welcomed this kind of disguised sexual attention from my father because she wasn't getting enough anywhere else.

Matilda was always tougher-minded about everything. This gave her an unfortunate penchant for idealizing purportedly tough, emotionally strangulated, semi-criminal types, especially in the way of movie anti-heroes; first Lloyd Nolan and then a few years later Humphrey Bogart, and godnose who and how many more later, since this type of anti-sexual emotional cripple is now the only sort of media-hero left. But other than that, her feet were always on the ground, where the rest of us kids — and certainly Ruth and me — were impractical romantic dreamers. The next time my father pulled one of his private panty-raids when Matilda came home late with her date and was necking with him quietly in the parlor, the scene was improved by my father suddenly appearing in the darkened doorway between the dining-room and parlor in his flannel nightgown and bedroom slippers, snapping on all the overhead lights unexpectedly, and standing there in tableau holding a big alarm-clock accusingly in his hand.

When the evidence of his disappointed eyes told him that his daughter was not, as he had feared and/or hoped to catch her at, getting fucked, he announced loudly: "Young man, are you aware that it is TWELVE-THIRTY in the morning?" And he threw her date out. My father *then* started the examination of her underwear and so forth, in the usual fashion, with Matilda screaming and fighting him off and trying to push down her skirt. The whole family came running, rubbing the sleep out of their eyes, to save her. The next morning, when my father had gone to work, and the rest of us were having breakfast, Matilda summed it up, I thought, very well:

"All he wants is what the rest of the fellows want," she said.

What was my surprise, many years later, on receiving a free book through its author, the transactional psychoanalyst Dr. Eric Berne, who said he liked my books and wanted me to read his — the book he sent was called *Games People Play*, which is only the first part of a three-volume *summum* of Berne's shrewd and powerful, and terribly funny and slangy way of sizing up the crooked motives behind many of the strange behaviors of people, that suckers like you & me think are interacting with us as honestly as we are with them (and which may be truer than we think!) the other two volumes being called *What Do You Say After You Say Hello?* and *Sex in Human Loving:* terrible titles both, but terrific books that take the skin right off wherever you touch them or them you, so be careful! — what was my surprise, I say, to have *Games People Play* fall open in my hands to the following dishonest "life game" very simply described in the chapter on Sexual Games, which is taken much further in the last volume of the three:

208

"Uproar." *Thesis:* The classical game is played between domineering fathers and teen-age daughters, where there is a sexually inhibited mother. Father comes home from work and finds fault with daughter, who answers impudently; or daughter may make the first move by being impudent, whereupon father finds fault. Their voices rise, and the clash becomes more acute . . . both retire to their respective bedrooms and slam the doors. In any case, the end of a game of "Uproar" is marked by a slamming door. "Uproar" offers a distressing but effective solution to the sexual problems that arise between fathers and teen-age daughters in certain households. Often they can only live in the same house together if they are angry at each other, and the slamming doors emphasize for each of them the fact they have separate bedrooms. *[Now notice:]*

In degenerate households this game may be played in a sinister and repellent form in which father waits up for daughter whenever she goes out on a date, and examines her and her clothing [!] carefully on her return to make sure that she has not had intercourse.

209

The slightest suspicious circumstances may give rise to the most violent altercation, which may end with the daughter being expelled from the house in the middle of the night. In the long run nature will take its course — if not that night then the next, or the one after. Then the father's suspicions are "justified," as he makes plain to the mother, who has stood by "helplessly" while all this went on . . . This game is not as distasteful to the father as he might like to think . . .

WHEN I found out the enormity of my father's lie about me to Tia's mother, on Hitler's "Great Lie" principle, telling her that his divinity-trained teenage son was now a white-slaver, and doubtless was going to sell her fifteen-year-old daughter into an Oriental whorehouse, I was sorry I had become an atheist so soon. It would have been a comfort to me then, to believe there was a yawning Hell somewhere below the turning earth, a Gehenna of pain and punishments that would one day rip wide open with a horrible scream like an earthquake, and greedily swallow down my rotten, lying, misbegotten crackpot of an ugly, illegitimate father into its burning depths.

Like Caliban, the hellborn rapist, or Shakespearean equivalent of a teenage white-slaver in *The Tempest*, "You taught me language, and my profit on't is: I know how to curse." *Sheol! — Sambatyon! — Accursed, accursed, accursed!!* Yes!! And his tongue would be nailed to a flaming board sprinkled with burning acids: the proper punishment in the world-to-come of all liars and tattlers. Maybe I'd even nail it to the board myself! No, I wouldn't actually want to *do* it, but I'd be willing to stare at it and gloat sadistically after it was done, maybe by some sinless, impersonal, computer-operated cybernetic torture machinery, like watching horror t.v.

I was almost ready to rush back into religion in my new and fierce delectation over the idea of Hell. I would have made a great Dominican torturer for the Inquisition — in the refined intellectual 1984 cat-&-mouse style, of course. Lots of people have told me that I'm nothing but an over-reacting sadistic censor — a mere modern Savonarola turned inside-out like a French tickler. Yes! Yes! Yes!! And now I wanted it all tucked back rightside-in the other way. So *I* could enjoy the sadistic thrill of torture and screams and blood and dismemberments and disfigurements and

211

agony and castration and pederastic rapes and stuff and shit and everything awful I used to complain about and want censored and burned and buried forever in Japanese "art" movies and French *dernier cri* philoslopical novels and Mafia-patriotic gangster and horror and atom-bomb movie gloats! — While YOU bullshit me for a while about how terrible a social scourge sadism is, when it's *me* that's the sadist; instead of how artistic and beautifully done and technically admirable and aesthetically valid and excusable and everything & nothing and authentic a part of life it is, after all, and how you don't really feel a thing and have never walked out on a horror movie or turned off a t.v. atrocity program in your life — when it's *you*.

Yes, it certainly would be wonderful if there were a real and palpable Hell for all those inexcusable sinners, naturally not including you & me because *we* always have an Extenuating Circumstance. Just like Hitler, who was a poor, neurotic, maybe pre-psychotic and epileptic guy who had hallucinations and chewed the carpet when he felt upset about the, er, Jewish Question — and its Final Solution. But alas, I knew that there was no Hell. Hitler got away with one bite into the cyanide capsule, just like Goebbels and Frau Goebbels, who also had the thoughtfulness to inject deadly poison into their children's veins a few minutes before, so the poor kids wouldn't be exposed to public scorn later in a bullet-proof glass cage like Eichmann. And my father would get away with everything too.

And when my father would die one day — and that rotten off-spring of Satan and Lilith *would* die one day, I supposed — it would be in all the odor and dignity of his usual phony sanctity, doubtless wrapped up for the voyage in his white woollen *tallis* and lace-trimmed *keitel* shroud he always wore like a princely dressing-gown every spring, presiding over the Passover table — and for the orphans at the Jewish Home for the Friendless when his own children all moved rapidly away. And wholly imagining himself ready to shoot straight up to Heaven, on the Guardian Angel Express, and to sit in Paradise in the world-to-come and eat of the great fish Leviathan, prepared since time immemorial especially for him and the rest of the thirty-six Secret Saints. And how would I be able to deprive him of his imbecilic certainty of his reward in the world-to-come, when now I wanted to believe in Hell myself?

One thing was sure, though; and a petty revenge it is. If the reason he had ever wanted a son, and a son who could speak Aramaic Hebrew, was to have some superstitious sucker to light a memorial candle in a fluted drinking-glass for him every year, and

213

intone the special Yahrzeit prayer for him ostentatiously at the synagogue that day, and quietly over his grave, he had positively lost that forever, that selfsame wintry February day when he crucified two innocent children in love, whom he caught kissing on a bed.

And I spat on the ground — believe me — and rubbed it triumphantly into the dust, the day I learned, forty years later, that this hypocritical Yiddish art-theatre Tartuffe had just died at the age of ninety-four. "For God so loved him that he kept him out of Heaven till the last possible minute." It's just lucky I don't know where his grave lies, or I would certainly not wait an hour to go there and shit on it. In fact, I *was* there about a month ago. I had it planned. And only the fact that I had a friend by my side, who was photographing the room I was born in, and the cellar where Merry and I invented the sixty-nine, and all the rest of my ridiculous childhood memories and victories and disasters, and whom I was hoping to keep convinced that I'm really quite a nice fellow — and not the cruel and vengeful bastard I really *am* — kept me from suggesting that we should now get back into the car and find our way to the local Jewish cemetery, so I could defile my father's grave.

Sometimes innocent third parties don't entirely understand the artless authenticity of a gesture like that, ridding oneself finally and forever of the parental spook that has clung like a vampire on one's back for half a lifetime. Yet everyone understands, and finds nobly sentimental, the exact same gesture if it disguises itself hygienically as burning to ashes your mother's or father's corpse, and scattering their ashes — with the sick program they imprinted on your naked childhood mind — into the winds of night. "Adieu, adieu! Hamlet, remember me," cries the Ghost — the one part Shakespeare played himself onstage — programming Hamlet for the aborted revenge that destroys him. No, no! *Break* the Machine. Forget! *Sheol! – Sambatyon!* — *Be thou accursed, accursed, accursed!* Let that be all your Yahrzeit. *"Yisgadal, v'yiskadash, sh'mei rabbah* . . . Magnified, magnified and sanctified be Thy Great Name . . ."

NOW I KNEW. That was what my insane father had told them. I was a white-slaver — a cadet. I was a white-slaver, was I? At sixteen. Young Lefty Legman, King of the Girl-stealers and Red-Bandanna Gypsies, the youngest Talmud-translator and white-slaver in

America, and with the highest I.Q. But there wasn't anything funny about it. My father was really crazy, I saw now, and wouldn't ever change. So now I was a white-slaver, was I? Break in little girls and treat 'em rough — like *him* pulling up Ruth and Matilda's skirts when they went out on dates! Make a better white-slaver than I ever would!

So that was what he had done, just to ruin things between Tia and me. When he rushed off, that day in the snow, to tell Tia's mother on us. I knew he'd told her he found us laying on the bed together, and kissing. And surely pretended he'd found us making love the whole way too. But how could I have ever dreamt — imagined! — that he'd embroider it into anything as crazy as criminals and white-slavers? What kind of stuff must be going on all the time in his mind, I asked myself? Like the time he wrote the letter to the Emperor of Austria-Hungary and got put out of the country. What a really bloated idea he had of himself! And those letters now to Walt Disney about Mickey Mouse, and to Henry Ford and President Roosevelt. But this time he wasn't fooling me. He was just jealous about Tia and me. You couldn't fool me about that. Jealous, disloyal, *and* a lunatic. He had rushed out into the snow to bear false witness against me — his only son. And Tia too.

216

That night, when I got home from running after Tia's mother and trying to talk to her, I walked through the house without speaking to anyone, surly and dark as a thundercloud. No one noticed it anymore except my mother. My scowl was permanent. Everybody was in the front room listening to the radio, except one of my older sisters who was out as usual. I got the family *Bible* out of the sideboard by the phone as I went through the dining-room, and took it with me into my bedroom. Sitting on the narrow cot under the naked light-bulb I looked up the passage about false witnesses in the 19th chapter of *Deuteronomy*. That was the Ninth Commandment:

> "Thou shalt not bear false witness against thy neighbor. . . "Thou shalt not go up & down as a tale-bearer among thy people: neither shalt thou stand against the blood of thy neighbor: I am the Lord . . .
> "If a false witness rise up against any man to testify against him that which is wrong . .
> .
> "Then shall ye do unto him, as he had thought to have done unto his brother: so shalt thou put the evil away from among you . . .

"Thine eye shall not pity him; but life shall go for life, eye for eye, tooth for tooth, hand for hand, foot for foot."

I put out the light and stared out the window with the Bible still open upon my lap. They knew, those old geezers that wrote the *Bible*. They knew. *"Thine eye shall not pity him. A life for a life, an eye for an eye, a tooth for a tooth: I am the Lord!"*

I decided my father ought to die. Anyone could see that. And I knew what I had to do. I went back into the silent kitchen and routed out the big *fleischige* carving knife that we never really ever used except at Thanksgiving for the turkey, and hid it under the pillow of my bed. When he was good and asleep I would creep into my parents' bedroom right next to mine and plant it in his heart — if he had a heart! Just like the silver stake you had to stab into Dracula's heart, because vampires sleep all day forever in their tomb. No blood would even spurt out, not with a guy like my father. Just bossiness and lies. Red ashes, maybe, like out of a dead volcano.

I realized perfectly well that I'd go to jail for it, and get the electric chair of course. I wouldn't even try to run away. I'd be proud of what I'd done. The cops would arrive by noon, I figured, maybe earlier, so I

218

went back out into the parlor where they were all still listening to some drama on the radio, and kissed my mother goodnight and hugged her very tight. I didn't want our very-last-kiss-ever to be spoilt by cops in blue uniforms, and handcuffs, and me being dragged away to burn. I was perfectly calm. I did not even look at him, as he sat fiddling with the radio dials. The sound of the frequencies or something was never quite right for him — he always had to be diddling with it. That was over now. He would be better off dead.

But I fell asleep the minute I crept into bed, and when I woke up in the morning my father had already gone to work. I felt like dumb Hamlet, swearing to the Ghost to *sweep to his revenge,* and then fumbling it. I just shrugged and went to breakfast. The next night would be plenty time enough. No angels were going to be waiting for him.

While I was finishing my shredded-wheat and milk and brown sugar in the kitchen, my mother called me from her bedroom where she was making the bed. She took me wordlessly by the hand and led me into my own tiny room and turned back the mattress under my pillow. There was the butcher knife, gleaming flatly, silver grey and broad, and twice as enormous-looking as it really was. We looked into each other's eyes, and I broke into tears.

"Who are you going to kill?" my mother asked. "Both of us? The girls too?"

"No, only him," I whispered. "I love you." I stopped crying and stared ahead stonily.

We sat down together on the side of the bed and I told her what Tia's mother had said. That Daddy told her that I was a white-slaver and a criminal, and that was why I could never see Tia again. My mother said she knew all about it already — he had explained it carefully to her too. And nothing she could say would make him realize it was the most ridiculous thing in the world. Nor understand the enormity of what he had done.

The reasoning that led my father to this strange conclusion about me — for which I was still intensely determined to kill him — was as follows. One day the winter before, my mother told me, she'd sent me to take my father his lunch that he forgot on leaving the house. I was to wait till he came out of the Lackawanna Railroad offices at lunchtime, and hand it to him. When I delivered him his lunch-bag I told my father I had been waiting for him in a little grimy candy-store across Lackawanna from the railroad station, where I went to keep warm while waiting. And what had I done there, he asked? Nothing, I said; just watched the fellows playing the pinball machine. I

220

guess that was the detail that tore it. It appears this grimy little shop on the wrong side of the street was the main hangout for all the railroad office's horse--players and gamblers, and doubtless a few pimps as well picking up the cheap after-office-hours trade. Birds of a feather play horses together. Ergo: I was a fledgling crook and white-slaver. That didn't prove I was already selling any innocent girls into the Buenos Ayres circuit, but I was clearly on my way.

After my mother explained the whole incredible stupidity to me, we sat awhile on the bed without talking. It was very Talmudic, wasn't it? Irrelevant evidence, and a fore-ordained conclusion. But all perfectly logical. I stared out the window at the big white oak branches in the Israels' backyard. The young oak in the Edwards' yard next door was now getting very tall too. I could remember when it was only a sapling that didn't even come up to my window. When I'd have come back from college, on my ten thousand dollar scholarship from Old Isaacs, the moneylender whose wife died, it would be an enormous oak. I reminded my mother about the lost scholarship, or maybe it was her that reminded me.

"That's why he stole my money," I told her bitterly. "He was jealous of me that time too, like this time with Tia."

221

"No," my mother mumbled, looking away. "He really thought he could double the money for you gambling. He was going to use it *all* for you. What was left you went to the *chalutzim* camp in Long Island with, and to the *yeshiva*."

"Sure," I said. "To be a Leader in Israël. And so now?"

"He always loses," said my mother helplessly. "He doesn't know how to concentrate. But he still thinks someday he's going to win. That's his craziness."

Yes, I thought. That, and ever playing pinochle at all with those card-sharks in the backroom of the hat-factory down on Penn Avenue. Where he and everybody else *knew* they were cheating him blind. Meaning that it was him and not me that was really hanging out with criminals, wasn't it? To be sure.

"And this time," I said finally, "his craziness was to steal Tia from me, with crazy lies. So why should he live, and me die inside?"

"Don't say that, honeybunch," my mother told me quietly. "You're not going to die inside. You're young. You write beautiful poetry. You'll have *lots* of girls." She smiled. Her voice was soft and cajoling. Permissive . . .

222

"I don't *want* lots of girls. I want Tia! I *love* her."

"You ought to go on a vacation this summer," she said after a pause. "Why don't you go hitchhiking like all the other boys, and get a job somewhere? You'll be out of high school soon now. You could save up money for college."

College didn't interest me anymore, I told her. I'd probably become an arctic explorer instead, or in Asia somewhere to look for dragon bones, or a forest ranger out West where I wouldn't ever have to talk to anybody. I hated everybody except her. And Tia.

"Well," my mother offered, "if you want to go, I can always loan you five dollars for grub-money. I have it saved up from the shopping."

I knew how she had saved that money. By walking fifteen long blocks to town on her bad ankles, for months, every time she went shopping, instead of taking the streetcar. And every other kind of mad economy like that. After all, it was me that forged the phony transfers for her, for years, with a ticket-punch and a toothpick, so she could at least take the streetcar home when heavy-laden with shopping, as far as Quincey Avenue by the hospital. Yes, and walk all the rest of those seven blocks uphill, with her swollen ankles and the heavy packages. Or maybe she'd sold

223

one extra set of tablecloth embroidery after working months on it every night by artificial light, and hadn't poured all the money into the family budget. My father's gambling losses over the years had finally made her wily. She hid her extra couple of dollars now. Why not? She earned it.

How far was a five-dollar crash fund supposed to take the family in an emergency, I wondered. Well, far enough to get me out of town. I guess I was the emergency this time, with a carving knife under my pillow. We were partners in crime now, because now my mother knew. And I got her to phone Tia for me, and told her to pretend to be a girlfriend named Julia if Tia's mother answered.

"I'll say Yolanda," she offered. "Maybe she knows my American name."

Tia was home and we could talk. My mother vanished discreetly into the kitchen and closed the door, and I leaned up against the colored burntwood telephone pedestal, straining to hear every note of Tia's voice. Her family was going on vacation in hardly more than a week, she said, to Asbury Park or Long Branch in New Jersey, along the Atlantic Ocean where they went every year. It was like Atlantic City, but smaller. Tia assured me she would write to me, but I

224

wasn't to answer as my letters would surely be intercepted.

"I won't be here," I told her. "I'll probably go hitchhiking somewhere and earn some money for college. But I'll come back every weekend for your letters," I hastened to add. We kissed over the phone and arranged to meet less than half an hour later at the old quarry. She'd have to stop at Mildred's house first, and slip around by Pine Street in case her brother watched where she went from the upstairs porch. Everybody was in the plot now to keep us apart, except Mildred.

When we met at Stipp's Quarry, Tia said she could only stay for a few minutes, because it was Saturday and her mother expected her downtown at the store at ten-thirty, to go pick out a new bathing suit for Asbury Park. I kissed her hungrily. There were no cars, ever, along the unpaved road in the daytime, and I felt her body all over with my hungry hands while we kissed. Tia said her mother hadn't told the whole family I stopped her at the streetcar the night before, because she was afraid her father or brother might kill me for pestering them.

"I wouldn't care," I said, and thought I meant it too. "The way I feel, I wish I'd died that time the lightning hit me, right there in that cowfield throwing

225

quoits." I pointed. Tia kissed me, and let me pull her bodice open and kiss her titties too. Then I promised her I'd design a bathing suit for her myself, made entirely of turquoise blue ribbon and full of diamond-shaped holes. That'd stop all the traffic on the ocean highway, if there was one.

"Yes, and get me put in jail the very first day," Tia objected. "Wouldn't you be jealous of all those other men, looking at me?"

I hadn't thought of that; I was still only a novice as a white-slaver. "Sure, I'd be jealous," I admitted. "But I have to pretend. Otherwise I won't be able to say goodbye to you at all."

I ate up her breasts with my eyes, and almost as avidly with my mouth. We kissed & clung, and each kiss was to be our leave-taking. But I wouldn't let her go. I kept kissing Tia — her breasts, which she was now hiding away in the cups and straps of her bra: her mouth, her eyes, her hair, her ears, taking little pretended bites at the high swell of her cheekbones and straining her to me every time she said she really had to go now. Finally I became very tense and told her to stop trying to disengage herself, because I didn't intend to let her go. I wrapped both my arms tightly round her like two angry pythons — a favorite image of mine then.

226

"Look down there," I said grimly, pointing with my chin to the long drop beyond the cliff where we were standing over the edge of the quarry. "That's twenty yards straight down." It was too, or at least ten. "Maybe I'll just throw us over together, with you in my arms. If we can't live together, we'll die together!"

Tia didn't struggle a bit. She just smiled sweetly and kissed me again. "If that's what you want, darling," she said, "that's what we'll do."

"Don't humor me!" I grated. "You don't think I mean it, but I do." It wasn't suicide I planned: I wanted to *murder* everybody — me included.

"Of course you mean it," said Tia. "But let me go and buy the bathing suit first." She smiled winsomely at me. I was glad she didn't fight me, because then I might have done it. I really might've. I was that crazy by then. I felt as stiff as a board; my chest and throat all clogged up. Our breaths were alternating as I kept Tia wrapped tightly against me, her breasts swelling against my chest and then falling back.

"Yes," I agreed finally, loosening my arms. "Mildred can wear the bathing suit to our funeral."

We both began to laugh a little, ruefully. Then we climbed back out through our special hole in the wooden fence around the quarry cliffs, and trudged back up to the top of the hill through the cowfield hand in hand. This would be the end for us, I knew. Our love story was over. The old, abandoned Loop-the-Loop tracks were still there as we walked by, twisted and busted in the field as they had been the day of the lightning, years before. How stupid, I thought, for us kids to have imagined they were from a carnival ride, when they were so obviously mine-shaft rails from the colliery right in front of our eyes at the foot of the hill. It was still working, the big wheel turning slowly at the top of the breaker to pull the coal-cars up. The breaker-boys were gone now, on account of the Roosevelt Law, but they were still getting out coal there.

Old Mrs. Mittleman, only a block down from us on Harrison Hill, had gone to answer the phone the year before while she was frying eggs in the kitchen, and when she got back her whole kitchen and back porch were fifteen feet down below the ground, from a mine-fall in a shaft passing too close, right underneath their house. She could still see the eggs frying in the pan on the stove, down at the bottom of the hole, she told my mother. Lucky for her she wasn't down there too, sliding along to Oakwood Place.

"Don't go back to the quarry when I'm in Asbury Park," Tia cautioned me at the top of the hill where we had to part.

I glowered at her. "You don't think I'd bring any other girl here, do you?" I bristled indignantly, ready to be furious again, and wishing we had gone instead to Stipp's stone mill and fucked like waggle-assed minks in the stone-dust.

"No. I mean don't go there alone."

FOR THE NEXT couple of days I wandered around like a poleaxed beef, conscious that I had suffered an overwhelming trauma but without the slightest idea of what to do to straighten myself out. The trauma wasn't actually yet, when I knew that Tia and I would be separated, probably forever, and that our unachieved love-affair was really over before it had begun. That hadn't even hit me very hard at first, when we were separated by force months before. I was still sure then that we could see each other and talk to each other on the sly; and we did, no matter what our parents may have wanted. What made the iron finally enter into my soul, like the Psalmist with his feet in the stocks and fetters, was understanding now, months later, just *how* it had been done by my father, and how impossible it would be to remove the treacherous stone he had flung between us and into the

229

well of our happiness, Tia's and mine. And he seemed glad of it too! Grown-ups were perfectly crazy. Crazy! Never mentioned it; never said a word to me of what he had really done. Loving Tia now no longer made me feel so happy and complete, as hating him made me feel storm-tossed inside and unable ever to come to rest.

I slouched dispiritedly into Stück's bookstore one afternoon, early in June, and my uncle Joel studied me in some concern. "Whatsamatter, kid?" he asked. "You look as *verblunget* as a wet fart bouncing about in a blanket." I didn't even smile. *Verblunget* was Yiddish for hopelessly lost: I knew that much, and that was exactly how I felt. I wondered if I could confide in him. He was my mother's cousin after all.

"What would you do, Baron," I asked, putting it to him in elevated terms as a hypothetical case, "if some sneaking, smirking, penis-jerking monstrous bastard — not even up to a rattlesnake; that at least gives you a warning! — snuck up in back of you and struck you down, in his monstrosity, with the girl you loved?"

"Are you kidding!?"

"Not kidding. Just a monster — and a close relative of mine."

230

Joel gave me a very long look, and moved his mouth into a figure "O" several times as though he was about to say something, but then thought better of it. He finally struck a completely theatrical perky smile, his mouth watermelon wide, and both forefingers uplifted like an orchestra conductor about to give the signal to start. "I'd just *laugh it off,*" he stated, lying in his throat, as we both knew. A pause. "Better than crying, ain't it?" He then began cornily reciting some inspirational Pennsy-Dutch dialect poem to the effect that "Shmile und de Vurrld shmiles vit you; Laugh und de Vurrld will roar; Howl und de Vurrld vill leave you, Und never come back any more. . ." But I wasn't in the mood to listen it out. I knew its lies by heart anyway: Yeh, yeh. ". . . But a shmile is not exbensive, Und covers a Vurrld of voes!" To hell with that!

"Sure," I snarled. "But what about sucking out the snake venom instead, and spitting it back in his face?!'"

"Dot's good too," Joel conceded. "Just be sure you got a good spitter. Lotsa times you piss at the moon, and it falls in your coat-collar instead. Take it easy, kid. Try laughing, like I said. That little girl is just as crazy about you as you are about her. *Nobody* can break you up."

231

I knew of course that he was lying just to cheer me up. For Gripe's sake, we were broken up already! He added some further happy homily of warning, about "never getting into an ass-kicking contest with a three-legged man." I just stuck out my lower jaw like Mussolini, said nothing, and left. Three-legged man, my ass! With a three-faced Emil Legman? Huh? What about that?! Those old boogers that wrote in the *Bible* about false witnesses, *they* knew. Old King David in the Psalms, he knew too: *"Deliver my soul, O Lord, from lying lips and from a deceitful tongue. What reward shall be given or done unto thee, thou false tongue? Even mighty and sharp arrows, with hot burning coals."* Right? Burning coals!

Everything is right there, in Maimonides' old medieval code — The Table Is Set. If I drop my *yarmulke,* I say a penitential prayer. If I drop my prayer-shawl, two penitential prayers. If I drop my prayer-book, got to fast all day. And him? What about *him!* Got to wait for heaven, for those "mighty sharp arrows" and those "hot burning coals," hey? And me? What about me? I get my heaven & hell right here on earth, don't I? He fixed it for me.

Maybe there are sins too awful to be punished for. The first time they let me hold the spare Scroll of the Torah, sitting very erect in synagogue on the platform while they read out of the other one, I asked old Mr. Ganz, the *shammos,* what the punishment would be if a person dropped the Scroll. He just looked at me funny, sucking on his moustache menacingly, and said, "Nobody could ever drop a Scroll. You would die first, and it'd fall on your body." He was right too. I looked it up in Graetz and *The Legends of the Jews.* When Rabbi Akiba got involved in the revolt of the Jews under Bar-Kochba against the Emperor Hadrian, the Romans caught him and crucified him and flayed the entire skin off his body while he was still alive. And when he called for a Scroll of the Law so he could glorify God's name with his dying breath, it fell helplessly from the cut muscles of his martyred arms. But it never hit the ground. The book says the angels held it up till Akiba could finish his prayer.

I suppose that's partly an exaggeration, but it's what I'd do if *I* were an angel. Some sins you don't need to be punished for. Akiba's prayer is the one you say standing up on Yom Kippur: The Great Pardon, "Kiddush ha-Shem." That God's name is sanctified by accepting martyrdom for your faith, rather than abjuring it to save your life. Nowadays they credit that high principle to *La Passionaria*, Dolores Ibarruri, the egeria of the Spanish Revolution: *"It's better to die on your*

233

feet than to live on your knees." But the idea is old, old, old, and always the same.

FORTUNATELY, there was all that idiotic brouhaha just then about the white shoes I was supposed to wear at my graduation, now only a few days away, and I tried doggedly to involve myself in it. The idea was that the girls were to wear whatever they liked, but the boys were all to be dressed exactly alike in blue wool jackets and white icecream pants with white shoes to match. Any kind of shoes, as long as they were white. Black-&-white were acceptable — just — but black shoes were absolutely out. And black shoes were all I had, or all that my mother was willing for me to buy a new pair of, with my share of the little chunk of family money set aside for practical shoes: one pair for each of us each year. Her emergency fund of five dollars would certainly not go for anything so frivolous as white shoes, and to be worn only one night!

Our family was always more or less poor, owing to my father's large gambling losses and only very moderate earnings at his job. And never were we poorer than now, just after the crest of the Depression, when my father had only recently swung a job as rate-

234

clerk in the Delaware, Lackawanna & Western railroad offices. For two years before that, after he lost his butcher-shop because of dangerously cutting his hand, he had been going from door to door all over Lackawanna County, buying up old gold for resale: mostly from mothers of families desperately hit by the Depression, whose last asset was their wedding ring. And my father would be there at the door, tremendously polite, to offer to buy that ring, or heirloom gold watchcases. And to scratch them on the inside with his little assaying touchstone strips, to find how many carats the gold proved, and then to weigh it meticulously on a tiny little brass scale fitted with its minuscule Troy weights into a polished yellow wooden box.

Quite a lot of men were out there then in America, buying up old gold that way, especially the simple broad wedding rings every woman wore. It was a lot higher-class work than selling spit-&-polish red apples on street corners, the way many men did during the worst years of the Depression from 1930 to 1933; and there was plenty of material available. The population was 120,000,000, which meant fifty million wedding rings, of which half were probably for sale if you pushed the newly-poor women just a little bit. Just old-fashioned flat gold bands. Obviously, millionaires' wives didn't have to sell their diamond-studded wedding rings for old gold; and the best figures available showed that four percent of the population had (and still has) ninety percent of the wealth of the world. Nobody will ever know how many millions of wedding rings were melted down then, to tide over us others, the newly-poor American families.

Ten years later the Germans netted about three million such rings from the assassinated Jewish population of Germany and Eastern Europe, but they used the far simpler system of just cutting the dead Jewish women's rings off — or fingers *with* the rings, if necessary, and knocking the gold teeth out of their skulls — after gassing them to death. My father didn't have to cut any women's fingers off. He was very polite about it. Anyhow, he preferred that, he said, to having to get the husbands' and grandfathers' gold watchcases separate from the timekeeping works inside, which was always a real hassle and took him a lot of time. To get the woman's wedding ring, you just had to convince her that her family needed the money — which she knew damn well — and that this was her last resort. And she slipped or yanked it off her own finger with a sigh, and maybe a little soap to ease the passage.

236

The way he described it at supper sometimes, it reminded me a lot of a simple seduction: not much different from talking a girl into slipping off her bloomers. But of course, I never made any such remark. My father evidently had lots of charisma that way, and could talk the legs off a wooden chair. But after sweeping my mother off her feet twenty-five years before, and into marriage, he never used it again for sex. I guess that would be my inheritance. I never got any other.

Anyhow, that's why there wasn't any money for white shoes for me then, even though my father had landed a steady job in the middle of the Depression as a railroad rate-clerk and by heroic methods. Not a very high-paid job, you may be sure. But Roosevelt's New Deal had just made thirteen dollars a week the compulsory minimum wage for full-time work for men or women — no children could now work full-time — and plenty of jobs, including my father's, had to be raised a couple of bucks to come up to that minimum. That's $670 a year, fella, including a two-week paid vacation in the "poverty line," that I'm below, being pegged now at $15,000 a year, it says here.

Of course, $13 a week would buy 130 loaves of bread then, at 10 cents apiece, and I don't know exactly how much a loaf of baker's bread costs today. My wife,

Judith, bakes our whole-wheat bread in the kitchen stove, and it is marvelous! So find out what the current price of a loaf of bread may be, and work it out in "constant dollars," chum. It may surprise you. And we've lived here that way on this olive-ranch in the South of France for twenty years, without running water, electricity, car, telephone, or toilet, and brought up our three kids here, and left all that rat-race behind us. Go thou and do thou likewise — if you have that luck. [Editor's Note: Hey! Wait a minute! No running water at first, but it was obtained from 1963 on.]

In any case, the white shoes weren't all there was to it. The high school graduation exercises were to include a couple of slices of unison singing by the whole class, in particular a gucky parody of a current popular song called "Wagon Wheels," itself an impudent plagiarism of the famous slow movement from Dvorak's "New World" symphony. I can't remember all the godawful words set to this piratical mess, except the final climax on the second *"You-oo!!"* There the presumably original Wagon Wheels were twice transmogrified and transported bodily up the scale — into "Cen — Tral — *High!!*" and beyond. And then down again, in mercilessly slow and treacly sincerity, like a particularly sadistic dentist drilling grimly into your back teeth:

238

Cen — Tral — *High!!* — We — Hail — You-oo!!
Thanks — Are — *Due* — To-hoo — *You-oo!!*
Central High! —We-he — Hail — *You!!*

As openers, there was also to be Sir Edward Elgar's ultra-corny "Pomp & Circumstance" march, with specially composed words sung by all the graduating girls, to the accompaniment of the school marching band. Meanwhile the graduating boys, lined up as a blue background on the stage, were to link arms and stamp out the rhythm, up & down, in unison — evidently with our new white shoes — while grunting out a sort of Indian war-chant responsory, or rhythmic sexual howl of dogged frustration, to wit: *"Unk-Gunk! Unk-Gunk!"* We were told just to "make sounds" but Unk-Gunk! was what came out.

Since the class numbered something like a hundred postulants of each sex, the result, which we were all required to practice together for the final three days of school, was to finish with us arriving onstage in the school auditorium *en masse,* singing and stamping our brave little adolescent hearts out something like this, with occasional spasmodic riffs & flourishes of the wild-scream variety by the band. These I believe were adapted from "The Stars & Stripes Forever," the patriotic Portuguese-American outpourings of that well known bandmaster-composer John Philip Sousa, and aren't Elgar's fault at all. The band begins, *presto marcato;* then settles into a sort of slow, surging jelly, as backdrop for the girls' ultra-slow singing and to pace us boys' manly footwork and grunts:

Band: Blankety-blank! Blankety-blank! -
Blankety-blank! Blank! Blank! - *BLANK!!!!*
Woo — Woo — Woo — Woo —
Girls: We — AMER — Ica's DAUGHH — Ters
—

GRAD —Joo — Ating — From HIGH — School
—

Boys: Unk-Gunk! — Unk-Gunk! *(white shoes, up &
down)*
Girls: WEEE — Welcome — You — HEEE —
Eere! —
PARR — Ents — And TEA — Chers — So —
DEAR!!

Boys: Unk-Gunk! Unk-Gunk! — Unk-Gunk! Unk-
Gunk!

Band: (Indescribable.)

I know you're not going to believe this, but it is an authentic fact that Sir Edward Elgar swole up and died authentically dead that very same spring in England. This was unquestionably — in my mind, anyhow — the direct if occult result of our graduation song, perhaps at an earlier rehearsal. If it were me, I would've died too. Just in a frenzy of shame. I've never admitted this to anyone before.

Things then got serious, as I knew they would, on the second morning of rehearsal when we were all supposed to be in our blue jackets, white shoes, and so forth. And there I was, the one & only rum-bum in black shoes. I ran around desperately, asking all the other fellows beginning with a rather nice quiet guy named Landis, who stood next to me alphabetically onstage, whether he had an extra pair of white shoes, or even black & white, that I could borrow just for the one night of the graduation ceremony. But it was no go. I even asked the two class closet-homosexuals, including plump, grinning Blatthofer, who played the piano and was the life-of-the-party on all possible class occasions; and thin, tight-faced Robert Higson, an early hifi buff whose father was a surveyor, and who tried to feel my ass unexpectedly while playing me my first Sibelius record (long-playing *and* hill-&-dale, at that early date) in his back yard.

241

I had wanted to leave at once but Higson reversed direction quickly and begged me to stay, his thin face all screwed tight in desperation. Then he played his *best* record, a hill-&-dale transcription of Borodin's "Polovetsian Dances" from *Prince Igor,* performed by some unknown New Jersey Ukrainian Church Choir, with organ, which was in fact one of the greatest orgies of recorded sound I ever heard before or since. We had to attach pennies to the back of the needle arm with a twisted rubber band, to get the needle pressure light enough to play. And he kept dropping the pennies on the floor in his terror that I would leave owing to his unintentional erotic lapse. But the music seduced me, and I stayed, and he was the soul of sexual restraint all the rest of the afternoon. Poor guy. But even Higson didn't have any white shoes to lend me now. No one could help me. Poor guy, me too. All us lost souls.

At the very last, when the rehearsal was breaking up after the second time around, with parodied Dvorak and apotheosized Elgar pouring out of everybody's ears — *Unk-gunk\ Unk-gunk* — a tall ugly boy I hadn't even asked came over and mumbled apologetically in my ear that he knew a way for me to get the white shoes I needed. And needed pretty desperately now, as I could see that some of the other

242

guys in the class were fixing to beat the shit out of me if I ruined their graduation ceremony, as they saw it, with — BLACK SHOES. Talk about being an honorary Negro! Now I knew how it felt, if I hadn't known already since the incident with the horseshit balls, in the alley behind William Prescott School, years back. Perhaps I should also mention I can't remember a single Negro boy or girl in my high school class, or public school either, for all that Scranton lies a good 100 miles above the Mason & Dixon line. In fact, I don't remember seeing any Negroes at all, until I came to live in New York, except maybe old Charlie, the combined janitor and *shabbos-goy* at our synagogue.

The boy who offered to help me get the white shoes was a big, funny-looking kid named Meyer Goldberg, one of the bright lights of our English class with the modern-minded Miss Oldham. Everybody in class was crazy about his act, on the days when Miss Oldham required us all to "Speak or Sing or Do Our Thing." Meyer's thing was a sort of wild, unintelligible patter, half talk and half gibberish, recited incredibly fast, and during the course of which he would simultaneously emit a fabulous counterpoint of assorted loud whistles, beeps & boops from between his front teeth. — "All with my mouth," he would announce innocently, pointing at his slightly gapped

243

front teeth with an enormous chessy-cat grin. This specialty of his invariably had all the other kids, and even staid, ears-laid-back Miss Oldham and her gold pince-nez rolling in the aisles.

Nobody could figure out exactly how Meyer Goldberg achieved this whistling-cum-bleeping production with just his tongue and teeth, and while talking a-mile-a-minute too, but we all found it grand and applauded him like mad, me louder than anybody else. Even though I knew bitterly that my own best and most emotional recitations before that very same class never could or did net the wild applause and laughter Meyer Goldberg's whistling act got — every time. And at the end of which, each time too, he would pull out of his pocket and hold up an amateurishly hand-drawn sign showing a small yellow bird with a big beak, inside a rickety cage, proudly lettered: "GOLDBIRD!" And we would all grin and wildly applaud again.

And so when you see today seething crowds of mesmerized kids and adults, tens of thousands strong, weeping and screaming in public arenas over some goony sex freak or non-singer like Bobby Dylan or David Bowie or Madonna or Mick Jagger or Prince or Michael "skinless" Jackson, on the television today, and from as far afield as Sydney, Australia, or Bergen,

244

Norway, or Osaka, Japan; don't imagine for a minnit that mass hysteria over imbecilic shit like that is anything new. Not at all, whether in entertainment or politics, or religion-shouting; nor in the worship of plain clay idols and the Golden Calf. Just try to figure how to keep your kids out. And yourself.

So, Meyer Goldberg was the boy who confided to me, in a shy and apologetic undertone, that he thought he could help get me the brand-new white shoes my soul thirsted for. It would be easy, he said. I simply had to meet him in my oldest work-clothes the very next morning, early, right on the corner of Gibson Street near my house. And we'd get to work immediately, by seven a.m. at the latest. "Before it gets hot," he added. "It's outdoor work."

And he was there right at the corner, as promised, promptly at a quarter to seven. And we pitched in. Just a block or two away from my house, there was a truly enormous trash-dump, house-high, that covered the whole city block between Gibson and Myrtle Streets, just before you got to the little mine-colliery, and cater-cornered from Stipp's Quarry. The trash trucks would arrive at that dump every Friday all day, with the dry trash, mostly house furnace ashes and assorted tin cans and cardboard cartons and wooden and metallic junk, all of which they would dump over the edge, helter-skelter, from high up along the alley, halfway up the hill. They'd been at it for years at that location, and the whole hill, opposite my old cowfield on the other side of Gibson, was a crumbling jungle of trash, including old twisted machinery, lots of busted ventilating fans, and even a few junky old Model T Ford cars, in among the mountains of caked ashes, collapsed cartons and rusted tin cans.

Our cue, Goldberg told me, was to manage to find the couple of dozen still useful — and therefore valuable — chunks of metal or whatnot mixed in at random among the junk. Whatever we found that looked possible we would stuff into two folded burlap sacks he had brought along, cutting it loose when necessary with a small metal hack-saw he had also provided in one of the sacks. He had done all this lots of times before, he assured me. When we would have enough, by the middle of the afternoon, we'd take our salvaged junk downtown and sell it to a wholesale junkman he knew, out toward Green Ridge. We'd make plenty, Goldberg assured me; at least three or four dollars each, if we had any luck finding the right kind of junk. It was really a lead-pipe cinch. He was full of cheerful assurance and I was willing to believe every word he said. It was my last chance.

246

Yes, indeed, I was very bucked up, and certain that he was right. We'd be back downtown from the junkman in Green Ridge and buying my white shoes by five o'clock easy. The stores all stayed open till six, at least, to get the trade from people coming out of their office jobs at five. And the white shoes surely wouldn't cost even as much as three bucks. And I would find some way to sneak off after the graduation ceremony and meet Tia on the sly — she had promised surely to be in the audience — on some pretext, and buy her a big chocolate icecream soda on my leftover cash.

But it was tough, dirty, hot work out in the early summer sun, hour after hour, grubbing filthily all morning through the rusted metallic junk that was to be miraculously transmuted into crisp new white calf shoes. Well, it was surely a lot better than exactly the same tough, dirty, hot work I'd done those Sunday mornings all through every summer for the last five or six years, ridiculously cutting down and hauling home in my express wagon great bales of ragweed, to stack right under my father's bedroom window, presumably to prevent his August hay-fever! And hauling home all the other kids' cuttings too, who I'd inveigled into the same imbecilic work — except that they got paid two cents a pound and I got paid nothing. And I had to weigh off their ragweed too!

As Goldberg and I worked and searched, crouching and stumbling with bent backs over the junk, I kept glancing up toward Stipp's Quarry. To me that quarry meant *Tia:* her open-mouthed kisses, her pulled-up skirt and bra, and her naked breasts for me to kiss and maul. Of course, I couldn't really even see the quarry, which was nothing but an enormous stone trench blasted out of the ground, blocks long and wide — and deep — like a miniature Grand Canyon. But I could see the busted old unpainted wooden fence around the high run, winding down, bumpy and unpaved, along Colfax Avenue, where she and I would sneak in after dark to lie on the high cliff and hug & kiss and yearn, our hands avid and groping inside each other's underwear. Dumb, damn, shy kids! And I was thinking bitterly and compulsively too, how I certainly ought to kill my father now for what he had done. But then I'd get the electric chair, wouldn't I, and never see Tia again. That was the bad part. I wouldn't really mind dying for the revenge I knew would be deeply right; but never to see Tia again? — not even to hear her voice over some celestial telephone? No! that was more than I could bear to imagine.

248

By noon Goldberg and I were pretty darn hot and dirty, and went back to my house to wash up. The sleazy damp ashes had filled our sneakers by the end of just the first half hour, and our socks were floating in a marmalade mush of gray ash when we took them off. I gave him a pair of mine to change into in the bathroom with me, while my mother was calling us to come to lunch. She knew we were skipping school, but it obviously didn't matter. It was practically the last day of the school term and of high school. Damn 'em all! She wouldn't say a thing like that, but she knew what we felt.

Goldberg and I sat on the front porch steps after lunch, and dumped our metal swag out of the burlap bags onto the yard-wide sidewalk. It looked like a pretty sorry lot of twisted chrome and junk to me.

"How much do you figure all that's worth?" I asked dubiously.

"Well, to tell you the truth," he said, "maybe about a buck."

We stared at the pile. Pretty grim. At that rate we'd only have two bucks' worth at most by the end of the day. And here it was nearly one o'clock already. You couldn't ever really get a good pair of white leather shoes for only two bucks; a dollar ninety-five, the way the customer-brainwash prices in the stores' advertisements slyly expressed it.

"White sneakers?" Goldberg suggested without much conviction. "Low ones would only be about a buck." I didn't answer. We both knew I'd never get away with going to our graduation wearing sneakers, even white ones. The other guys'd kill me. They'd *mobbilize* me.

"I'd give you my own pair, and maybe not go," Goldberg offered heroically. "I'm not going to college anyhow, the way you are. But I got real small feet, and narrow. Prob'ly a size-'n'-a-half smaller than you. Mine'd never fit you."

I looked at his feet. It was true too. "I really appreciate that, Meyer," I said dispiritedly. "But let's just forget all about it."

"No, sirree!" he insisted. He smacked one fist into the palm of the other, like a baseball catcher preparing for a real fast pitch. "I got an idea! We're going at this the wrong way. You just follow me an' do everything I do. And *ixnay ackenray!* — y'unnerstand? Don't say one word."

We trotted all the way down Harrison Hill now on the double, with our jute sacks over our shoulders, and across the bridge, me following blindly. Popped into the first beer-joint we came to on Moosic Street.

250

They were all open again for a year or so, since the repeal of Prohibition that everybody said was responsible for Franklin D. Roosevelt and the Democrats winning the election. Nobody wanted fat-faced Herbert Hoover anymore anyhow, and everybody figured he was responsible for the Depression. Well, maybe not responsible, but he sure had done all the wrong things to try to stop it. Most of the beer-joints were now newly equipped, after being shut tight since 1919, and doing a landoffice business. Especially at noontime and evenings, when the working-stiffs rushed in clamoring for their first glass of beer after a long day of work.

A glass of beer: that cost a nickel. A schoonerful was a dime. And lots of places still had free lunches at all hours, like in the Good Old Days before the War. Of course, adolescent kids like Meyer and me couldn't drink standing at the bar at all, but we could still go in with our twenty cents jingling in a bucket for the barman to fill, and that way rush the growler home for grownups. If we took a couple of sips of beer on the way home, nobody knew or cared. I myself could never stand the taste of the stuff until years later, and found it horribly bitter.

Meyer asked the barman very politely, if we could go down to the cellar to look around for old junk. The man inattentively pointed to the inside door down, and nodded sure. Two kids. Down in the cellar my mentor & guide suddenly seemed galvanized, and rushed around wildly, obviously looking for some very special thing which he did not find. He pulled me up the stairs immediately and we hurried on to the next beer-joint. The second crack out of the box Meyer found what he was after right away: a sort of small L-shaped piece of gray pipe sticking out of a dusty old beer-barrel, seemingly attached to nothing. He tried violently to unscrew it, getting me to help him. We sweated over it like stinkpots, the veins bulging at our foreheads, but we couldn't budge it. Finally Meyer snatched out his metal hacksaw from the burlap bag, and sawed that thing through in a jiffy, casting alert sideways looks the whole time up at the top of the staircase to the bar. He threw the pipe-end into his bag and we scrammed out of there fast, with a quick "Thanks, mister," to the barman upstairs.

It was clear that this pipe we had found was something valuable, but I couldn't figure out exactly what it was, and was somehow shy about asking. By the end of the afternoon we had bagged three of them in all: two L-shaped, and one quite a bit bigger, in a long lazy-S shape. On our way to the junkyard now, way over on Capouse Avenue by the railroad tracks, to

252

cash in our haul, Goldberg finally explained to me what they were. Three block-tin joints from the old beer-barrel installations from before prohibition, and worth plenty.

"We stole them, didn't we?" I sort of demurred.

"Nah! They don't want 'em anymore. I bet they don't even know what they are. They have barrels with a pump now under the bar upstairs. It's just junk."

The man at the junkyard on Capouse was as grimy as we were by now and pretty rough-looking. I couldn't miss noticing a big ear-ring he wore in one ear, and he also sported an absolutely enormous gold wristwatch. He seemed to know Meyer very well. Later Meyer told me he was a Gypsy and used to be King of the tribe, but now the other Gypsies wouldn't talk to him because a woman had poured a pisspot on his head out of an upstairs window and disgraced him forever. Gypsies were very proud, and had a whole code of honor like you wouldn't believe. All their women were whoors, and only pretended to be begging or telling fortunes; but only to outsiders — not Gypsies. If they ever fucked another man of their own tribe, besides their husbands, their husbands would cut off their nose with a butcher-knife and kill them; and then the two men would have to fight it out to the death with knives. It all seemed perfectly reasonable to both of us, though pretty dangerous.

The Gypsies all came from Hungary — everybody knew that — just like my parents had. That's why they were all such good musicians, when they weren't being junkmen. My father's family had been horse-butchers for ages, I knew, and he had told us kids many a story about how incredibly sly the Gypsy men were as horse-knackers and stealers. Two Gypsies snuck over once from the Rumanian side of the Carpathians and stampeded all the horses of an entire Imperial Mounted Regiment through a mountain pass in the night, and no one ever saw a single one of the horses again. And one of the two Rumanian Gypsies had been a cripple and a hunchback too! Tom Mix and the rest of the mere cowboys at the Nickelette, Saturday afternoons, just weren't in the show.

My father said the Gypsies were all descended from Lank Timoor — it took me decades to find out he was talking about Tamerlane — who was also a hunchback, and had come from China centuries before with his horde of wild-eyed horsemen who killed half the people in Europe, worse than Napoleon! But they stopped when they got to Budapest because it was so beautiful there, and they made a deal with Don John of

254

Austria, who beat the Turks at the Battle of Lepanto — a sea-battle as it happened — that the Gypsies would supply the whole Austro-Hungarian cavalry with horses. When they didn't steal them, that is. In fact, they *did* steal them, but only from the other side of the mountains each time. They were also incredible riders and could stand on their heads on the saddle while their horses galloped along at full speed, and juggle knives at the same time! My father said he saw that himself when he was young man in the Austro-Hungarian army. Well, I knew now that he was just an insane liar, but I also suspected that our mangy couple of, well, er, *promoted* beer-pipes weren't going to impress the Gypsy junkman much.

"What'cha got this time?" he asked Meyer dourly.

"Three joints. Just like you said. And one of them is pretty big." He dumped them out of the sack carefully right on the ground at our feet, with the rest of our morning's junk.

The Gypsy pushed at the pipe-ends contemptuously with his toe, his mouth pursed out in a disgusted look. That was so he wouldn't have to give us what they were really worth, I knew. Old Mr. Stück, the second-hand bookseller on Washington Avenue, had pulled the same trick on my sister Ruth and me,

255

the one & only time we ever went to sell him back some books — I was just there to help carry them — to buy a big present for my mother on her fortieth birthday. The junkman got out a one-hand sword & buckler scale and weighed our block-tin pipes very carefully, until the sword-scale swayed into balance in his upthrust fist. He looked like a statue representing Justice. Then he gave us the astounding sum of twelve dollars, all in silver dollars. I nearly fell over. Twelve bucks for three pieces of pipe! More than a man could earn in a week! And just for three dirty chunks of tin pipe!

Meyer and I divided the money outside at my insistence. He actually wanted me to take it all! He didn't need any money, he assured me, anyhow not this week. He was only trying to help me. I wondered silently how often he had visited the junkyard before. The Gypsy junkman seemed to know him well. We rushed back downtown, with Meyer telling me about Gypsies the whole way. When we got to the Endicott shoe store, they were already shut. So was Thom McAn's up the street. All shut. It was past six o'clock. Well, it didn't matter. I could get the white shoes with my six dollars the next morning, easy.

"Can I tell my mother this money is honest?" I asked worriedly as we parted, eyeing the six silver dollars in my hand. We were standing at the streetcar stop now, waiting for the Petersburg trolley. I was tired out and sweaty, and planned exceptionally to ride home. I was rich!

"Sure it's honest!" Meyer laughed. "We worked all day for it, didn't we? And you saw the junkman weigh it on the scales, fair & square. Just don't tell your mother *anything!* I never do. What are you, a little kid?" And off he went, up the street, in an arpeggio of miraculous whistles, burps and beeps, to end the day in glory. Now there was a great guy, I thought, staring out of the window of the Petersburg trolley home. A really great guy.

A FUNNY thing. Here I'd gone to high school for four years in New York and Scranton, and the first *real* male friend I ever made was on the very last day of school. Well, I guess the Ratajski brothers were my friends too, but only about music. And their mother didn't really like me either; I guess because I was Jewish. She had this big plaster bust of the anti-Semitic Polish dictator Pilsudski right on their parlor table, and practically idolized it. And they never did succeed in teaching me to play the Chopin Polonaise from notes,

257

the way they could. Yes, and read off which was which, just from Leschetizski's thematic index at the front of the music book, the way you'd read a cornflakes box. Well, what about Mel Cantor, and Jack and Larry, and all those kids in the Bellamists' Club? And Cy Endfield and Izzy, and Jimmy Kennedy? No, not real friends: just guys I knew and talked politics with. That's not the real thing. Sweating over all that greasy junk all morning with Meyer Goldberg, and getting ashes in our shoes, that was something else. I could see that now.

Yes, a funny thing. His saying about loaning me his own shoes made me decide not to buy any white shoes at all. My mother was right. It was idiotic to spend that much money on a fancy pair of shoes I'd only wear one night for a fleeting ceremony. What kind of fashion snobs were those high school teachers trying to turn us into, anyhow? Like girls! I didn't even *want* the shoes now. White shoes. Ridiculous! Didn't care a darn about the whole blinking graduation either. Goldberg was right about that too. Just an empty ceremony for wet-behind-the-ears kids and their sentimental parents. Ceremony or no, I was out of school now, wasn't I? Who *cared* if I went and marched up & down and grunted "Unk! Gunk! —

258

Unk! Gunk!"   And who ever heard of anything stupider?

My own parents would be terribly disappointed, of course, if they couldn't be out there in the auditorium at that cruddy graduation ceremony, with old Jonesy, the leftover wartime chemist-principal, handing you your rolled-up diploma with a ribbon around it, and all that middle-ages baloney. Yes, and me going "Unk! — Gunk!" and stamping up & down in time with about a hundred other boys. Oh, well. Though I no longer gave a stinking damn what my father might want — not ever, nevermore! — I felt I probably shouldn't disappoint my mother. I knew I meant the whole world & all to her, being her only man-child and all that; and me "going out in the world," as she saw it. Anyhow, I knew my mother certainly did love me and would put her hand in the fire for me; and I loved her very much too.

So I did go downtown again that last morning, but not for the shoes. I simply went to get a short haircut, which would use up the odd 25¢ change from my sixth silver dollar, after I'd bought a clutch of 8¢ streetcar tokens the night before and gave all but the one I'd used to my mother for a present. That way she wouldn't have to walk home from the shopping all the way uphill from the hospital on Quincy Avenue, seven different times, when I'd be away working all summer, the way I'd planned. My sisters would never be able to fake the punch-hole dates in the streetcar transfers for my mother with a whittled matchstick the way I could — my main fiscal dishonesty so far in life, until those dubiously boosted block-tin pipes just yesterday. Sawed loose from the beer-joint barrels with a hacksaw; I couldn't deny that.

But the place I usually went for my man-style haircuts down on Penn Avenue, where my father used to go to, and had showed me, was already shut for vacation. Some kids had their mother cut their hair — just all around with a bowl, when they were really little, in grade school. It made them all look like greenhorns, immigrant kids fresh off the boat. My mother hadn't cut my hair since I was twelve and going away to the Yeshiva in New York. When I came back, and was Bar-Mitzvah, she said I was legally *a man* now. And she refused even to trim my hair any more, on the brilliant pre-Freudian grounds that *"Men hate women who cut their hair."* That meant both ways to her: women who cut the men's hair, or who cut their own hair short, the way tons of girls and women were now doing in America, and it always looked as lousy to me as it did to her.

After all, hadn't she run away from Europe so as not to have to cut her hair off when she'd get married? She also told me that men especially hate women who cut men's hair, "because they stand in back of them and *scare* them. But the manicurist-girls sit in front, and hold their hands, and all the men are crazy about them." She knew. My mother wasn't just smart about bidding at contract bridge. She knew about lots of other things too, and was never afraid to say what she thought. But she also knew when it was diplomatic to shut up, something that my father never learned to do. Me neither, I guess.

Wandering around town, my last morning as a high school student "on the hook," I fell into another barbershop just behind the Hotel Jermyn that looked extremely bright and clean. And what was my surprise when I found there another of my classmates, about to graduate with me that same day, named Danny LoJorio, dressed in a gray cotton utility jacket and glumly sweeping the cut hair up off the floor with a large pushbroom. We talked in undertones while Danny's father, who was the barber, worked briskly on another customer in the big, whirling, pump-'em-up chair, occasionally turning to snap an irate order at Danny in Italian.

Danny said he wouldn't be going to the dress rehearsal at school that afternoon, with the entering march and stamping garbage. He had to work, he said. We talked over the graduation ceremony briefly. How the only one outstanding person was the valedictorian, who got the highest marks in the graduating class by blinding himself with homework every night for four years. That meant he'd now have the honor of giving the main speech to the parents, and wearing a pleated black academic gown with long full sleeves and a black mortarboard hat! The valedictorian, and the class president, who also gave a speech, were the only ones who counted. The rest of us were just marching robots. Who wanted it anyhow? To be a greasy grind and a glad-hander for years — yes, and never skip a single day of school, either! — just for the right to be dressed at the ceremony for one evening in a medieval black pleated gown, like an old lady, and a funny hat.

This time the valedictorian was to be Frank Shoemaker, a typical studious grind. Nobody in the class liked him much. He was nearly as unpopular with the other boys as I was, even though he had lopsidedly tried to launch himself in school politics too. But you didn't have a showing in school politics if you weren't really very popular, or on one of the varsity athletic teams. Not Frank! He wanted the worst way to be

262

class president, but couldn't make it owing to the other students' classic hatred of high academic achievers, something I knew painfully all about, practically since kindergarten. My own marks in high school hadn't been anything sensational. I did manage to get on the honors list, but that was all. Too busy dreaming about Communism and girls, to do the necessary swotting and studying. The half-year I spent in College later, I did disastrously worse, and for the same reason. And that was all the academic education I ever got.

Danny's father cut my hair. Very crisp and capable, he was, spouting only a few of the usual barber's bromidic remarks about the weather, etc., but whirling me around in the chair often and with much extra snapping of his little long pointed scissors in midair. At the end he dusted my shoulders off with the big brush — and my neck with the talcum brush — that was to hide the dirt on the back of your neck if you'd forgotten to wash there first — and he tried to talk me into letting him put stinkadora in my hair, with me doughtily refusing of course. All barbers had that nuttiness about wanting to make you smell like a whoorhouse. Or maybe it was the extra ten cents for the hair-goop that they were after. Anyhow, I hated to have my hair plastered down flat, even with water. Still do.

Danny's father then commanded his son to shine my shoes. "You wanna shoeshine, don'tcha?" he demanded of me as an afterthought.

"Naw! No shine."

"Sure you do. Gonna gradjuate today, ain'tcha? You an' my son Daniel." Then virulently, *"Danny! Shine his shoes!!"*

Danny stood there like Lot's wife in Sodom, turning to a pillar of salt with the pushbroom in his hand. He was turning green and red too, like the painted statues in a sideshow, but not reaching for his brushes and cloth and polishing paste.

"Ya deef?!" his father almost screamed. "Give the customer a shine!!!"

I jumped out of the barber-chair and flung my quarter down briskly on the counter to pay for the haircut. "No shine," I assured this tragic Italian Abraham and his not-yet-sacrificed son Isaac. "We'll be wearing white shoes at the graduation."

"Danny! Shine his shoes!!" I could see my father wasn't the only struggling European immigrant, lost between overweening pride and uncontrollable jealousy of his educated neo-American son, Mr. Success. "I want my son to be all things and have all the things that *I* could never have or be!" Oh yeah? And suddenly I could see myself again, so clearly in the

264

intense slanting sun of those early Sunday mornings for all those years before — my father's pride & joy, the Leader in Israël in-the-bud — with my big coal-shovel and filthy brown-wet broom, bagging up the newly-slaughtered beeves' still-juicy bullshit, in the deserted killing-pens of the Franklin Beef Company in Minooka, P.A. to fertilize our kitchen garden. *"Danny! Shine his shoes!!"* Blessed shall be the beaten and the humiliated, for they shall be all their fathers' joy.

THE GRADUATION dress-rehearsal that afternoon went off without too much of a hitch for me personally. As I knew would happen, my classmates were more than ready to beat me to a pulp, especially the couple of athletic jocks still sore at me for having accidentally kicked their football hero Carle Aldren in the balls when he had me on the ground. At the very least they were anxious to bloody my nose and doubtless my newly-bought creamy white icecream pants, thus to be dripped upon for my unforgivable sin in not having white shoes to wear.

Instead of expressing my due remorse about the shoes — and by implication for desecrating their idol, Aldren's, sacred balls, also with a sinful shoe — I tried to swagger it out, and told them boldly that *they* were all wearing white shoes because they were Capitalists, and the couple of guys amongst them in black-&-white shoes were Socialists. Whereas, I, the Class Communist, was appropriately shod in black like an honest working-stiff. In other words, — "A plague on both your houses," and Damn you all! Things then began to heat up for me on the sidewalk outside the main entrance to the high school, where we were all milling about waiting for our signal to march in. I was saved at the last minute by my next-in-line mate, Landis, telling everyone in a loud undertone behind his hand that my family was too poor to afford white shoes and I already tried to borrow a pair from him.

Then we marched in. *Unk! Gunk!* — Up & down! — Buzz-fuzz! Fuzz-buzz! Gunk! Gunk! *Gunk!* Like the perfect little brainwashed soldiers they were preparing us to be. The band played. The boys marched. The girls sang. Everything right on signal. *Date:* First day of summer, 1934 — just five years till World War II. Yep, everything right on signal.

(The Band:) Blankety-blank! Blankety-blank!
Blankety-blank, Blank, Blank, Blank, *BLANK!!!!*
(The Girls:) We — Amer — Ica's — DAUGHHHH —Ters —

266

Grad —Joo — Ating — From HIGH! — School!
(Us Boys:)   Unk! Gunk! Unk! Gunk!
Unk! Gunk! Unk! Gunk! (Stamp! Stamp! Stamp!)

I could hear it all transmobulated inside my head, just like in *All Quiet on the Western Front.* "Shoulder Armmmms!! Fix Bayonets!! CHARGE!!! — Whatsamatter, you yellow-bellied fag bastards? Ya wanna live forever?! Charge!! And turn that bayonet in your fellowman's guts, so you can rip them out blue on the ground!!" I could hear it. I swear I could hear it! Just like Joan of Arc: the very words. Over that pitiful, maddening Unk! Gunk! — Unk! Gunk! — *Unk! Gunk! Gunk!!*

And there, to close the actual ceremony just a few hours later, was our victorious Valedictorian too, the big winner in the lesson-studying sweepstakes. Resplendent now, leaning triumphantly against the lectern at stage center with the Salutatorian, in the flowing black gown befitting his four hard years of never-missing-a-single-day study. Rehearsing over in their minds surely the brave openings of prepared speeches. How would it go? "Our Respected Teachers and Beloved Parents! Here, With Grateful Hearts and Open Arms, We Welcome You. . ." Yes. Our Beloved Parents especially.

267

Secretly I felt I owed it to myself to louse things up somehow, at the real ceremony that night, but there wasn't much I could do as just one cog in the marching line of blue jackets and white icecream pants (and shoes). I did my best, though — and little enough it was — by slouching in as I came onstage, instead of marching in phallically upright, stiff & strong, and *with a snap!* as we were admonished to do by Coach Bob Fitzke, to be sure, who had been drilling us and giving us our cues.

Unfortunately, there were only two lines of boys, so me and Landis, at the "L" in the middle of the alphabet, were all the way out at one end of the stage. And standing right in the wings there, too, to monitor the show, were Coach Bob Fitzke and a bald, elderly, heavyset math teacher I didn't know except by reputation as the main anti-Semite in the school. Next after football captain Carle Aldren and Miss X, that is, who was still competing with me to the death for my platonic Polish *shikse* girlfriend, Nadja.

Well, I hadn't hardly started sinking into my intended disruptive slouch, in among all the stiff & strong and snappy other diploma-marchers, when I felt a terrific punch in the small of my back that nearly turned my slouch into a vertical leap, like a powerfully administered rectal goose. And a cold-steel whisper

268

hissing behind me, "Straighten UP! you red-assed son of a *bitch!*" It was ramrod-me from that point on. Unk! Gunk! — Unk! Gunk!

Never really knew positively if it was clean-living, right-thinking, vitamin-crunching Coach Bob Fitzke or Old Baldy, the anti-Semite, that hit me in the back, but I can't believe it was Fitzke. I'm pretty sure it was Baldy. Coach Bob Fitzke never ever swore with a big-big D, or any other way. The worst he'd ever even say to his football team when he found them insufficiently aggressive was to call them pantywaists, the fellows said. Or to round them up, after the half-time break in the game, with a barbed *macho* shaft-up-the-arse of, "All right now, let's go, Girls!" Anyhow, Coach Bob Fitzke would certainly not be capable of hitting even a class-traitor like me with his back turned. Unsportsmanlike. In the end — no kidding — that right-thinking son-of-a-gun Fitzke was the most inspiring teacher I ever had. Unk! Gunk! — Unk! Gunk!

CHAPTER 12

BREAKING OUT

I COULDN'T stay in the house when evenings came. It wasn't the heat; it was just that nothing interested me anymore. My hundreds of cards of pasted-up jokes from the *Literary Digest* were just kid stuff. And translating the *Talmud* into English was pretentious bosh. Who wanted the *Talmud* in the twentieth century anyway, besides me? — Maybe. Swing into that singsong tune now, nasal and querulous: "An *aig* laid on a holiday, asks Rabbi Shamai, is it sacred or profane?" Bunkum! What crap! But when I asked Rabbi Tannenbaum something sensible, like whether menstruation is *fleishige* or *parvah*, that was the end of my *Talmud* lessons. Those guys with their combed black beards were living a thousand years ago in their heads — two thousand years ago! There was no more time for that. It was high summer now.

I padded out of the house in my little white shorts and big sneakers. My mother was reading the *Saturday Evening Post* on the porch-swing in the failing light.

"I'm going over to Manny's," I told her.

"Wear a shirt. The mosquitoes will eat you alive."

I went back and put on the brown pongee shirt with long balloon sleeves that Ruth had given me. She swore it didn't look like a girl's. I knew it did, but I didn't care. It made me feel like Athos, Porthos and d'Artagnan. I only wished it had a ruffled jabot at the neck. The Scarlet Pimpernel! — Reaching down from my powerful white, shaggy-maned Arab steed to pluck a wayside maiden up onto the saddle behind me, her soft titties plunging up out of her tightly-laced thingummy and squeezing tight against my back as she hung on for dear life. Gal-lup, gal-lup, gal-lup! — cheating the red-stained guillotine of its wonted prey! And then, on the greensward, by the light of the stars . . . Wow!

As I got to the corner the streetlight came on. Peewee Smith and sharp-faced Vince Hopkins, the postman's son, were talking baseball with the most

271

terrible earnestness, teetering on the curb under the streetlight. I just waved and turned down Gibson. At Jaffee's store on the corner of Prescott, I could read the marquee on the Nickelette halfway up the block: Claudette Colbert and Clark Gable in *It Happened One Night*. You betcher ass it happened one night! She was French. Wasn't she the one that had the nerve to show her tits bare in *Henry the Eighth?* No, that was *The Sign of the Cross*, that my father didn't want us to see. Anyhow, nobody had that incredible, faraway Chinese face except Myrna Loy. Just like Tia — the spitting image! She was the one I always jerked off over, imagining her stark naked. Wow!! Well, Sylvia Sidney looked a lot like Tia too, with that little heart-shaped face, but she was always suffering so. You wouldn't catch Myrna Loy making a fuss like that. She'd get in there and poison 'em, or stick 'em with a long hatpin, or I don't know what. Anyhow, she wouldn't just suffer. I turned down the alley right before Irving Avenue and into the Grossmans' big back yard.

The whole tribe was sitting out in the grape arbor testing Manny's great new electrical idea. He'd run a long wire out from the parlor porch, and now they had the table radio inside the arbor in the dark. And the music was pouring out of it! Manny's touch of genius was that the iron arbor itself was the aerial.

You had to hand it to him. The Symphonette Strings: that was their evening program, advertising automobiles. I had seen their picture in the Sunday paper rotogravure section once. The main violinist was completely bald. I knew it wasn't true you couldn't get an erection if you were bald, but I'll bet girls didn't like bald heads much either.

The Symphonette Strings, with Lily Pons' husband conducting. I couldn't remember his name. I didn't know what they were playing, but it was very beautiful. I slipped into a corner of the big wooden sofa-swing, and mumbled hello to everybody whose face I could make out. There was Manny, and his father and mother in the big chairs. The old man was great; leaning back in his expansive European way with his legs stretched out and ankles crossed, his pants-belt unbuckled and his thumbs in his armpits, clipped under imaginary suspenders. Mr. Grossman was the leading light of the miners' union in Scranton and Lackawanna County, and proud of it! He only worked in the office though; I wondered if he had ever chopped coal. Their sexy daughter-in-law Eleanor was coming down the kitchen steps now with her other sister-in-law, Sharon. They had the porch light on but only for a minute, just enough to see their way. They were carrying big lemonades with ice and spoons in

273

them, on a tray. I said hello, quietly so as not to spoil the music.

It was very dark, and lovely in the dark except for the mosquitoes. Eleanor sat down with her lemonade in front of the radio, churning her ice around in the glass to make it tinkle. Sharon sat down in the wooden swing next to me. That was the only place left. I don't know why I did it — it was absolutely insane — but I dropped my hand, face up, on the flat pillow on the swing beside me just as she sat down, so that without knowing it she was sitting on my hand. Sharon did not realize what it was, and wriggled her ass slightly, expecting to smooth out the bump in the pillow that was me. I didn't move at all. But after a moment I began tightening and loosening my hand, like a velvet claw, right under the soft crumpet of her crotch. This time Sharon knew it wasn't a bump in the pillow, but she said nothing and didn't resist. When my hand became wholly insistent, she turned her face to look at me in the dark. The music had come to an end and they were announcing something else. Sharon's eyes searched mine profoundly.

"The music is beautiful, isn't it?" I babbled.

"Beautiful!" Sharon agreed, this time arching her butt backwards slightly when the music began again, so that my fingers were now slipping into that

274

long, flat groove I was making in the thin stuff of her dress where she sat. In the dark she began waltzing her ass with the utmost delicacy against my hand. I curled my center finger into a knuckle and squeezed it up into the groove. It was pitch dark now. Somewhere a car went by out on Irving Avenue. I don't know how long this went on. I was mesmerized by the slowness of my own motions, and the slow, definite rhythm of Sharon's response. Suddenly the back door opened on the brightly-lighted kitchen, and I could see the silhouette of Manny's elder brother Arnie, Sharon's husband, coming down the back porch stairs.

"We're out here, Arnold!" Sharon called, waving to him in the dark and giving a couple of extra bounces on my hand for good luck. "Come on out; I've saved a drink for you!"

She got up then, giving my shoulder a tremendous squeeze as she stood up, as though using it to help her rise. Under cover of her motion I put my hand frankly up her dress, clutching at the back of one silk-clad knee. But she ran away, and up the stairs, giving Arnie a dutiful peck on the lips as she passed into the Grossmans' kitchen. The arbor-party broke up soon after that. And I was hooked. Sharon was a lot older than me, of course. Married too, but I didn't care. The next day I came round in the afternoon to see Manny again. Sharon was still there, sitting in the parlor reading a novel. I put a record on the phonograph. We talked. She explained to me that they would soon be moving into this big subdivided old house on Mulberry Street. Arnie worked late almost every night — he was getting to be a big lawyer around Scranton — and Sharon wanted to know if I'd consider coming to baby-sit for them Thursdays, which would be the maid's night off, so Sharon and Arnie could go to the movies together. Maybe one other night too, if the maid took an extra evening off. The baby, Alex, was only three years old. He'd be no trouble, really. I could read — they had all the latest books — and eat anything I wanted out of the refrigerator. I said yes to everything. Sharon would come by my house that evening in her car on the way downtown and tell me if it was all settled. I explained eagerly just where I lived. How much money would I want, she asked?

"Money?" I said stupidly. Who cared about money?

"Arnold will give you union rates; that's a dollar and a half. But you'll have to stay each time till we get home even if it's late."

"You bet!" I agreed, enthusiastically. I wanted to grab her right then & there, but Sharon evaded me

276

easily and tripped upstairs. At the landing she turned and smiled down at me charmingly. I was too young to recognize it as a smile of triumph. Nor would I have cared if I had. I was thinking how lovely she looked, with her halo of soft brown hair — sort of like Sylvia Sidney.

When Sharon slid along in front of our house about seven o'clock in their big family car, and gave one discreet honk of the horn, I was out of the house in a flash: long pants, sleeveless sweater, hair slicked back. I was ready. I jumped in beside her, and she put the car silently in gear and started down the hill. We were both suddenly embarrassed. She told me about the car. It was Arnold's old red Stutz Bearcat, that he'd had since he went to college at Princeton. All coal mine organizers' sons who went to Princeton, I assumed, drove Stutzes. But it was Sharon's car now, for doing all the shopping. Arnold had a new Auburn sports model to run around in for his work. It had beautiful lines, didn't I think? Actually I liked the red Stutz better: it looked roomier, in case it rained or you had passengers in the rumble-seat.

We drove around Nay-Aug Park a while trying to think of something to talk about that we had in common, other than what we both knew damn well we had in common. Sharon asked me about my name, and

277

I told her Gershon was my Hebrew name. On my birth certificate it said George. My father had lost his nerve on the way to the vital statistics office. Well, Sharon was her Hebrew name too. She liked it better. She had been, er, christened Shirley. We both laughed cozily. My family had wanted me to be a rabbi, I told her, but they were just about over that. I myself planned to be a psychologist. Or maybe a musician. I was crazy about music, although I didn't know very much about it. Sharon said she had an uncle who was an orchestra conductor in Germany, a very good one. He'd had to leave because of the Nazis. He was in Amsterdam now. That reminded me that I had an aunt in Vienna who was a concert pianist. My mother often mentioned her. She was really my mother's aunt. Her husband was the concert-master of the Philharmonic Orchestra there. Well, actually, he wasn't really her husband.

"Oh, what does that matter?" said Sharon. It didn't matter a bit, we agreed. Sharon said they'd probably have to leave Vienna too.

We parked in the dark near the entrance to Lovers' Lane, though I didn't tell Sharon that's where I was piloting her. We walked down the long unpaved walk, past the caged buffalo and the big boulder-covered bear-pit. The buffalo was standing there,

278

humpbacked, rubbing up against his iron fence in the half-light, his head enormous, his fur all shaggy and moth-eaten and fitting him rather poorly. In front of the bear-pit was a broken bag of peanuts on the ground. I wondered idly what dumbbell had tried to feed peanuts to the bears. Bears eat people.

At the bottom of the walk, just over the Falls and the little twisting wooden bridge, was the stone seat outside the safety railing, where Tia and I used to sit. I was going to invite Sharon to sit there with me now, but something stopped me. Too dangerous at that hour, in the dark. Instead we walked back up the path halfway, and silently paused by a tree to kiss. Her mouth was lovely, and alive with motion as she kissed me back. I took hold of one of her breasts through her dress; it was very soft, and made me quite wild. We stumbled further away from the path, and fell together in the underbrush.

I was all for ripping her panties away and fucking her right then & there, but Sharon slowed me down simply by refusing to let me stop kissing her. I got my hand inside her crotch, and was lathering her up practically into a foam. My own state was beyond discussing, my long pants all bulging and dripping with my overflowing juices. My fly would be stained. Sharon unbuttoned me daintily, to the degree it hadn't

279

already happened by itself, and wound her soft hand and fingers around the tip of my prick, only half drawing me out through my undershorts. I wriggled like an insane porpoise trying to get free of my pants, but it was no use. She began stroking and massaging the head of my prick with her cupped fingers and hand, and I knew I would come soon if she kept it up.

"No!" I muttered against her cheek. "Not this way! Lay back!"

I was prepared to shove her back and rape her if she resisted, but she didn't resist at all. She lay back willingly, her fingers still holding my prick. But instead of sinking it into her as I should have, I remembered suddenly that it was my duty to be gentle and romantic, and began kissing her soft belly. Her panties had fallen away somewhere by now. She opened up her knees wide, like the pages of a book, and I was nuzzling her pussy-hair with my nose. Soon I was splayed out before her on the ground licking her cunt wildly, and drinking her juices which were wonderfully plentiful and marvelously perfumed.

"Oh, God!" she kept moaning. "Oh, my God!" Then without meaning to, I shot all over the ground, and Sharon wouldn't let me fuck her after that for fear I'd give her a baby.

The next night was just the same — the Stutz Bearcat softly honking for me at sundown, and us making love in the bushes of Lovers' Lane, but this time I ended in her hand instead of on the ground. I didn't want it that way, but Sharon's practiced fingers were like a baby octopus mouthing my prick.

When I got home my mother was waiting up for me. She was sitting knitting on the sofa, with the big afghan around her legs.

"What was that horn-honking?" she wanted to know, without preamble. "I don't let the girls run out when fellows honk for them, and you can't do it either. Let your date come in the house."

"That wasn't a *date*, Ma," I lied. "That was Mrs. Grossman. You know — where I baby-sit for them Thursday nights."

"Some hot-looking baby," my mother commented, tying another ball of yarn into her work. "A real cradle-snatcher, if you ask me."

"Look, Ma, I'm the baby-sitter! They're going to pay me a dollar-fifty."

"Who ever heard of a boy baby-sitter? How come they don't want Ruth or Matilda for that work?"

"Ruth and Matilda wouldn't take it. They earn more at their jobs. Listen, I wanna go to bed. I don't want to talk about it anymore. I'm tired. I went to the movies."

"With her?" I didn't answer.

My mother put down her knitting and folded back the afghan, swinging her legs to the floor and motioning me to come and sit by her side. I sat down with her, and hugged her around the shoulders.

"Why are you trying to fool me, honey?" she asked softly. "I know why a young boy goes around with a married woman. Things must be different now. When I was fresh married I didn't make goo-goo eyes at anybody. No boys, no men, no boarders, no young rabbis — nobody! You think I didn't have lots of offers? But I loved my husband. Your Mrs. Grossman don't. If she's not honest with him, she won't be honest with you. She's old, anyhow."

"She's *not* old! She's only thirty."

"And I'm only forty," my mother snapped back. "Why don't you take *me* to the movies and hold my hand?"

I held her hand in mine. Half an hour ago I had been holding Sharon's pussy in that hand.

"You can get a nice girl your own age, easy," said my mother. "You're good-looking; you're smart. You've got everything, if you only knew it. You don't have to go around with a married woman with a baby."

282

"Yeah," I snarled, suddenly rigid. "I've got a girl my own age too! But I'm a white-slave gangster! Gonna sell her into a whoor-house in Buenos-Aires. I'm gonna *debauch her purity*, and disgrace her family! So at least I'm not gonna debauch any married women's purity, am I?"

"Sure you are," my mother said calmly. "Even worse. Maybe you're not making a whoor out of her, but *she* is."

I flung up from the sofa, and stood facing my mother with my face working. Was touching Sharon's body and she touching mine really whoredom? Like the old prophet Ezekiel and the sisters Aholah and Aholibah: *"For in her youth they lay with her, and they bruised the breasts of her virginity, and poured their whoredom upon her."*

"I don't want to talk about Sharon Grossman to you," I snapped. "You're just jealous."

"Sure I'm jealous," my mother said slowly, reaching out one hand to smooth my tortured face. "But the difference is, I love you."

"And I love you too, Ma," I almost wept. *"I really do!"*

IT WAS a whole spy-story operation, like something out of the Baroness Orczy's *Scarlet Pimpernel,* to get to see Tia on her graduation day. She got out of the house on some pretext of having to compare dresses with Mildred: the girls were all to wear party dresses of any color they chose, because there'd be a dance afterward to which of course I wouldn't be allowed to take her. We met on the walk hidden behind Mildred's house, and Tia showed me the dress she'd wear: a gorgeous thing of green and yellow Scottish tartan, but actually of taffeta or I don't know what, that rustled like a live thing as she held it up for me to see thrown over her arm.

I was bitter because I wouldn't actually see it on her, and made some remark about how beautiful she'd be for all the other guys but me, who'd also all get to feel up her body politely at the dance.

"I won't dance that close," she promised me.

"But they'll still have their hand on your ass."

"On my waist."

"I love your waist," I hissed. "I want to be biting it *right* now!" I grabbed her and started mauling and hauling her to me by the hips where we stood.

Tia extricated herself politely but firmly, and promised she would dash out of the school before the graduation procession started, and meet me across the

284

street up under the portico of the Christian Science Temple, the usual tall, cold, imitation-Greek structure with the usual pillars along the front portico. The graduation was to be in the early evening, so no one would see us, and I would see the dress, and be able to kiss her for good luck. I would throw the dress up over her head, I promised grimly, and kiss her right on the belly-button.

"Anywhere you want, darling," Tia assured me, in her sweetest, most mollifying voice.

She got out as planned, on the excuse of having to go to the little girls' room, as the girls quaintly called it, and dashed up the steps of the Christian Science Temple where I was skulking like an assassin behind the pillars. The dress was indeed very beautiful on her, though I hardly looked at it as we flung ourselves into each other's arms. As opposed to my wild threats about her belly-button, I only tried to pull down the rather high neck of the dress to kiss Tia's breasts bare, but she wouldn't let me do it. She made no objection, though, when I frothed up the taffeta skirt in front, dragged her panty-crotch aside and kneaded her bare pussy frantically as I kissed her mouth again and again. I was wild with frustration — with love and horniness. *They'd* all dance with her, squeeze her, smell her!! I kissed her wildly, our teeth striking together dangerously.

"Oh, darling," Tia moaned, a little theatrically, "what's to become of us?" And then she was gone, another girl having darted across the street signalling frantically to get her. I didn't hang around to see her come out after the graduation ceremony with her family, to go to the dance. Or maybe on some luckier swain's arm. I didn't think I'd be able to stand seeing that.

Walking home up the hill, my head down and feeling very fierce, about a block away from the school I heard someone hailing me by name. It was Gwen Schwab, Manny Grossman's clever girlfriend. Gwen wasn't pretty, with a slender little sad face that only lit up when she spoke, but she had a sweet character and a magnificent contralto voice that spelled S.E.X. all over it. She was the only girl in our bunch who could play chess well, and obviously had more brains than Tia or any other girl in our gang except Jane Jacobs Butzner. And my sister Ruth, of course, but Ruth was a lot older than us.

Gwen told me that her younger sister was graduating too, that night, but the family could only afford one nice dress, which the sister was wearing. So she hadn't gone into the auditorium either, just like me.

We walked on up together, and when we passed the corner of Quincy Avenue where she lived she invited me to come and sit on the porch and drink some of the family cordial, which was schlivovitz, a kind of prune brandy her aunt learned to make in the Old Country.

"No one is home," she said. "They're all at the graduation."

I hated drinking liqueurs because they were so sweet, but I was just in the mood to agree. I remembered again with a sick feeling, that the cloying liqueur didn't improve, that masochistic spring night on the restaurant mezzanine, drinking *crème de cacao* with Jimmy Kennedy and Tia, and how it had been him that kissed her in the taxi home, and not me, while I paid the driver extra — sardonically, 1 thought — to slow down rather than interrupt their goodnight kiss. Some guys are crazy, I admit, but what *do* you do when the woman you love wants to show the power of her sex and beauty over every man? And has the bad taste to do it in front of you. Wait until it happens to you, you son of a bitch, and then you'll know how it feels! And little recourse you have, to acting jealous, especially when you've been preaching to everybody the way I was: "Love & sex are beautiful. They are the

287

only real purpose of human life. And your body is your own."

I wanted to get drunk now, something I had never in my life done. That dance was going to be in the ballroom of the Hotel Jermyn, downtown. And there'd be rooms there, available, upstairs, with beds. Somebody might get Tia drunk — I was getting drunk, wasn't I? And how could you know what she'd do then? Those high school boys weren't as enterprising as the college men that came up from Philadelphia for the prom dances, but plenty of them knew which end was up.

Gwen and I sat in the increasing darkness on the swing, under the brooding, overhanging eaves of their narrow porch, sipping our syrupy cordial in tiny glasses she'd brought out. After three of four of these I lost my grouch and became rather elevated and expansive. I began warning Gwen loftily against Manny, who I assured her was totally insincere about everything including his Socialistic beliefs, did not appreciate her brains, and probably only wanted her "pale pink body." I was gagging that up to make it seem less narrow-minded for a red-hot rebel like me to be saying.

"Is it wrong to want my body?" she asked quietly.

288

I started explaining to her very precisely how there was a right and a wrong way to feel sexual passion for girls, and that Manny Grossman surely did it the wrong way. He was in reality no better, I cautioned her, than the gross highschool boys from whom I was assiduish- wait a minute, assiduously collecting erotic slang terms for my dictionary, and bawdy songs, most of them dripping with hatefulness and contempt. For who? — for girls! Some of the songs were really disgusting, I told her.

"Sing me one of the nice ones," Gwen said. The opposite of me, Gwen believed in Accentuating the Positive.

I couldn't remember any of the nice ones, and the liqueur was beginning to get to my head, making my tongue stumble. The only song that ran through my mind went:

When you take it in your hand, Mistress Murphy,
You'll find it only weighs three-quahrters of a pound.
It's got feathers on its neck like a turkey,
Will you take it standin' up or layin' down?

I sang this boldly for Gwen, in its proper mock-Irish brogue and lilting tune, though not very loud, as it would be too easy to rouse the neighbors, some of whom were also probably sitting on their porch-swings right across the street in the lovely June night.

"If that's one of the nice ones," she said, "the bad ones must be *terrible!*"

We both began to giggle, and I suddenly realized I had never sung a dirty song before a girl since I was a kid up at Lake Winola. Except maybe that one about "Bye-Bye Blackbird" to my sister Ruth. But that was different; weren't we thinking about that *scientifically?* I offered now to make up a song in Gwen's honor on the spot. Maybe there wouldn't be any acrostic on her name — it had too many letters for a sonnet, I explained, counting and spelling out all the letters, which I suppose has the same flattering effect on anybody — but I'd be singing it, and that ought to count for something. I modelled my song on the British army's bawdy "Kathusalem," but the words were nobly chaste as I had no desire to hurt or shock her. If I hadn't already been a little drunk I wouldn't have sung "Mistress Murphy" for her either. I stamped out my song in half-voice to the fast rhythm of "London Bridge is Falling Down":

> Oh, Gwendo-line, if you'll be mine,
> I'll make you Queen of Palestine.
> So cast no pearls before the swine,

290

Thou daughter of the Rabbi!

Right on cue her father came trudging up the porch stairs in the dark. A quiet, grieving man — a workman furrier, not a rabbi — who had recently lost his wife, and was left with two teenage daughters to bring up. He informed Gwen quietly that her sister Nan had gone to the graduating students' dance, peered vaguely at me, and went in the house, where we could hear him continuing to trudge upstairs and doubtless to bed. Gwen didn't present me to her father, and he had acted almost as though she were alone on the porch. When he said the word "dance," I was immediately conjuring up Tia in her crinkly green tartan taffeta, her fine breasts panting; dancing, whirling, wriggling with the whole rotten stag-line of ardent young bucks exactly like me, and I began scowling again in the dark.

The lights her father had lit in the house all went out now. Gwen wanted me to make up more verses to her song, but instead I asked her gruffly if there was any more prune cordial. I didn't feel able any longer to pronounce a word like *schlivovitz*. For answer she slid to the floor on her knees at my feet, and to my astonishment she began gently biting my penis through the cloth of my fly. I was dumfounded, as I don't believe I'd ever even linked arms with her walking up the street, or ever dreamed of kissing her, let alone having her kiss my prick. I was madly in love with Tia, and Gwen was somebody else's girl.

The average person might think that she could be forgiven for thinking I was leading her on, what with that song about Mistress Murphy taking the singer's three-quarter-pound prick, whether standin' up or layin' down; and, perhaps even more directly to a young girl's heart, making up an impromptu song on her own name recommending to her under a transparent veil not to cast her pearls before her swinish current boyfriend, and instead "Oh, Gwendoline, if you'll be mine. . ." Well, she was willing. What was so surprising about that? But me, I was dumfounded by her response. I guess it never occurred to me that songs and music mean *sex* to a woman — in fact, that's exactly what music means to me too — or that anyone would take the words of a folksong so seriously.

I took Gwen's head in both my hands, and tried gently to push it away from my fly. But she wouldn't stop. She was now kissing up & down the length of my prick, which she'd outlined all stiffened through the cloth of my pants. She looked up at me with her eyes very wide in the dark.

292

"I could make you forget her," she said gravely, in her darkest, huskiest voice. And she rolled my prick between her palms through the cloth, trying to make it even stiffer, and making an unmistakable kissing or receiving gesture with her open mouth as she stared into my eyes.

Then she started unbuttoning me and drawing my prick out, and I pulled her up violently and back on the swing with me. I grabbed her around the shoulders, kissing her crushingly on the mouth and kneading her soft small breasts with my chest from side to side. How savantly I did it, I thought to myself sadly, when I wanted so much to be caressing somebody else. I did not feel anything at all inside for Gwen, except that I appreciated her quality as a woman in being willing to suck me like that without preamble. And I knew I wouldn't lay her, as she kept urging me to do with the swaying of her body and her soft, inarticulate preliminary moans as we kissed.

"It wouldn't be *fair* to you," I choked, at a pause for breath between powerful soul-kisses, dropping her head and sitting up against the swing with Gwen plastered to me. "No one will ever make me forget her. I'll love her when I'm clay!"

293

This was the phrase I heard the Irish salesman at the store mutter, and it was written in fire in my heart.

Gwen stopped trying to pull me down flat with her on the mattress of the swing, but kept my hands on her breasts in the grip of her own. "You've got it bad," she said. There was a pause.

"Love always makes a person unhappy," I said finally. "It's all lies about it making you happy." Another pause.

"I could make you happy," Gwen said. She was pushing her hair back out of her face.

"Yes," I agreed. "Because we don't really love each other. Love is like chains on me," I added. "I'm chained to her — for life!"

"I don't think so," Gwen said, giving my prick another squeeze with her hands. I suddenly realized she had it out in the air now. It was standing up like Cleopatra's Needle in the park — another phallic fetich for women to idolize. She went down on me frankly now, getting the head of my prick between her lips first and then sinking her mouth slowly down around my shaft and coming up again even slower, her eyes wide open and continuously staring up into mine.

I knew I wanted it, and real bad, and my hips were beginning to jazz up against her mouth

294

convulsively to drive my prick deeper in, while she savored it just that way. But I couldn't go on. I felt that I was crucifying myself, and that I would kill Gwen if she made me shoot in her mouth this way. It was absolutely crazy, too, because here I was having a red-hot affair with Sharon — for a year now, while loving Tia to the bottom of my soul simultaneously. Well, that was it.

I kissed Gwen's hair and pulled her mouth up off me, and took her in my arms again trying to act brotherly. That was it. To be crude about it, I was just getting my nuts off with Sharon. Well? Gwen was drooling on me right now. She wanted to get my nuts off too, and I could just see she was going to drink it and lick her lips. That'd be the best method of birth control we'd have. — No! I wouldn't do it! Gwen was a real sex-job, all right, but that wasn't all she wanted. She said it already: she wanted to make me forget Tia. And remember *her.* No! Tia was who I loved.

I tried to cool us down, by stages. I pulled up Gwen's bodice and bra now, licking her tiny nipples and fencing with them with my tongue. Then I'd stop — and get up — and I'd say goodbye and thank you for the prune brandy — and — Gwen was writhing like a fresh-fucked fox in a forest fire when I sucked on her nipples. I wasn't cooling anybody down. Me

295

neither. But I knew I couldn't go on, and felt as cold inside as any icicle, no matter how tense and curved upwards my prick was standing. What did *he* know? *I* knew! *I loved Tia,* and that was all there was to it. I wasn't going to fuck Gwen because I wasn't going to!

She was laying there now really all splayed out, with one leg flung over the back of the porch swing, and pulling my prick towards her with both hands. I wondered vaguely how she had gotten her pants off without me noticing her doing it. I hadn't taken them off her, had I? I guess she never wore any. Really sexy girls almost never did. That way you could drop to your knees and kiss their cunts and bury your nose in the hair whenever you had a secret minute alone. Like Tia and me, as I dreamed it. Gwen was writhing her bare belly and her free leg up & down against mine, murmuring encouragingly in a voice so throaty it seemed to be coming up from underground, "Come *on,* come *on!*" I can't remember any more except that I kissed her mouth again and pulled away, practically jumping off the dark porch, and walked home in the night, buttoning up my pants-fly as I went, and feeling like the fool I was. One thing I knew was that if I ever saw Gwen again in the library she'd be liable to kill me; at least cut me dead. Why was I so crazy? — Why? Why didn't I just turn back, the way I ought to, I asked

296

myself? And throw Gwen back down on the swing again, if she wasn't still laying there right now rubbing herself, and fuck her till her ears flew off! But I didn't. I just tramped on home, block after block, my head filled up blindingly with images of Tia in her taffeta dress, dancing . . . dancing . . . turning . . . And her breasts . . . I could actually taste the salt of their sweat on my lips. Then I remembered it was really Gwen's breasts I was tasting. I began to cry, and kept my eyes on the moon at every cross-street, hoping an automobile would come along and kill me.

THINGS didn't work out the way Sharon and I planned. Everybody was too crowded at the Grossmans' big house on Irving Avenue, in spite of its ten rooms, so Sharon and Arnold and the baby went to stay with her parents in Philadelphia while waiting for their new apartment on Mulberry Street to be available in the fall. Then they went for a vacation to the seaside. So now I was receiving brief sustaining notes from both Tia in Long Branch by the sea, and Sharon in Atlantic City. Sharon's were discreetly signed with her initial only — just a long squiggle for the "S", with wild "Xs" underneath representing kisses. When you looked at it, it seemed to say "SEX," but that was all the sex I was getting.

Berta Parrott phoned a few times, still asking — but without saying so — why I never came around anymore Saturday afternoons. A day or two later Jimmy Kennedy and I turned up idly together one afternoon to see Cy Endfield, who wasn't home. So instead we dropped in on Berta, who was terribly flushed and surprised with two gentlemen visitors. Her thin older sister was there too, but fortunately not her parents, and we kidded and lallygagged with the two of them for half an hour. Nothing was said about Kennedy being an Irish Catholic and the two girls Jewish. It was understood. Then Kennedy suddenly announced that we had to be leaving, and dragged me out. Berta was visibly crestfallen. Her sister hadn't been playing along, and wasn't too sorry to see us leave. But Berta really looked as though she was going to bust out crying. And here she'd thought everything was fixed up now and going to be fine; while the sister had been watching us obliquely, laughing but obviously so suspicious of everything the whole while.

"What's the matter with you?" I asked Kennedy in an undertone, the minute we were on the porch. "Shouldn't we invite them out?"

298

"Nah," he said, waiting till we were out on the sidewalk to explain, "I can tell just looking at Berta that she isn't That Kind of a Girl!" I knew he was right. Berta was forgotten. Sex is King.

Endfield knew all sorts of people, but he never knew any girls. His mind was too full of amateur magic and prestidigitation, along with an endless and terribly verbose concern with his own personal Cyrillic intellectual state and development. He had a friend visiting from Los Angeles named Israel Shapiro, who was just as talkative as Cy was, and about the same vaporous bullshit. They were being red-hot radicals that summer, and that was worth listening to. But they would never talk about coalmine dynamite caps, the way I wanted to, and continuously got off into philoslopical discussions of the educability and perfectibility of the Working Classes.

During one such discussion, when I had the nerve to interfere, making the remark that all the workers *really* cared about is getting more money, fucking, and spectator sports, I was practically shoved into the outer darkness. History repeated itself here a few decades later when the Secretary of Agriculture, Earl Butz, was "allowed to resign" in 1976 for having stated in a published interview that the Republican party can't attract the Negro vote *"because coloreds* [i.e.,

299

niggers] *only want three things: a tight cunt, a pair of loose shoes, and a warm place to shit."*

I compounded my crime by observing that, as far as I could make out, neither of them had ever had a job in their lives, so what the hell did they know about the Working Class? They then fell on me verbally for half an hour, kittle-pitchering me back and forth as I fenced first with one and then with the other. They adored that kind of verbal glup. I could hold up my end in it, but somehow it seemed too Talmudic to me, and just not worth while. A little like wrestling in a tub of perfumed butter. It might be fun with a girl, but not with two youthful male intellectuals eager to show off how erudite they were in all the latest fads. One thing was sure, I could see: this kind of discussion would never successfully result in the Revolution as planned by Marx & Lenin. We went out and had ice cream in a little bakery nearby that Cy knew.

The bakery was just across the street from the Scranton Conservatory where my sister Ruth used to go for her elocution and toe-dancing lessons. The baker was alone in the shop except for a sallow boy in a big apron working in the back. I wanted to point out to Izzie and Cy that *that* was the working class, but we were too busy with our own ice cream Revolution in eight flavors, with sugary cinnamon buns. The baker was a fascinating man: a middle-aged Czech named Henk Barbush, who had been in both the Austro-Hungarian and Russian armies during the World War, and was like somebody out of Jaroslav Hasek's *The Good Soldier Schweik*. Maybe Schweik is who he was. He came over and stood by our little table and told us about the War: about the dirty Polack girls who each used to whore for fifty soldiers in a night — sometimes more — laying splayed out like a figure X on a straw pallet on the ground, and who they called *gruzhenkas*.

I got a sheet from the lined order-pad on the counter, and began writing down words from his bawdy vocabulary in three languages, with Barbush correcting my spelling. He said he knew German too, and reeled off a long litany of scatological filth in rhyme in that language, all about the *klapusterbeeren*, which he explained carefully were the grummets of mixed shit and hair and gism around the unwashed asses of the *gruzhenka* whores. We listened to him with great interest as we poked daintily at our ice cream with little spoons: vanilla, chocolate and maple-walnut for me — that was my favorite.

When the time came to pay I claimed I didn't have any money. I knew Endfield had plenty. After all, his father was a rich furrier and they lived in a mansion. Both Cy and Izzie considered it very

301

uncultivated of me to try and sponge like that on more fortunate persons, who had nothing but their weekly allowances. And I began singing the *Internationale* in my best voice, with them shushing me:

> *"Arise! ye prisoners of starvation.*
> *Arise, ye wretched of the earth!*
> *For Justice thunders condemnation;*
> *A better world shall come to birth!"*

After that I would always walk down around to the little bakery, coming home from the Public Library. The baker was flattered by my writing down his reminiscences of the War, and began telling me more and more awful things. Sex was long since behind us — that had just been the humorous part, to get the audience hooked in. And he flung us both into the real horror of war, sitting with me at one of the little tables in the back of the shop in his white apron and sometimes a funny, round white cap, his shoulders hunched forward and his eyes boring up into mine as he told of shooting prisoners in the back of the head over graves they had to dig themselves at gunpoint; of the soldiers shitting in their pants when the big guns slammed and screamed overhead during bombardments; of shells ripping off a man's arm or head, or tearing out his guts in a puddle of blue muck at his feet in which he fell and suffocated; of "accidentally" shooting unpopular officers in the back during attacks; and stealing guns and pocket-watches from the dead & dying; raping peasant girls, and fucking goats when there were no girls because the officers had dragged them all away shrieking, to gang-shag them privately in the little wooden drinking dens and *estaminets*, which were of course off limits to common soldiers.

It was endless, grovelling, gruelling, pitiful, horrible, filled with overpowering stinks and smells, mostly of death and terror and unburied corruption; all braided together in cold coagulated blood and ghastly screams and explosions as men and animals died. I wrote it all down, not knowing exactly why, in scrawled pencil notes that later I could hardly read. Every once in a while a customer would come in, usually a woman with a child or children, and Barbush would leap up from our table and bustle over to pick them out half a dozen Vienna rolls or square sugar-buns in a bag, handling them with bright shiny little tongs, or ladling out double dip icecream cones for the kids. Then he would skid back to our table in the half-dark in the back of the shop, and the rapes and blood and explosions and the terrible screams of wounded horses and dying men would start again, while I hunched forward now too, and wrote . . . wrote . . . wrote . . .

303

After a while I hated Barbush, and I certainly hated his stories. But I went back again and again to hear more and more. We were accomplices somehow in a horrible, dirty thing that he was rolling off his shoulders onto mine like a *dybbuk*, and I was too dumb and fascinated to stop him. I began having bad dreams, in which Barbush and his tales of the war on the Eastern front figured as a great black bird of prey with a cut throat, croaking dismally like Poe's Raven as it swallowed down my blood along with its own. I decided several times not ever to go back to Barbush's bakery again, but I always went, explaining to myself weakly that after all he had the best icecream anywhere around. But I didn't eat his icecream anymore. I just sat writing down what he told me, in a sort of rapid shorthand of the main words and subjects, as afternoon would turn to evening, and I would stagger home filled with horrors and unable to eat my mother's piping hot supper, nor to explain why.

The most awful thing Barbush told me wasn't something that had happened to him but that he himself had done. And he wasn't the only one. But he found it difficult to admit to this atrocity, and circled around it several times, interrupting himself to recount various hilarious shit-house jokes and anecdotes before telling it straight out. To get higher pay and better treatment he had become a corporal and trained to be a marksman. He and the other marksmen would stand on the raised firing step in the trench, behind a sandbag parapet, in the very early morning as the mists were rising off the ground, waiting for the morning bombardment to end.

When they would see incautious enemy soldiers in their telescopic sights, squatting to shit anywhere in view, or tearing off their beshitten pants and underdrawers and trying to wipe themselves clean if they had unloaded in fear during the bombardment, my baker friend and the other marksmen would make a special point of trying to shoot off the squatting soldiers' down-hanging balls, and would congratulate each other and hit each other on the back with gross laughter and jokes when they succeeded. I wrote it down but I felt sick and disgusted looking at him, when our eyes met. He read the expression in my eyes. — How not? It was the same as his own.

"The Cossacks did worse stuff than that," he muttered, defending himself from the accusation in my eyes.

"To guys' balls?"

"Sure, to their balls! That's where it hurts the worst, don't it? Sandwiches; cracking 'em with two bricks . . ."

305

"Don't tell me about it," I begged him, holding up one hand. "That stuff is awful, Henk! I'm going to have enough bad dreams about all the rest of it."

"I have bad dreams too," said the baker slowly.

CY ENDFIELD knew all sorts of people; you had to hand him that. He sort of collected them, as though he knew he was so lifeless and unsavory himself. It was always somehow through his family that he met people, so there was always some connection with Russians, furs, and even a couple *of ci-devant* Russki nobility, or so they claimed. One day, for no reason at all that I could see, since he didn't take piano lessons himself, he took me along with him to see a young music teacher named Basil Dolgoruki, down on Linden Street, who had long, poetic blond hair, wore a cape over his business suit tied with a bow of silken cord at the neck, and long, pointy brown suede shoes which I considered extremely *distingué*. I guess he thought so too. Dolgoruki gave piano lessons in a big drafty studio over a building that served as a boxing-and-wrestling arena, halfway between the courthouse and the police station, where all the ward-heelers hung around to enjoy the bloody fights. Dog-fights were forbidden, as too ghastly, and cock-fights too, but there were supposed to be both, secretly and at night, up in a big garage somewhere beyond Dunmore, where the blood-sport bettors all went. You had to know somebody to get in, like a speakeasy.

Dolgoruki's studio was about the bleakest, shabbiest thing I ever saw, except for the basement photographic atelier of a guy with buck teeth that I knew in New York who used to pick up girls in Greenwich Village bars in the late evenings and then take them there to photograph their cunts. Because Dolgoruki's studio was dedicated to music, there was a large grand piano prominently in the center, with some of the black enamel chipped off around the edges here & there, and a mournful-looking gilt harp that had seen better days. That was the main, or musical part of the studio. As a waiting room for the students there were a couple of kitchen chairs by the door, partitioned off behind a plasterboard wall covered with photos of Dolgoruki in various poses at the piano and with his students — the successful ones, I assumed — thumbtacked on crookedly but in great profusion.

Naturally I told Dolgoruki that I was trying to teach myself to play the piano, and he assured me that I would never succeed that way. He was thin and rather odd-looking, with an enormous globular forehead and long, prematurely graying blond hair hanging over his eyes. He told me to come back and bring some music that I could play. If I had talent, he told me, he would give me lessons free. He only took money from middle-class families, for giving their ugly daughters lessons, he said. He reached over to the piano and walked his fingers up & down a few notes, contemptuously. *"Plink, plink, plink! And for this did Mozart die?!"*

He then smashed into the tremendous opening fanfare of Grieg's Piano Concerto, leaping violently down the scale, after a sinister, cymbal-like rustling, in great claw-fingered octaves, several times over: *DOH!!!* — Sol!-Mi! *DOH!!* — Sol!-Mi! *DOH!!* — Sol!-Mi! *DOH!!* taking both the piano and the orchestral parts somehow for those first crashing heroic bars, so slavishly imitated by Tchaikowsky. After that, Dolgoruki invariably swung into this Grieg Concerto fanfare whenever I walked in through the door, perhaps as representing his nobilitarian dream or delusion about himself, or maybe just to flatter the ass off me. In which you may be sure he was wonderfully successful. What an artist in hokum! Maybe he should've used Louis Moreau Gottschalk's wholly cornball *Bunker Hill Fantasia,* or Beethoven's even worse *Wellington's Victory.*

Dolgoruki was altogether very theatrical. At my test lesson or tryout or whatever it was, which I could see excited him only to boredom and pity, he told me something of the glorious history of the Dolgoruki family in Russia. The Dolgorukis had been real king-makers, and for hundreds of years. The Romanoffs were nothing but weaklings and lunatics, except for Peter the Great, of course. Catherine the Great was a German whore. The only thing she ever did right was to have her lovers Orloff and Potemkin strangle her husband, Mad Peter the Third. He himself, Dolgoruki told me, was a direct descendant of the illegitimate child that Peter the Second, the grandfather of Peter the Great, had fathered on one of the Dolgoruki girls he was madly in love with at the age of fifteen. That hit me right where I lived! But the enemy faction at court had poisoned him before he could marry her, to prevent the Dolgorukis from gaining even more power.

The last Czar's step-grandmother, just a few years ago, had been a Dolgoruki, but she died without writing her memoirs telling half the secrets she knew, her husband being the Imperial Chief of Police. Otherwise he, Basil Dolgoruki, would probably be the Czar right now! Under the title Wassily the Fifth, he added, looking angrily at his fingernails, his lips grim

309

and twisting. And there would never have *been* any Russian Revolution, neither in 1905 or 1917, which were both part of the same Secret Plot, and were caused solely by bad management on the part of Count Witte, who betrayed his country during the Russo-Japanese War by restraining the Cossacks when they might have saved Russia! Which was being destroyed systematically by the Czarina Alexandra, who was also a German whore and a hysterical cunt, who couldn't think of anything except sucking the mad monk Rasputin's prick. Which was over twelve inches long and as thick around as your fist. Also stiff *all* the time, but Rasputin would hold it against his body when in public by strapping it against his stomach with his belt, hidden under his embroidered tunic. It was very educational.

In Dolgoruki's waiting-room, just about every time I was there, a poor ugly rawboned country-girl would be waiting for her piano lesson. I think Dolgoruki purposely took students that ugly to give him an excuse for his endless anti-woman insults and remarks. This girl's name was Rosanna Trimmler, she told me, and she came in by bus each time from Moscow, P.A., just up the road. I know this sounds as though I'm inventing it, to fit in cutely with Dolgoruki's noble and imperial genealogy, but it's the plain truth. Just one of those little coincidences life is full of. I've had lots funnier ones happen to me than that. I could have said she came from West Tunkhannock or Equinunk or Moosic or Minooka — or some other American Indian town-names, all in the neighborhood — if I wanted to be funny. And what about the incredible group of towns, also in Pennsylvania, near Harrisburg, which sound like someone's venereal history as you pass through them one after the other on the roads: Peach Bottom, Gap, Intercourse, Paradise — and Blue Ball! I hear they've cravenly changed the name of Intercourse to "Jim Thorpe," after the Indian runner. What next?

Rosanna fell in love with me instantly, owing to my pretty face, no doubt, as she was heart-rendingly ugly herself and certainly needed some kind of dream to live for. Or perhaps she was impressed by the princely airs I was picking up listening to Dolgoruki's outrageous lies. She used to follow me around like a heart-struck poodle dog, waiting to be either kissed or kicked, and obviously didn't care which, as long as her demi-god — that was me — would pay her some attention. When she spoke to me, and even more so when I answered her, she would wreathe her craggy face in a sappy expression halfway between an ecstatic smile and an idiotic smirk, and twist up her ungainly

311

body practically into a spiral, beginning by twining one leg and ankle round the other in a kind of vertical Half-Gaynor, or Front Developpé. It was not necessary to be a gynecologist to recognize that her problem was about six inches below her navel, and deep inside.

If I tried to get away by saying I was going around the corner to Stück's bookshop and would be back later, Rosanna would thoughtlessly follow me right out of the studio like a shadow, missing her piano lesson without a qualm, and turning up behind me wherever I went. She didn't bother to give any explanation. Like the unclimbed peaks of the Himalayan mountains, she was *there*.

I tried to shake her off by telling her, with as much kindness as I knew how to muster, in response to her frequent wide open invitations to come and visit her family in Moscow, PA., and roll her in the hay, that I already had a girlfriend with whom I was deeply in love. I didn't bother to say anything about my mere physical infidelity with Sharon, which would have confused the issue. The only result of my telling her even this much was that I then received to my home address, which she got from the phone-book, a series of pathetic letters and invitations, in a childishly large and angular handwriting very similar to her own gawky bone-structure, I thought, and sometimes decorated

312

with hearts & flowers, ornate birds, etc., both inside and on the envelope, for the edification of the mailman.

In these letters — and I was very glad she restrained herself to them, because what would I have done if she started telephoning at all hours of the day & night? — Rosanna finally told me flat out that she could make me a lot happier, any way I wanted, than any darn girlfriend I already had, *if I knew what she meant.* I knew what she meant. Gwen Schwab had already made me the same offer, on Tia's graduation night. I'm still sorry I didn't take Gwen up on that. She had fingers that touched me like a moth's wings, fluttering on my prick. Love is love, but in the end you have to take care of your prick too. Below and beyond the heavy sentimental talk, I'll bet a lot of women feel the same way about their cunts. Rosanna certainly did.

My pretty face in those days is also not something I'm just making up. I looked like one of those pensive angels playing oversized theorbos in the background of musical paintings of the time of Vivaldi and Bach. Aside from attracting a goodly number of high school girls, identifying with me like mad as *the boy they would have wanted to be if only they'd been born a boy,* I was apparently overwhelmingly attractive then to homosexuals too. I'd already had a lot of trouble being followed by them in the streets of New York, especially in the evenings, and on the East River bridges when I foolishly slept there, since I was twelve years old.

As it turned out, Dolgoruki was homosexual too, aside from being the rightful Czar, and was less interested in my piano playing — or even the ridiculous couple of marches and country dances I'd already composed, and brought for him to see — than in getting me away from my family and alone with him out on the road. He filled me up with a line of bunk about how he needed a companion and concert-manager, for the series of high-class concerts he would be giving all around Pennsylvania, New Jersey, and as far south as Atlanta, Georgia, during the rest of that summer and fall.

He saw no reason, he told me, his stringy hair falling into his eyes in utter sincerity, why a clever young man like myself, with musical interests and all that, couldn't serve as his concert-manager. All it really came to was answering the telephone and writing publicity handouts for the newspapers in the towns where the concerts would be. I'd also handle all the cash; take care of the railroad tickets and reservations. I would get my meals and transportation and hotels free, plus twenty dollars a week as wages. When I told my mother ecstatically about the marvelous job I had

314

swung, it was the twenty dollars that made her suspicious of the whole thing. That was far too much money to pay anyone my age, she pointed out, when you could only get ten dollars a week working in a store, or fifteen at most after working there for years. And then I was supposed to get hotel, meals and train-fare in addition.

"Yup!" I said triumphantly. "And I get in to all of Basil's concerts free, too. And any others on the circuit, if I want. And Chautauqua lectures, if there's any in town. All free! It's like a college education." It was certainly the greatest first job any boy had ever swung. And me only one month out of high school, too.

My mother was too wise to attack head-on about this, in spite of her suspicions. Or maybe she was too kind, when she saw how enthusiastic I was. This wasn't like condemning my affair with Sharon out of hand, simply because Sharon was a married woman. Instead, my mother started asking around, without saying anything to my father, to whom she also warned me not to breathe a word or he'd be sure to spoil everything, as usual. I promised her Daddy would know *nothing*. As I had mentioned that I met Dolgoruki through Cy Endfield, my mother phoned up Mrs. Endfield first, and asked a few pointed questions,

315

mother-to-mother. Mrs. Endfield must have asked Cy about it, and then phoned back.

The very next afternoon, when I got home from the library, and from conferring with Dolgoruki about our first planned concert swing through the Jersey beach resorts — where I was of course going to stun both Tia and Sharon by walking in on them dressed to the nines, in my new character as operatic impresario — my mother broke it to me. I told her we had been conferring in his apartment up on Linden Street, this time; not in the studio with the piano and harp. Too many ugly girls there, I said airily. They bothered us when we had to discuss important plans.

"Yes," said my mother, sort of looking absently away, "fellows like *that* think all girls are ugly." Her tone would have etched steel.

"Fellows like *what?*"

"Your friend Cy Endfield is making a joke on you. This Basil — " she said it with poison in her voice — "he's just a fairy! Like in Sodom and Gomorrah! He wants to get you alone with him out of town somewhere in a hotel room. And you're so dumb you want to go!"

I didn't answer. I just stood looking at my mother like a felled ox. Everything had clicked into place at the deathly words "Sodom and Gomorrah."

316

There was no mistaking that. I knew instantly she was right. I felt a terrible shame and confusion welling over me, as though I had been sodomized already. She was still speaking.

"Fellows like that ought to be in jail! And he will be, too, if he doesn't leave you alone. I called him up and told him so."

"You called him up, Ma?" I asked, practically strangulated.

"Sure I did! Who is he, the Emperor Francis-Joseph?! I told him my son wasn't for sale for twenty dollars a week. No, and not twenty hundred a week, neither." She was beginning to tremble as she spoke. "I told him if he tries to steal you away from your family, he should kindly remember you're exactly sixteen years old, and it ain't going to happen to you like Loeb and Leopold that killed that boy! He don't even have to take you across the first state line for the Mann Act, and he's going to jail for *life!* They should only give him the electric chair, that dirty rotten skunk!!"

There was more, but I wasn't listening. My mother had her tongue very well-hung in the middle when she wanted to let go. But I didn't need to hear it all. It was the detail about the Mann Act that clinched it for me. Now I understood why Dolgoruki had

317

explained to me with so seigneurial an air that he was too much of a cape-wrapped artist to bother with hotel reservations and train tickets, and that I'd have to take care of all that. The poor slob imagined that would clear him of the Mann Act, or maybe he thought he could accuse me, if he had to, of transporting *him* across the state line for immoral purposes.

The funny thing was, every single thing he told me about the Romanoffs and the Dolgorukis turned out to be exactly true. I looked it all up later and it was historically true. Except maybe his claim to being the rightful Czar himself. But who knows? Of course, the one thing he had forgotten to tell me was that he was a pederast. Well, actually, that's not the funny thing. The really funny thing is that I never felt grateful to my mother for breaking up the plot. I admitted she was right, but to me she had just spoiled things. I could have taken care of myself. I wasn't a child anymore.

"What if he got you drunk?" she asked, when I told her that.

"I don't drink."

"Is that an answer? And when he tells you all the big theatre-managers drink like fishes — so are you going to say No?"

Yes, she was right all across the board, but it was too close to the way my father had crashed in

318

ruthlessly, and broke things up with Tia. Tia, whom I would now never see, with me dressed as a concert-manager in my grey suede vest with pearl buttons and pointy shoes, there in Long Branch or Asbury Park.

WELL, the net result was that I left home "for my vacation," and was very soon out on the road hitchhiking. My mother made me two monstrous-sized omelet sandwiches on rolls, to take with me for the first day or two on my own. She also made me eat another omelet drenched with ketchup, right then & there, and a pile of lettuce. I packed my stuff in a small cheap cloth suitcase she gave me, after emptying her powder puffs and stockings out of it. I was all set to go.

"If your money runs short," my mother told me, "drink milk. Milk will give you the most food for your money. And eggs next. Eggs are always cheap even when they're expensive."

"Yes," I agreed with a ferocious grin, "and you don't have to eat them with a *knife!*" I was in a hurry now to be gone.

My mother gave me a five-dollar bill which she took out of her bosom, folded so many times it hurt, and we kissed goodbye. I gave her extra kisses for my sisters. Within the hour I was somewhere on the highway in the direction of Tobyhanna and the Delaware Water Gap — summer camp country. The suitcase was heavier than I expected. I'd stuck in a couple changes of socks and underwear, another shirt, and especially a large, thick, one-volume edition of *The Complete Plays of Eugene O'Neill*. It weighed a ton as I walked slowly along beside the highway with my bindle in hand, my thumb pointed vaguely east.

To my surprise I felt wonderful and very light-hearted. Every mile I got away from Scranton was falling off my back like the millstones on the chest of the poor wretch being tortured, with weights crushing him, in Victor Hugo's *The Man Who Laughs*. I purposely screwed up my face into my now-standard contemptuous snarl of mock superiority. That would be my defense — my pretended laugh, cut into my own living flesh. Afterwards I couldn't get that surly snarl off my map for the next five years or more, but that's another story.

There was something indescribable in the air that day. I couldn't quite put my finger on it. Later I understood it well. *The smell of freedom!* It carried me up into the air, and I simply laughed at things that would have ripped me into bits just the week before. Most of the cars and trucks passing on the road wouldn't pick me up. I didn't care. The drivers laughed at my outthrust thumb, or actually thumbed their noses back at me hatefully, or made vague, mendacious gestures of having to turn off the road just up ahead. I didn't give a damn. I was *free!* I felt as if I was growing wings — big ones.

Admittedly, *The Complete Plays of Eugene O'Neill* was dragging me down a bit, or trying to, but I had resolutely made up my mind that I owed it to myself to at least attempt to read it. O'Neill was certified by all the book-reviewers and George Jean Nathan, the best dramatic critic, to be the most important American literary man alive, other than writers in the relatively low activity of fiction, to which I no longer desired to sink. I must have believed at that time that stories told in dialogue form are *not* fiction. How I could have believed that, I don't know, since I myself told jokes all the time, which are certainly fiction in dialogue form.

Why fiction, containing descriptions of the scenery and written-out excogitations by the author and his characters, should be a less noble literary form than plays, in which all the descriptions of scenery are grouped briefly in italics at the beginning of the scenes, while the author and his characters thereafter do nothing but excogitate *aloud,* I am no longer able to say.

I had already gone rapidly through the equally large volume of the *Complete Works* of Shakespeare and found it difficult though very inspiring. I read it again later, but slower. But Shakespeare was an Englishman, and Eugene O'Neill was an American writer and that was what I planned to be. A serious writer. No fiction. Henk Barbush — a pseudonym, as you will have understood — the little Czech baker in the icecream store, had given me my baptism of fire.

Be that as it may, there I was out on the highway, with my bindle crooked over my shoulder in classic style. I slung it on a small branch plucked from a leafy tree after I got tired of carrying it in my hand. I was industriously hitching all the infrequent rides anybody would offer me, on trucks and passenger cars, in the general direction of the Delaware Water Gap, a great mountain cut-through with visibly upthrust geological strata along the broad river, and halfway between Scranton and the Atlantic seaboard. Because, very close, somewhere along that coast at that very moment, Tia French was right now dunking her sweet little ass in the ocean wave. And I was bloody-well going to arrive there, somehow and soon — and with a couple of bucks in my pants pocket too, to take her to the movies and neck her pants off — or bust a gut! For me, that put things in focus.

Old Man Grossman had given me the idea, by telling us not so long before that a young fellow could always get a paid vacation any summer by hitchhiking up to the Catskills or Adirondack Mountains and taking a couple of weeks' work as a dishwasher or waiter in one of the many summer resort camps along the rivers and on the hills. There were always jobs like that available, he assured us, a fact which I stressed in getting my mother's grudging permission to go, but of which I did not then understand the unpleasant significance: that nobody really wanted such jobs, because they were gruellingly hard. I soon found out. Maybe waiting on table wasn't too bad, but dishwashing then was pretty close to Hell. I immediately landed a job as a dishwasher the minute I hit the Delaware River beyond Lake Wallenpaupack, somewhere around Matamoras. A summer camp, with the usual polysyllabic mock-Indian name. No experience was necessary, I was told.

"If ya ever washed yer hands, kid," the kitchen-boss told me, "ya know how to wash dishes! Ho-ho-ho!" I would receive eight dollars a week in cash, three meals a day — whatever the guests ate — and a bed. As to the washing of the hands, etc., the difference was in the soap. The soap-powder that had to be used then for dishwashing on a large scale like that, was powerful

323

caustic stuff, intended to cut through the grease in a hurry, and reeking of free alkali. It burned through the skin of my hands at the second meal's dishes. By the third day my hands and wrists were turkey-red all the time and grotesquely swollen halfway up to the elbows. The almost boiling water in the dishwashing tubs also kept intensely raw and agonizing every crack opened in the skin of my fingers and palms by the lye in the soap-powder. All my fingers & thumbs looked like Dutch sausages.

The worst was, I could barely hold up before my eyes the large, heavy volume of *The Complete Plays of Eugene O'Neill.* This I tried nevertheless to read in the few afternoon hours I had free every day — mine was a ten-hour work day from six a.m. to eight at night — sitting on my little folding cot in the small tent out behind the kitchen, where I was lodged with the other kids who washed dishes with me. We were not given beds in the dormitory with the waiters, who were all lively college students and pre-meds from New York and Philadelphia, because they wouldn't allow us in the place. For all the strong soap that reddened and bleached our skin and tore our fingers, there was a heavy fungoid pall upon us that came from dealing with dishwater all day long. It clung to us, and we stank.

The O'Neill was getting to be almost as much of a calvary for me as the dishwashing. I had begun with *Mourning Becomes Electra,* which had a lot of publicity then, but I couldn't go it. Too heavy sledding for me. *Strange Interlude* too. I yearned for my one-volume Shakespeare instead, where even the longest speeches went off like magic if you read them aloud, and you could clearly see the meaning of the whole thing and the feelings of all the actors in every line. Reading O'Neill was more like climbing backwards through blue mud. But I pressed on regardless. I knew that nobody would accept me if I wrote like Shakespeare in the twentieth century. I even wondered why they kept the revivals going all these centuries. No help for it, I would have to write like O'Neill, unless I was willing to *sink* to mere fiction. I turned the Bible-paper pages with the eraser-tip of a pencil held in my teeth; my hands were too swollen then to do more than hold the book up.

The Emperor Jones and *The Hairy Ape,* in the same volume, were a lot better than the *Electra* I'd been trying to plod through, and almost readable. Maybe plays looked good on the stage, I decided, if the dialogue was natural, even if they read on paper like the gabby shit I knew they were. I tried *Desire Under the Elms* which I wrongly assumed from its craftily misleading title would be about sex. More gabby shit, and not enough sex to give a nymphomaniacal flea a hardon. Well! I shouldn't've complained. O'Neill hadn't even written yet his last and worst stinker, *The Iceman Cometh* — meaning the Man of Ice, or cool cat — with its final, orgastic monologue over twenty minutes long, for the benefit of the drunken bums and other women-haters assembled onstage, explaining how the travelling salesman had killed his wife "because she was so *good!*" Meaning, I suppose, because she was so bad in bed.

That was the first paradoxal lesson every writer was supposed to learn then: reversals and tergiversation — uncourageous silence and cunning misdirection. Very appropriately, nobody liked to say that right out. After all, why be a writer or speaker if what you're going to do is tell lies or say nothing? You had to pick it up silently from watching what your mentors and teachers did and didn't do; where they spoke, and where they shut up. All writers ran shit-scared and the prevailing color was yellow. Otherwise you had to be published abroad, like D. H. Lawrence and James Joyce. In those days — which had already lasted since the invention of printing, and maybe before — almost everything about sex, in books or plays you didn't plan to go to jail for publishing, had to

326

be written and understood backwards or in a carefully veiled code, a sort *of lingua franca* everybody understood but that even the most trenchant critics like George Jean Nathan and H. L. Mencken could hardly do more than allude to. They certainly never used a dirty word themselves, though everyone — man, woman & child — seemed to know them well.

The essence of the writing art, under the censorship system, was that the writer castrated himself and his intended message, not *on* paper, but before he even put pen to paper. In other words, in his mind. The censorship that mattered was internal, as with everyone else, and being a successful writer meant accepting and rejoicing in a self-inflicted brainwashing and prefrontal lobotomy. After you dropped your balls in the censorship basket and bowed down to the floor, the money would come rolling in. It replaced your missing balls. While you replaced the missing sex with sadism.

The French erotic poet and novelist Pierre Louÿs pinned the whole thing to the wall sardonically in his little *Manual of Good Manners for the Use of Well-Bred Young Ladies,* where he explains that in the bed of a properly brought-up young woman you never hear a dirty word. Everything anatomical is "you", "yours", "it", "me", "that," and so forth. When a well-bred

327

young lady means: "Oh God! I really need to get fucked before long, or I'll be climbing on the walls!" she says: "I feel rather *nervous* today." — Not: "He has balls like a bull!" But: "He's quite manly." — Not: "I came like a queen — three times in a row!" But: "We had a very interesting conversation." None of that has changed very much. Don't believe everything you hear about some New Freedom, which will surely turn out to be only a temporary blessing after all. The real censorship is still inside: when things are dropped or turned into meaningless polite code before they're ever spoken or written. Or never said or written at all. After that, what does it matter what rare and outlandish specimens the smut-sniffers ban or the cops burn? While the internalized censorship substitutes sadism for sex.

Sitting with my big club-like swollen fingers balancing the O'Neill before my sincere young eyes, I decided that if I never could write plays — and I was pretty sure by now that I couldn't — I could always get a job writing humor for the radio with my file of jokes pasted up from *The Literary Digest* for backlog. That's what everybody else was doing. My mother's cousin, Joel Friedman, the dialect-comic back home, had another cousin who was the joke-writer for Eddie Cantor on the radio. Joel said the guy had a filing

328

cabinet of jokes and situations, arranged by subjects, as big as the catalogue in the public library.

It was well-known. All the big comedians on the radio and in the movies and musical comedies were really deaf, dumb & blind — especially dumb — and stood there with their thumbs up their ass until somebody came out and wrote out the jokes for them on a slate. Funnymen! Everybody knew that. But how could I call myself a serious writer if all I'd write was jokes?

Well, Shakespeare went in for some pretty crude comedy banter too, didn't he? All in code too, every time, but obviously not too hard for the groundlings in the nickel seats to understand. Most of it was just to lighten the atmosphere between murders. Like the Porter's soliloquy in *Macbeth*, which they'd cut out of the text they furnished us in high school. Or *Titus Andronicus,* a real horror story and too rough for me, with murders and tortures galore, and even cannibalism, and a raped girl with her hands cut off and tongue cut out so she wouldn't be able to tell who raped her. But the sex in Shakespeare was all in jesting code. Even *Romeo* & *Juliet* had a lot more murders in it than love, and the two lovers never got laid at all. Like Tia and me. They just die. I had thought about that often. No, Shakespeare was very bloody, and had no

329

real guts when it came to sex. If that was Shakespeare, what could you expect of the others?

Down by the river there were a dozen big wooden canoes and a rowboat, for paddling up & down the Delaware. The guests at the summer camp did their swimming at the wooden dock there, and the college students who were the waiters did their serious flirting with the girl guests — who outnumbered the men two to one — and prepared their late-evening rendezvous in the girls' cabins. I seldom came out of my tent in the afternoons, because looking at the girls in their skimpy bathing suits made me very *nervous*. I just mentioned this a page or two ago. I knew I had no chance of getting anywhere with the girls, the way my fingers were all swollen up and my hands looked so grotesque. What was I supposed to squeeze their tits with, my foot?

At night, after I'd got the last big pots walloped, I'd gobble up a couple of extra desserts I'd have slipped off the guests' plates at dinner, untouched or half-eaten, as they came back to the kitchen on the bus-boy's tray. Then I'd go out and sit by the water in the dark, under a tree somewhere. Very late, when the neckers and petters would stumble away from the dock to the girls' cabins, to finish their lovemaking in beauty, I'd climb into one of the canoes and lay and look up at the mocking moon, feeling miserable and bitter. My first job, eh? *Pure slavery!*

Now if only my mother hadn't ruined things — I mean, I knew she meant well, goddamit, but she ruined it, didn't she? Then instead of being, as I now was, a crudely exploited member of the Downtrodden Working Class, I'd be a highly-paid, easy-riding concert manager and culture-vulture. And at that very minute, instead of laying there in a canoe with a hopeless hardon, I'd be entertaining Tia in a fine restaurant in Long Branch and then making savage love to her on the deserted sandy beach at midnight, under the same damn moon up there laughing at me now! Or to Sharon, in Atlantic City — or both! Why not? My harem of two! But would it really be like that, I wondered? Or would I be running down the corridors of second-rate hotels, holding up my pants and desperately fighting off Czar Wassily Dolgoruki V, with his long hair hanging over his eyes like a gorilla, and a footlong hardon like Rasputin? Well, one thing was sure, which solaced me a little. If I hadn't been anybody's prat-boy on the Brooklyn Bridge at midnight, when the homos threatened they'd kill me if I didn't, I wouldn't be doing it now for anybody just for money. Nor because they got me drunk! Money like that would never bring me any luck with girls. You had to be either *front* or *back* — A man couldn't be both.

BY ABOUT the end of the first week I had formed a plan of escape, wholly criminal and deplorable, of course, but there wasn't any other way out. They'd told me I would have to finish through the second week, or at least the day of the week that I'd arrived on, in order to get paid the sixteen bucks coming to me. And I would need money. I told them already I was leaving, and the knowledge that my escape was imminent made it a little easier to endure the last days of torment, and the incessant torture of my alkali-lacerated hands.

The day I got paid off I hung around after lunch and made myself scarce out in the woods, but I didn't leave. Mainly I stayed away from the kitchen, and my old tent where another dishwasher kid was already being installed. The camp director had driven into Port Jarvis early that morning and found another victim at an employment agency. It was like the whoors walking up & down the street on the Bowery, when I lived in New York — anybody that had the money had their choice. That's the way it was during the Depression. Money talked. And not *much* money either.

I watched the new dishwasher for a minute, unpacking a couple of pants and shoes from a frowsty little canvas suitcase just like mine. One more dumb kid, like me, looking for a free vacation. Well, I would have mine! I dabbed my swollen hands with soothing vinegar from a little bottle — the only medicine I had — and waited. Then on a sudden inspiration, I went and spoke very briefly to the new kid for a minute.

"Listen, fella," I said, showing him my little bottle, "this is vinegar. If you have any trouble with your hands — with the soap — rub vinegar on 'em!" And I stumbled away, choking up with everything I could not say.

When evening came, I was still sitting at the edge of the woods. I ate the sandwiches I had surreptitiously made up at lunch, of meat and bread and a few leaves of salad-lettuce salvaged from the guests' plates as usual before I washed them. My cloth suitcase was stashed unobtrusively behind a tree. This wouldn't be anything like Casanova's well-publicized escape from the Prison of the Leads in Venice, that Ruth and I had read in his *Memoirs* and agreed he'd probably bribed his way out and was just making a story of everything that hadn't really happened. There

333

were probably just as many autobiographies that were really fiction, as there were books pretending to be fiction that were really autobiography! If I'd have known about Henry Miller then, he would have been my best example. As far as my own escape was concerned, all I had to do was get one of those big canoes out into the river.

When it got to be good and dark I ventured to wander out and around the camp, for all the world as though I were a paying guest. Nobody paid the slightest attention to me. The Invisible Man. This was the first time I'd ever actually observed the camp's nighttime activities, except listening to the sexual promise of the opening & closing of the girls' cabin doors late at night. Usually I'd be completely knocked out with tiredness when night came, and sprawled like a dead animal on my cot, or I'd be out laying in one of the canoes where it was cool, trying to find relief in sleep from the aching and burning of my hands and wrists, trailing them over the edge of the canoe into the river.

A few fellows & girls were going up the steps of the big wooden pavilion that served as the camp meeting-hall. I thought vaguely they might be showing movies that night, and followed along. There weren't any movies, but one of the camp activity directors was beginning the reading of a play. It was obviously a very good play, full of strange fantasy, but he read it so abominably and flatly, with voice and gawky gestures as heavy as lead, that I fell asleep several times listening, and had to jerk back awake so as not to miss the end. Near me, at the edge of the hall, some of the couples were necking instead of listening, sitting on their folding chairs right in view of everybody. More power to 'em, I figured! Years later I learned by finding it in an anthology, that the play I had fallen asleep over was Ferenc Molnar's masterpiece, *Liliom*. That's what a bad reading can do for a great play.

Then another, younger fellow took over and began reading us another play. This was very definitely a second-rate piece of pure hokum called *Chicago!* by Ben Hecht & Charles MacArthur, the only professional writer I'd heard of who came from Scranton. It was evidently written as a tryout or first draft or cast for their later, greater collaboration, *The Front Page*. Bad as it was, though, the chap who read us *Chicago!* was a real actor. He was so lively, so ebullient, so joyous and bouncy in the way he read all the parts in various voices and even acted out all the stage directions, that he made this cheapy clinker of a play sound like a million bucks. He mugged, he laughed uproariously, then suddenly stopped and fixed us with a baleful, leering eye. He stamped, he hopped, jumped up & down like a jack-in-the-box; even shook his shoulders in an imitation hula dance to show his excitement. He mugged, he slugged; he shouted, mocked and wept, pretending to fall against the wall and clutching imaginary saviors. At one of the hoked-up climaxes — and he hoked them to a frenzied fare-thee-well! — he fell to his knees and lolled out his tongue at us like a clown, to catch his breath. He grabbed us all by our shirt-collars and fly-buttons and dragged us into the act. The way he performed it, this third-rate chunkajunk came off at least ten times better than Molnar's *Liliom,* still hanging unsuccessfully in the air behind us.

I believe this was one of the most important professional lessons I ever learned. To sexualize the message, as I like to do: that art is like sex, and sex is an art. It all depends on *how you do it* — How you do it, and whether or not you know how to use whatever you've got. Real emotion always helps too — again, just as in sex. That's the message. And if you haven't got it, FAKE IT!! Rabelais' *Gargantua,* Shakespeare's *Falstaff,* Cervantes, Quevedo, Lesage, Defoe, Diderot in his incredible *Rameau's Nephew,* Swift, Smollett, Twain, Whitman, Joyce, and as far back as Aristophanes and Petronius Arbiter, are all trying to teach the writer and

336

artist the same lesson: *Shoot . the . works! Overdo!!* And do it *now!* To HELL with tight-assed polite restraint! *Time Is!*

I saw a record review a while back, that unconsciously takes the exact opposite position: of all the death-lovers, against life. It was a review of a stunning new recording of Beethoven's *Triple Concerto,* not usually considered one of his major works. The three greatest soloists in the world had combined to play it: Oistrakh, violin, Rostropovich, cello; and Sviatoslav Richter, piano — all three Russians — and with the best orchestra and under the greatest conductor in the world. The record had just won the Grand Prix in France, as the finest disc of the year. But this reviewer disagreed.

Working for a right-wing magazine, as he was, he could hardly afford to say anything nice about music being played by three Russians, not one of whom had yet "passed" to the West. "The new 'All-Moscow' recording, under the baton of von Karajan," he began snidely, "makes this rather inferior music sound *much better than it really is . . .*" There's no satisfying some people, is there? Of course, that's exactly what I just said about Hecht & MacArthur's *Chicago!* — and yet. He's against it, I'm for it. Maybe Beethoven didn't know he was writing "rather inferior music." Maybe

337

he was waiting for three smiling Russkis and one tiny, dynamic, white-haired Heinie to hear what he was really saying, almost two centuries later, and to say it *right* once again. *Shoot . the . works! Time Is!*

When the play-reading broke up and the lovers all filed out, their arms one-up-&-one-down around each other's waists and shoulders, I stayed behind a minute to stammer out my appreciation to the actor who had read *Chicago!* He told me his name but I didn't catch it. He said he wasn't an actor; he was a theatre director. I told him that listening to him and watching him read was an inspiration to me, and one that I would never forget. Nor have I.

"It was real — real *commedia dell'arte*," I said, mispronouncing it badly, as I often did with words I'd never encountered except in print.

He gave me a warm smile. "Are you an actor?" he asked. "We need actors here."

"No," I said. "I'm a writer." That was the first time I ever said those words. "I'll bet I can act too," I added with clumsy flattery, "now that I've seen how it's done. But I've never tried."

I hung around behind the meeting-hall, keeping out of sight for about an hour until everything was quiet. It was chilly when I got down by the river and I hugged my cloth suitcase to my belly for warmth. I was listening to the water rippling nearby and the nightbirds hooting and sometimes skimming up slowly into view across the water. There was a big moon. I hadn't wanted that, for fear someone would see me, uh, taking the canoe, but in the end it helped me too.

The canoes were all tied together at the shore, I knew, with a long chain running through, and going over & under the end strut on each one. But there was no lock at the end of the chain; it just hung down loose into the water. That was the detail I'd already noticed once, and that gave birth to my plan of escape. I slipped the chain quietly off the last canoe, and draped the rusty end back in the water. There were a dozen of them there. No one would ever miss one canoe.

At the last minute I nearly panicked when I realized I had no paddle. They must have taken the paddles inside at night; that'd be part of locking up the boats. But one of the rowboats mixed in with the canoes had a single boat-oar slung into it. The oar was pretty long and unwieldy, what with its metal rowlock attached, narrow handhold, and all, but that had to be my paddle.

I threw my suitcase into the canoe, climbed in and crouched down, and poled off from the shore with the rowboat oar. In another minute or two I was in the fast-flowing current, floating down the Delaware

339

River. When I came out of the shadow of the trees by the shore, I lay back along the bottom with my head on the suitcase, hoping to make myself invisible. If anybody saw the canoe they'd think it was just a floating log. I didn't much care where I was going, nor how fast. I just let the canoe drift downstream while I lay there and thought.

After a while I was afraid I might fall asleep that way, so I sat up again and tried to paddle with my oar. I'd never paddled a canoe before in my life and knew nothing about it, except the inspirational poem advising that in this life everybody has to "Paddle your own canoe!" Or *"Pas de lieu Rhone que nous!"* as our nervous French teacher, Miss Talbot, had told us; her one & only joke. The rowboat oar wasn't the tool for it anyway. I would dip it in on one side of the canoe and give the water a good shove backward; then haul it out and push it in the water on the other side for another good shove and swoop. Otherwise the canoe would go around in circles, I realized, if I kept paddling on the same side. I paddled and floated that way most of the night, sometimes lying down again in the bottom of the boat to rest. It was harder work paddling than you'd expect. Huck Finn says the sky looks ever so deep when you lie on your back in the moonshine, but what I noticed most was the long, high ridge of the Kittatinny Hills, sometimes on both sides of the river, with the moon beyond.

Very early in the morning, as I was rowing my canoe along as close to shore as I could hold it, a man hailed me from a small wooden dock where he was putting fishing tackle into a rowboat.

"You always paddle with an oar?" he asked, looking puzzled.

"That's all I've got."

"You wait here," he told me. I poled in to park along the end of the wooden dock and waited for him. He came back in a minute with a beautiful board canoe paddle with a red-painted end.

"Here," he said, "I'll trade ya." The earnest look he gave me said everything. I didn't answer. "You gotta feather it," he said, giving the paddle an odd turn as he held it at his hip. "You know how to feather, don't you?"

"Course!" I said indignantly. I'd been feathering for years! We traded, and I thanked him. Then, not taking any chances on doing it wrong, I pushed off from the dock with the handle-end of the paddle.

"Be careful," he called after me. "There's a lot of white water further down, when you get near the Gap. There's rocks there too."

341

In ten minutes I was an expert featherer. Natty Bumpo had nothing on me! I loved the delicacy of the motion, like carving butter with a hot knife or pushing a wilted noodle up a wildcat's ass. That's a joke, man! I loved the power of the water as you levered the paddle against it at the end of every catch, holding the canoe straight in the stream. I realized I'd have to disguise the canoe, and pretty soon too. The man with the paddle had been kind when he saw my total inexpertness. But somebody else might ask embarrassing questions. And what about the white water? That meant rapids — would I be an experienced enough canoer by the time I hit them? Hmmm . . .

The first town I passed was just a village, and I let it go by. The next one seemed big enough to have a paint shop, so I ran the canoe ashore and commissioned some little kids playing at the water to watch it for me while I had breakfast. I took my paddle with me on my shoulder. I got a quart of milk and drank it all down right in the grocery store without lowering the bottle from my lips. That was always good for surprising people, and all the breakfast I needed too. The grocery woman asked me if I were a health nut, but I told her no; that was just cheapest meal I knew of. Was there a paint shop in town, I asked? No, but there was a garage that did any kind of repairs.

The garage-man came back with me to the river and we lifted out the canoe on our backs and piled it onto his truck. The canoe was made of wood, not canvas, and weighed a ton. At first I said nothing about painting it, which would be pretty obviously admitting that the canoe was stolen. What I wanted, I told him, was to tack strips of heavy wire all along the broadest part of the keel at both sides from end to end, to protect me from the rocks when I'd hit the white water at the Gap.

"Yeah, those rocks are bad," he agreed. "They face upstream toward the middle of the Gap. If you hit one straight on you'll go right under. You alone? It's better with two people paddling."

He decided the best would be to use half-round aluminum trim instead of wire. The whole job would cost five bucks. Or three-fifty if I'd buy a reel of aluminum separately and leave him the rest of the reel. I agreed eagerly. Then, with elaborate casualness, I added, "She could use a good paint-job too, before you put the aluminum on. How much would that come to altogether?" Six bucks. They would supply the paint, and put it on with the auto-painting pump. The outside only. I chose bright blue. It would be ready in two days.

I couldn't help thinking, though not bitterly, about the strange operation of the economic system, where the garage-man was taking from me, for perhaps two or three hours of his work and a little paint, almost as much as I earned at Camp Na-Kee-Woo-Nah for a seven day week of chattel slavery, ten bitter hours a day, with my hands tortured with raw alkali, and not being able to sleep for my own stink, for a tip. He was also getting most of the reel of aluminum half-round, for *his* tip. Well, at least the canoe hadn't cost me very much. If I could overlook the dishwashing job that netted it, which I couldn't.

This taught me another very important rule or lesson: about honesty. That things that seem tough when you do them honestly go very easy once you begin to rob & steal and fake. That may be why there's so much robbing & stealing and fakery. It's honest work that's so hard, and so expensive. Being a crook goes fast and is very cheap. Of course, it's important to keep the cops off your back. That costs money too — sometimes more than you stole. Things are tough everywhere. That was why I was having the canoe painted, to be sure. The emotions of the victim — whether dishwasher or canoe-owner — don't matter a

344

damn bit to anybody except themselves. The main thing was *to rob & steal from either the ignorant or the helpless, who have no comeback and no defense.*

This valuable lesson, learned in adolescence, made it much easier over the course of the following years for me to understand the emotions, if not the activities, of most of my later friends, employers, booksellers, and publishers, who never actually seemed to hate me, in fact often showed something like real affection and even a splendidly insincere admiration for me, no matter how outrageously they robbed & cheated me blind.

For example, when *seven* different folksong collectors who'd generously offered me texts and music of erotic folk ballads, when I announced I was preparing a book of these, all then busted their asses rushing to get out exactly similar books and sets of phonograph records ahead of me. Two of them informing me that I could now no longer use the texts they had sent me, because they were now copyrighted by them, the new owners of folksong. Or when, many years later, three of my publishers — two in America and one in England — all holding signed contracts with me, simultaneously engaged in pirating my own books against their author (me), and cheerfully told me to go piss up a rope when I complained lightly. Owing

345

to a technical defect in my copyrights, they told me, I had no kick coming.

They were in the clear. And I understood them absolutely perfectly, because that was exactly how I had felt about the canoe. *My* canoe! Now you know too. Especially if you're just as honest as I am.

I hitchhiked back to Scranton in the two days needed for the paint job to dry, and spent my remaining money on buying army surplus camping equipment: a pup-tent and a rubberized groundsheet, a big felt-covered canteen for cooling water, an enormous jackknife with about six exotic blades, and an old army haversack which included an enamel dish and man-sized tin cup. My mother also got me my heavy sweater out of the moth-balls, the one she'd knitted me, plus a bunch of canned goods, mostly canned tuna and sardines, and the two rather worn gray wool blankets off my own narrow bed where no one would be sleeping now.

I also asked her for one large old bedsheet to make a lateen sail. I told her I didn't want anything too fancy, as I would be sleeping on Mother Earth from now on. That was intended as an affectionate joke, but she didn't like it. You can't always psych your audience's reactions. I once lost a lifelong friend because I couldn't restrain myself from telling a cruel

346

joke. I can now. I told my mother I only meant that I didn't want anything too good, because all my stuff might fall in the water once in a while. I didn't say anything about shooting any rapids.

Then I went into my mother's dress-closet when my father had gone to work, dived up under her perfumed petticoats and whatnots, and fished out blindly from my secret bookshelf there a few of my less favorite books, and my one-volume Shakespeare to replace the now wholly unreadable O'Neill on the canoeing trip. I also sort of snitched a couple of the books I was supposed to be keeping for my sister Ruth but which I knew she meant were now mine. Then I went downtown and sold the whole kit, cat & caboodle except the Shakespeare back to Orvie Stück. Again, I was stunned at how little he gave me for them, compared to what I'd paid — I mean paid *him,* at the very same bookshop — but at least now I had enough money to pay for the paint-job and the aluminum strips I knew I was going to need pretty bad. Anything extra I was left with would be my grubstake.

When I got back to the Delaware, I was staggering under the weight of the chockfull haversack and the blanket roll wrapped in my sister Ruth's old yellow slicker which still fit me because it was cut very big in fisherman style. My mother had forced this on me at the last moment, even though I assured her I wouldn't need it because I'd be sleeping in the tent.

"For an intelligent boy," she said, "sometimes I think I gave birth to an idiot. What if it rains while you're paddling the canoe?" I had told her vaguely about borrowing a canoe. "You're going to put up the tent with your other hand?"

Everything fitted like a dream into my gorgeously blue-and-aluminum canoe, and I pushed off into the stream. One other extra item I had stuffed into the haversack was a large roll of white court-plaster tape from the family medicine cabinet in our bathroom. With this, the first time I stopped by the riverbank to *eat my first meal as a free soul,* I lettered out the name I had chosen on the stern of the canoe at both sides: ESCAPE. Also a fine, large, overlapping five-pointed star in court-plaster at each side of the bow.

Jews are supposed to prefer the six-pointed Star of David, if only for its religious and magical significance, but I don't. As you can easily learn in the acid-etched satire on greedy wives that is "The Story of the Fisherman and his Wife" in the *Arabian Nights* — that's the one that begins with them living contentedly together in a large upside-down pisspot with a crack in it, which becomes a vinegar jug or even a rabbit-hutch

348

in the expurgated translations — wise King Solomon, also known as Lokman in Arabic, imprisoned all the evil genies in the world in blue glass bottles and threw them all in the sea, the genies being held captive for ten thousand thousand years by the mystic power of the Great Seal of Solomon imprinted in black wax on the bottles' mouths: namely the six-pointed star, or hexagram.

The mystical medieval Spanish work known as the *Kabbala* or *Zohar*, which of course pretends to have been written by Solomon himself, if not by the patriarch Noah on top of Mount Ararat while waiting for the waters to recede during the Flood, really goes to town on the six-pointed star, observing that its strange power rises from the symbol it openly offers, in its two interlocking triangles, of the Mystical Union of the Male & Female bodies: the triangle pointing upward representing the man's pubic hair, and the triangle pointing down being the woman's, as we all know. The six-pointed star is therefore *the* erotic sign or symbol that precedes and commands all others, alluding to God's first command to Adam & Eve: *"Be fruitful and multiply, and replenish the earth."* This can also be translated by a single word: probably the same Word that opens the account of *Genesis* according to St.

John: "In the beginning was the Word . . . " What is that word?

It's very wrong of me, I suppose, but in spite of all that — and a fig for the murky old *Kabbala!* Do your worst! — I prefer the five-pointed star. Perhaps because it can be drawn with a single unbroken line, just as I constructed my overlapping court-plaster star. It therefore beautifully represents the Golden Section, the Precession of the Equinoxes, the Music of the Spheres, Infinity, or anything you please. This last is usually symbolized much less elegantly as a figure "8" lying lazily on its side, which might better be used to represent the Mœbius Strip, that perfect symbol of modern futility and commuter repetition, or cloverleaf highway exchange, which is just the even *more* infinite figure "88" *in copula*. I'd love an erotically-interlocking Mœbius cloverleaf or hexagram.

There is also some secret delight for me in the hidden nature of the five-pointed star — the Pentacle, and just as magically powerful as Solomon's Seal, you may be sure — which I discovered accidentally through paper-folding but which I've learned other people have discovered too, before me. That is, that if you tie a simple knot in a strip of paper, and press it flat, not only do you visibly create a regular pentagon, for reasons no one has yet explained (which proves it's magical, doesn't it now?) but if you hold this paper pentagon up to the light, hidden inside it you will find a perfect regular five-pointed star or Pentacle, minus only one crossline at the apex. Be careful though: if you ever learn how to fold it with the extra crossline present, the world will come to an end. So don't mess around with Eternity! There's a mathematical formula for this, discovered by a starry-eyed Italian mystic named Leonardo Pisano Fibonacci in the thirteenth century, but I don't intend to entrust it to *anyone*. You saw what they did right away with $E = mc^2$. My navigation plan was simplicity itself, and based four-square on my total ignorance of canoes, canoeing, boats, water, sails, oceans, navigation, or in general anything aquatic except sinks & bathtubs. I knew nothing. *Nothing!* That was my strength. Otherwise I would have attempted nothing. This way I would do *everything!* I had planned it all in my head while hitchhiking back to Scranton from Port Jervis. I would simply float my canoe down the Delaware through the Kittatinny Mountains and past Philadelphia to Chesapeake Bay, using the paddle only to steer with, so as to save my main strength for later. No upstream slugging for me! Once I hit salt water in the estuary — which I'd notice at once when bathing in the river — I'd put up the big lateen sail I'd have sewn by then, and

351

the outrigger I planned to construct — therefore the large bedsheet and many-bladed jackknife — and I would turn left, or "port," and then sail due north, past Atlantic City to Asbury Park, TO FIND TIA!

There were admittedly a few details about which I may have been a bit fuzzy, but in the larger sense that was my plan. For one error, that I'll admit to: the name of the bay I was heading for was not Chesapeake Bay, which was several hundred miles further south, but what did that matter? The plan remained the same. Sitting like a teenage Neptune in the stern of the big wooden canoe with my red-bladed paddle trailing lazily as the water carried me smoothly and rapidly downstream, and feathering artistically from time to time, life was not very laborious. I could have sailed to Peru that way. All I needed was a map.

There was also the detail — merely psychological, not nautical — that at the first big bend in the river, down at Trenton, I'd be only forty miles from Long Branch or Asbury Park, where Tia was sure to be. I could ditch the canoe and hitchhike there, with luck, in a few hours. But you couldn't compare that with the glory of coming in, altogether unexpectedly, like Neptune from the waves, in an outrigger canoe flying my own big triangular lateen sail made out of a doubled-over bedsheet and already named in my mind

352

the *Walloping Window-Blind* though I hadn't started sewing on it yet. I'd be in all the papers, for sure. No, that wouldn't do any real good. I'd have to be discreet about publicity. I'd use a phony name for the newspaper stories: I'd think up a good one later. I'd have to. Otherwise Tia's family would be sure to find out it was me, and forbid her to pose with me for the photographers. I suppose they'd imagine this was the canoe I used for the white-slaving trade! The river kept taking me downstream.

When I stopped near towns to set up my tent, and people saw the canoe and asked me what I was escaping from, I'd tell them *"Work, Worry, and Women!"* which always got a laugh, no doubt because they thought I was too young to have troubles with women. A hell of a lot they knew! Anyhow, it was only a private imitation of that true &-copulative — the Intercourse of Language — "Wine, Women & Song." Irreversible &-copulatives are fun: I plan to write a dictionary of them one day. They're very ancient — there's plenty of them in Hebrew, especially in the *Book of Proverbs*. But triad forms are rarer than the simple "ham & eggs" kind. Especially when they're really irreversible: "High, Wide & Handsome", "Morning, Noon & Night — in Vienna," and "Fifty-four forty, or Fight!" If you look for them you can find them. It's

353

like the pretentious bourgeois in Molière who finds out he's been *speaking prose* all his life without even knowing it. Maybe the irreversible &-copulative I should've been trying to reverse was that even rarer quadruplex form, "Bewitched, Buggered & Bewildered — and Far from Home!"

When people would ask about the five-pointed stars on my canoe now, I'd just fob them off by saying it was an Indian decoration. Actually, the stars weren't pentacles to me; they were *really* stars, for navigation. They were Tia and Sharon — one on each side — the only compass I steered by. Or rather, just Tia — Tia on both sides! Sharon was nice, Sharon was sweet, Sharon had soft tits and a juicy twat — is that an &, like "tits & asses"? . . . "soft tits & a juicy twat"? — But I didn't love Sharon. *My compass was not fixed on Tia's cunt, but on her heart.* My heart too. And Tia was all my guiding star. The *Escape*, out of Camp Na-Kee-Woo-Nah, heading south for the Atlantic Ocean. Calling C.Q., C.Q. — Seek You! Calling C.Q., C.Q., C.Q.! The river kept taking me downstream.

PITCHED my tent and rested up a day at Bushkill. Weather good. Resting from doing nothing. A cow wandered by and knocked over my tent at my last pitch: meadow by the river. Simpler to stop by the towns from now on. It was a mistake to have my hair cut short like a toothbrush when I came on this trip. Makes me look like a German aviator, and the mosquitoes are biting me at night right up onto my scalp. I guess it was a kind of suicide — about T. Never going to do that again. People keep asking what I'm escaping from when they see the name on the canoe. I tell them, "Work, Women, and Worry!" But I worry about women a lot. Log-Book too small for these notes.

Got some kids playing by the landing to guard my tent and canoe, and wandered into the town to buy some provisions. Found the tiniest bookshop that probably ever existed. When I asked the bookseller how he made a living selling books in such a small town, he just laughed and said, "Well my shop is small too." Then he told me he was really a book-scout and went all over the state and upper New York too, in his car, finding books in the attics of farmhouses and other small bookshops, and then selling them to big dealers in Philadelphia, which he said was the best book town in the East and had been since the time of Benjamin Franklin. One day, he said, he was going to find a copy of Edgar Allen Poe's first book, *Tamerlane,* and make a fortune. It was worth thousands of dollars.

"Yes, but won't you have to pay a lot for it too?" I asked.

"Are you kidding? I'll give some appleknocker three dollars for it when I find it, and he'll be so happy he'll split his face smiling."

"And then you'll sell it for thousands?"

"You bet."

"You're just a crook," I told him. "You ought to be ashamed."

This made him bust out laughing. "You've got a lot to learn about bookselling, sonny," he told me. "I'm one of the most honest in the business. A real bookman'd *steal* the guy's *Tamerlane.* Maybe trade it with him for a *Farmer's Almanac* worth a nickel."

I browsed around. He had only two bookshelves, one on each side of his desk, and a box of junk outside. In the junk-box I found an old government publication about Eskimo string figures, which I figured would give me something to entertain myself with evenings. It was marked 20¢ but he gave it to me for a dime. He said he liked my attitude. Being a book-scout must be a nice business to be in — lots of fun and roving around in strange places. But you have to have a car. I met a woman book-scout once, hitchhiking. She paid for our motel and nearly fucked my brains out.

The string figures were great, especially the swinging, singing motions of your hands and arms after you got to understand the directions for the various figures and could do them *fast*. It was really lovely, even just to watch your own hands, like the Hindu dancers' *mudra* hand motions. Paper-folding was wonderful too, but in a different way. I'd been doing that off & on a lot recently, since Endfield showed me the Lotus fold. But paper had nothing kinesthetic and dance-like about it, the way string figures did. Paper-folding was the exact opposite: all slow and deliberate, with tiny motions sometimes, that you had to think ahead with care, and do with delicacy and exactness. With string figures there was none of that. You just hooked a couple of your fingers & thumbs into the big yard-wide loop of string, and you started waving and weaving your arms and hands symmetrically and back & forth. It was a joy. The kids by the river-landing loved watching me do it too, and I taught a couple of them some easy cats' cradles. They weren't very grateful and stole some of my equipment when I wasn't looking. Kids.

When I got my lateen sail cut out of the bedsheet and sewed, and hoisted it up & down a few times on the T-shaped mast I'd built out of a laundry-pole, I felt I was prepared. Next morning I struck camp, folded up my tent, and shoved off again into the river. A few miles above the Delaware Water Gap I camped again near some small hamlet. A man sauntered over while I was putting up the tent and began talking to me about canoeing and camping. He was very nice about it and didn't act like a scoutmaster, but he was obviously a real woodsman and knew a lot more about all of it than I did. He seemed to find some of my replies puzzling.

He took a particularly dim view of it when I told him I was planning to shoot through the Water Gap right after daybreak next morning, even though I admitted that I didn't have an inflatable life-jacket. I pointed out that Indians don't wear life-jackets and have been paddling canoes down all the American rivers for centuries. I guess that was a pretty snotnose remark, but he overlooked it and just repeated that there was a lot of white water just beyond the Gap and some of it was pretty dangerous. I explained that I had a good stout rope attached to the stern brace of the canoe, and if the rapids got to be too much for me, I'd simply steer over toward the shore, jump out, and sort of warp the canoe along by means of the rope, while I walked alongside on the shore. "Like a canal-boat," I finished.

This made him collapse suddenly in laughter, which he couldn't stop for quite a while, hitting himself on the leg and getting quite red in the face. I was a bit miffed, I had to admit, and got out the rope and showed it to him. This made him laugh even more, and he farted a couple of times too. When he finally calmed down and stopped guffawing, he apologized for laughing and for the farts too. Then he explained me a few things about shooting rapids in general and the Delaware Water Gap in particular, and its famous upward-tipped diagonal strata that people come from all around the world to see. And especially how the rocks in the Delaware right there are just the same way, and sometimes thrust upward against the direction of the river. So if you hit one you just don't bump over it, the way I assumed my heavy wooden canoe would simply do. Instead you were liable to shoot straight downward toward the base of the rock hidden under the water, with a sort of empty pocket right in front of it.

I informed him stiffly that I'd heard about that already from a garage-man upriver, and that my powerful wooden canoe wasn't likely to be harmed by any rocks, and was outfitted with expensive aluminum guard-lines to protect it. He started patiently explaining it all over again about the angle of the rocks — like the Water Gap itself, he said, gesturing toward the surrounding hills. He also added that what breaks up a canoe isn't exactly the hardness of the rocks but the force of the water wherever it narrows between them in the rapids, and that a wooden canoe would be busted up into toothpicks just like a canvas one or a birchbark. In fact, he said, the light canoes were less dangerous sometimes because you could maneuver them faster. As he talked, slowly the idea of the danger people were trying to warn me about began filtering into my bemused brain.

My benefactor also pointed out that half of the Water Gap had no shore, where I'd be able to warp my canoe along like a canal-boat, as I'd planned. He started smiling again here a little, but didn't begin laughing again. In parts the Gap was more like a fjord, he said, with high rock sides dropping sheer into the water. No shore. Altogether, he seemed to think that I was seriously underestimating the danger involved, and would probably end up dead & drownded, and very soon too. At daybreak. I thought that over a while.

"Do you really mean that?" I asked.

"Sure thing, boy," he said, dead serious now. "Unless you've got a special angel watching you, you're going straight to your death." Neither of us said anything for a while.

"Maybe you're that special angel," I said in a very small voice.

He looked away. "I've got a son just about your age," he said. "He lives with his ma now."

Not shooting the rapids on the Delaware brought me to my senses. I sincerely thanked the man who had talked me out of it, though this involved swallowing the bitter pill of admitting there were things I couldn't do, had no training or maybe even aptitude for, and didn't know a damn thing about. I noticed he hadn't said anything about my paddling and feathering technique, which he'd had a chance to observe when I was landing to set up my tent. Somehow I was just as glad he hadn't said anything about that. I believe this was the first time I'd ever made such an admission, even to myself, or been brought face to face with my own brashness and ignorant overconfidence, since that cloudy Friday afternoon when the lightning struck me throwing donkeyshoe quoits in the old cowfield on the hill over Stipp's Quarry.

Well, there it was. New Prometheus as I might be, and authentically heaven-struck, I didn't know *beans*

361

about paddling a goddam canoe, and would surely have drowned myself trying to bull it through the rapids, in my glaring ignorance of real paddling technique and how to read the white water. Every single word the man said came back to me all through the night, and I could also see very clearly — now that somebody had the kindness to point it out to me in an indirect way — that all I was, was a classic braggart, ignoramus, idiot, and all-around damned fool. Maybe I *belonged* at the bottom of the river.

And another thing, maybe I wasn't really the New Prometheus at all, but just Frankenstein's monster, brought alive with a few million volts & jolts from some cheap Crookes tubes, just like in the movie. Or not even the monster; maybe just Dr. Frankenstein's hunchback helper, Quasimodo, who capers around the scene stepping on his prick and gets a little shock too, and so he thinks he's King Shit. That was me.

I could hardly sleep the whole night, I was so furious with myself. The man had promised to come back next morning to help me portage the canoe past the worst part of the rapids overland. He was as good as his word too, and was there very early the next day with a light truck. I could read his unflattering thought, that he was getting there real early just in case

I tried to hit the river at dawn, the way I said I would, in spite of everything he'd warned me about.

We got the canoe out of the water and struggled it onto the back of the man's truck, lashing it down with the cords that were to have served to raise my lateen sail as I progressed triumphantly through Delaware Bay, turning left and north at Cape May into the Atlantic Ocean — I suppose I should've said "port," not "left," if I'd been oceanborne — and fold the blushing Tia in my arms at Asbury Park. Well, it was not to be. Not this time. The man laughed himself almost sick again as I explained to him about the sail, which was furled and stowed there under the slat-seat of the canoe. He certainly was an easy audience to get a laugh out of.

"Going to sail right out into the Atlantic, hey boy?" he marvelled, smiling like Santa Claus saying "Ho, ho, ho!"

"Sure. This is a pretty heavy canoe, you know. You saw when we picked it up. All wood. It's not made out of canvas like most of them." As I said it, the thought suddenly struck me that my bedsheet lateen sail wasn't made out of canvas either.

"What about the waves knocking you over?" the man asked. We got into the truck and started down the river road to the next town.

363

I explained that I'd already thought about the waves and was planning to build an outrigger a little further along, out of some heavy branches and the rest of the cord, just the way they do with catamarans in the Pacific islands. No wire, only cords. That way it doesn't cut through the wooden branches.

"Don't kid yourself, boy," he told me. "The Coast Guard would never of let you get past Wilmington with a rig like that."

"They'd never see me," I assured him. "I'd paddle at night and sleep in the daytime somewhere along the bank. That's the way the Negroes used to escape on the Underground Railroad before the Civil War. They'd get all the way north to Canada, to Great Slave Lake and *freedom!* Mostly they didn't even have a canoe."

He drove on a while with a big silent grin. I wasn't fooling him a damn bit, nor me neither. We stopped in front of a little railroad station, somewhere beyond the Water Gap, with a small sign "Railway Express" low down on the glass of the door. And he suggested mildly that maybe the best idea would be for me simply to ship the canoe home, and save us all a lot of trouble. I agreed. We unloaded the canoe, and I started making out the tag to send it home to myself —

364

express collect. That way the ticket agent didn't have to try to weigh it, nor me have to pay.

"You got enough money to get home with, yourself?" the man asked as we walked out, but I waved away his offer.

"I've got a little. I'll be hitchhiking anyhow. There's a girl I want to see at Asbury Park. That's why I wanted to sail up there in a canoe. But I'll get there."

"Yup," he said. "A hundred miles up the Atlantic, alone in a canoe. Lateen sail and outrigger. You know, I like you, boy. You're going to end up on the gallows or in the White House."

"Why not both?" I grinned. "First they'll have to impeach me for rape." There I knew all the answers, and was ready to start ripping out old jokes at high speed from the trash-&-trivia-laden clipping file in my mind.

"You don't have to rape those modern girls," he assured me. "They'll twist off all your fly-buttons just dancing with you."

"Don't I know it! And give you twenty cents change with their nookie."

Actually, I knew nothing whatsoever about dancing, and had never danced with any girls except my sisters. And even they'd given up on me after managing to teach me the rather stately waltz, when I

365

proved too dumb and unhandy for the simple cross-jostling of the foxtrot. And I had wanted them to teach me the tango! The truth is, dancing with them gave me a terrible hardon which embarrassed me with my sisters. And what I was certain-sure of now, in spite of my man-among-men wiseguy pose and bluster, was that I would never be seeing Tia again that summer at Asbury Park.

I thanked my benefactor and hit the highway. After all, I had no intention of arriving there like a hobo, hitchhiking with a bindle on my back, maybe in a red bandanna handkerchief — not after all my big plans! First as the youthful David Belasco of concert and theatrical booking, in my two-tone gray velour vest; or then at least as the waterborne conquistador, the Stout Cortez or Columbus of the Outrigger Canoe. Well, if not Tia, then Sharon would certainly be back soon, and I'd most likely see her the hot evenings meanwhile. I hitchhiked home to Scranton, mostly in passenger cars. I didn't have to get shook up in trucks, because it was easy to get rides. My close-cropped hair made the people in cars assume I was a college-boy coming home from summer school.

Yes, I would tell the drivers when they asked, I was coming up from Philadelphia, where I was a sophomore at Temple University, taking extra summer

366

courses to get into my pre-medical training as soon as possible. I was planning to be a brain surgeon, I assured them. Or maybe just a psychologist, if I found I couldn't stand the blood.

In among the lies I was churning out as fast as necessary, or faster, I was turning over in my mind what type of prizewinning whopper or champion tall tale I'd have to dream up for intravenous injection into my family when the canoe would arrive, which the Railway Express agent had said would be in less than ten days. I worked out a lovely, complicated tale of having found a temporary job taking care of dog-kennels at Pompton Lakes, New Jersey, for who but Albert Payson Terhune, author of *Laddie: Son of Lassie* and all the other grungy dog books. And I had accepted the canoe in lieu of part of my wages. So what was I supposed to accept, dog-shit?

Unfortunately, my father knew that area a lot better than I did, from taking the train to New York every two weeks for the wholesale meat auctions when he worked for the Franklin Beef Company. "But that's up in the Ramapo Mountains near Hopatcong," he objected suspiciously. "How did you get the canoe from Pompton Lakes to the Delaware?" Well, I explained rapidly, it wasn't the Terhunes, exactly, who'd given me the canoe, but a friend of theirs.

Another writer who was visiting them, Edgar Rice Burroughs, author of all the *Tarzan* books and bunches of others, I announced, pulling this name out of the air too. He had a big property along the Delaware, and half a dozen power-boats and canoes and all. He had been very impressed when I told them I was going to be a writer too.

"Humph," my father sniffed. "All the writing you ever did, I did for you."

"Yeah — in Hebrew!" I admitted. "But they write in English." This is the closest I ever remember coming to making an anti-Semitic remark myself, except about *Portnoy's Complaint* and Serge Gainsbourg, and I'd like to point out that I was trapped by the speed of the repartee. I'm not the only standup rabbi who ever said the wrong thing trying to come up with a snappy comeback. I admit this gives a nasty insight into my racial unconscious; so what am I gonna do — hang up my jock for a thing like that? I never liked anything about Hebrew but the sound of it, anyhow. And that's the last time anybody's going to ghostwrite *my* Bar Mitzvah speech for me in Hebrew, I'll tell you that. Throwing it up to me like that in public later!

My mother made peace between us by turning on the radio, and I stalked out of the kitchen. I was preparing to duck out the back door anyway, to meet

Sharon, who I'd already phoned. She'd be waiting for me in her car at the bottom of the hill. She didn't park the Stutz in front of our house and blow the horn for me anymore, since my mother had said she was a cradle-snatcher. My sister Ruth came through from the parlor on her way to the bathroom.

"I don't care myself," she said in a very quiet tone, "as long as you don't get in trouble. But the next time you make up a story, you better be sure you get your facts straight. Edgar Rice Burroughs lives in Tarzana, California. They named the place after his books. And I think his main home is in New Zealand."

"Of course," I replied indignantly. "He has houses everywhere! *Including* one on the Delaware."

When the canoe arrived, I set it up boldly out on the front lawn, on the two notched trestles I'd used all those years sawing the scrap wood for kindling for my mother's kitchen stove. Big sign on it: "FOR SALE — HEAVYWEIGHT WOODEN CANOE WITH LATEEN SAIL. $50." All the truck drivers slowed down passing the house to stare at the bright blue canoe, with its absurd triangular sail bellying proudly in the breeze, and my court-plaster insignia, "ESCAPE," still poignantly there at both sides of the vessel. Work, Women, and Worry.

The Ratajskis' snarky Welsh friend, Smitty, came by and got in a big argument with me about how much the canoe really weighed. I got irritated and told him if he could portage it all the way home it was his, free. He clambered underneath the wooden trestles and did manage to get the canoe up into the air on his back for a minute. Then he attempted to take a step forward, all crouched there underneath, stumbled and fell flat, with the end of the canoe falling with him. Fortunately, one of the trestles was still beneath it to take the weight, or it would have crippled him for life. He got up painfully and started hopping around, claiming that he had *half* carried it and so it was his, like I said.

"I said carry it all the way," I told him. "You didn't even carry it one step."

"Welsher!" he snarled.

"That sounds funny, coming from you." I was laughing at him, which I suppose I shouldn't have done, because he had really hurt himself on my dare.

"Awright," I agreed disgustedly. "It's *half* yours because you half carried it. Get a saw and saw it in half, and take your chunk home. You can saw it across or the long way, whichever you want."

What he wanted was for me to pay him twenty-five dollars in cash, since I had agreed just a minute before that it was half his. Or at least I should sign a paper stating that I'd give him half of whatever I sold the canoe for, when I sold it.

"What I'm gonna buy with my half is a bulldog," I told him. "And I'm gonna get 'im to bite your ass off if you don't quit shystering me!"

Smitty hobbled creakily away, sort of bent in half like a busted umbrella, and loudly complaining that I was a crooked cross and a welsher, "— And what else could you expect from a dirty Jew?"

"Yeah," I shouted after him, "Jewish welshers, the best kind! I ain't gonna fight you now, 'cause you're crippled. But the next time I see you at the Ratajskis', I'm gonna stamp you down and shit in your rotten mouth!"

At that, my mother surged out onto the porch to expostulate with me for disgracing her with talk like that in front of the neighbors.

"He called me a dirty Jew. I wouldn't stand for it from Carle Aldren, and I ain't gonna stand for it from anybody!"

"So what are you hanging around with *goyim* all the time for? Polacks!! What d'you expect them to be — human beings? They're not even greenhorns, just fresh off the boat. Wait till your married *shicksa* calls you the same thing too! In the first fight — every time!"

371

"Sharon is not a *shicksa*, mama, and you know it."

"The next best thing — and her a married woman too!"

"Mama, be logical. You're a married woman; does that make you a *shicksa?*"

"No, and you don't catch me honking my horn for no young boys when the sun goes down, neither!"

I beat a dignified retreat at that point. Everybody was against me. And all my purple hours after dark with Sharon, petting like mad in the Stutz and flat on each other's bellies in the underbrush of Lovers' Lane up in Nay-Aug Park, only had the effect on me of making me yearn even more for Tia. Well, not the *only* effect — I suppose that's just horseshit. But mostly. It really did make me lonesome for Tia, whose face I kept substituting for Sharon's, especially when Sharon would be coming and her face would go all slack in a sort of lovely wonderment. And I'd try to force her then to *be* Tia, by magical means no doubt.

I knew I was making a fool of myself, and dirtying my love for Tia by mouzling around lovelessly this way with another, older woman. But I didn't know what else to do. I wasn't about to join a monastery and translate the *Talmud* into Latin. Besides, Sharon was not conscious of my complex emotions, so at least I wasn't hurting *her*. She was satisfied to keep

372

things physical with me — because that was evidently in the area where her husband was letting her down and not satisfying her, for all the cut-rate diamond rings and brooches he kept giving her, as she told me.

One diamond ring each time he couldn't get it up, was that it? Like our watch-repair man who had to pay off his imported Hungarian virgin bride with diamonds every time he wanted to get laid. The thing that bugged me most was the far-too-clever way that Sharon always treated me with such elaborately discreet distance — even shaking hands with me with the sort of bent tips of her hand! — when we accidentally met at her in-laws, the Grossmans' house, and had to say at least hello & goodbye. I ended up being furious with her, and myself, and even with Tia. With everybody.

Tia was writing me pretty regularly from New Jersey; sympathetically too. She knew I was suffering, though she couldn't have known how much. I also noted carefully she never said *she* was suffering too, and I brooded lengthily over that. I was turkey-red emotional cuticle all over. Most nights I cried myself to sleep, if I could sleep at all. The only thing that seemed to matter to me now — to do — was to dash out to my assignations with Sharon. Getting into Sharon's pants calmed my soul, at least that long. And I never got any sleep at all the nights I didn't fuck her.

373

I had a notion she felt the same way about me. We never talked about love — how could we? What could we say to each other, "Belovèd soporific"? And what kind of future could we have, with her married to Arnie Grossman? And if I went away, how long would it take for her to replace me with some other ballsy young guy? "Belovèd sleeping-pill" — wow!!

In the end, I couldn't bear to have anyone near me or to talk to anyone at all for more than a gruff hello. Actually, I still loved everyone that I really loved — my mother, Tia, my sister Ruth, and Sharon too, in a way. I just didn't want to have to talk to them, or anybody. I hated everybody! I'd also long since lost my appetite and ate almost nothing, which upset my mother more than anything else.

The canoe was sold by now, to a family with a bunch of kids, who stopped in their car to look at it and concluded the sale within five minutes. I took the money and gave my mother half to bank for me as she begged me to let her do. I told her she could have half for the household expenses too, the way she always told the girls when they got jobs, but she wouldn't take it. I left her the half to do with as she liked, and she told me she would positively put it in the bank and it'd be there when I needed it.

374

The other half I stuck in my pocket. That would be my grubstake, the day I hit the road to go to college. I didn't know when I'd be back, if ever, I told her. I didn't know what I'd be doing. I'd be working my way through college, that's all. I'd write her a postcard every week, I promised. I didn't even have to *say* anything on the postcard, my mother assured me, if I didn't feel like it. She knew I felt bad, she said, and didn't want to push me to write cheerful, phony letters the way I'd had to do when I went to school in New York and spent all my time playing hookey — and writing them letters. Just an empty postcard every week, addressed in my handwriting, would tell her that I was still alive and all right. That was all she wanted to know. But you'd be surprised, how many people won't give that peace of mind to someone who loves them — not even that. I certainly didn't when the time came that I really left home.

WHEN AUTUMN came everything had changed. Tia and I finally had our chance and muffed it, one night in early summer when I invited her over to Sharon and Arnie's house where I was babysitting for them. Tia did not know that I was laying Sharon, because I never told her.   But she knew all about the mixup with "Prince" Dolgoruki the year before, and that other homosexuals were continually trying to pick me up when I'd be coming home from the library or from work.   Ridiculous as it seems, for a girl just seventeen, like me, she was then reading Krafft-Ebing's *Psychopathia-Sexualis* — it wasn't me that loaned it to her; I only wish I knew who did: probably Mildred or another girl — and later at one point Tia quoted to me laughingly from it over the phone, from a passage about homosexual prostitutes in Paris: *"Ne fais pas chanter les rivettes!"* which she more or less wrongly understood to mean not to let the homos get into my ass.

We had also agreed frankly several times that people our age shouldn't have to be masturbated for sexual satisfaction, but there didn't seem to be anything we could do about it.   Neither of us was able to come right out and tell the other that we agreed they should make love to some third party for hygienic purposes. *Damn* hygiene!   Besides, I would *never* have agreed. That's the Double Standard, all right.   So shoot me — I was in love.

This night when I was baby-sitting is easy to tell about, because nothing really happened.   Sharon and Arnie were going out to see a show in Wilkes-Barre, so they'd be gone a long time, coming home real late. I phoned Tia at once, and she shot through our Mildred alibi-chamber at high speed, and suddenly there she was at the door. I'd already put the baby to bed with his torn teddy-bear to suck on, and when Tia came into the parlor through the big French door my heart swelled up so much with happiness I thought I would die. We didn't waste any time. We turned out the parlor lights and walked hand in hand into Sharon's bedroom where I had already tossed the top sheet negligently back.

Tia wanted to undress but I wouldn't let her, and knelt before her and took every bit of her clothing off, kissing each bit of her body as I went. Then she wanted to do the same to me but I was too impatient and tore off my shoes and pants — she'd only had to step out of hers — and all the rest. And there we were lying naked together on a beautiful big bed, with soft nightlight coming in the window. A dream come true! And murmuring and kissing, and me pulling on her nipples with my lips, and crawling all over the bed to kiss and lick her everywhere.

And then I simply couldn't wait any longer, and started to crawl over her in that goddamn missionary position, which I knew was never any good, but I felt a vague shyness about using the great side-lying position

377

I had worked out with Sharon. I felt I ought to be giving Tia some virginity of mine too — even if only of the position we'd use — since she had just murmured to me to remember that she was a virgin and please to get a towel so she wouldn't bleed all over the peoples' bed. I dashed to the bathroom and brought back a couple of face towels, which I slid caressingly under her adorable little rump. Really not so little, and beautifully round and creamy, but that's how young lovers seem to think.

I had a hardon like a crowbar — this is not poetic reconstruction; I remember it well — and I can still see her lying there on her back under me, with her mouth fallen open in anticipation and breathing in slow panting breaths. And there I was, balancing on one hand and trying to direct my penis into her. Tia knew enough to spread her legs wide open frankly, but she really was a virgin and didn't know she'd have to raise her knees to tip her cunt up toward me.

"If you don't, I can't," I murmured, dropping my prick and pulling her knees up at each side. I wanted to tell her everything all in a rush — to pull my prick into her, just where she felt her opening, with her hand; to wrap her legs around me; to shake her ass like crazy when she felt it going in. But I couldn't say any more. She was a virgin, I loved her, and I wanted it all

378

to be a beautiful experience for her, even if I had to slow everything down to a snail's pace. Snails make the hottest love in the world, and in slow motion, like a nautch-dance. Because each two snails are hermaphrodites and they're really making four-way love, like a double sixty-nine and how can you beat that? They're fabulous to watch.

So there we were, slowly sinking into each other's final embrace after a year of heartbreak and waiting. And slow — slow — slow — And then it happened!! Not lightning this time, though I would have preferred it, because this time it would've mercifully killed me. — Car-lights! Sweeping in a curve across the driveway — a car stopping, doors slamming, and Arnie's unmistakable voice saying loudly, "I'll be in in a minute. Is there any coffee?" And Sharon answering.

"Oh, damn!" Tia breathed under me. "Is it them?"

I didn't even answer, but was out of bed like a shot and jumping into my pants and shirt, stuffing it into the belt all askew. When I got to the door, barefoot, Sharon was hardly inside and I blurted out to her desperately, "I have company — in your bedroom — keep Arnie out!"

379

The look that Sharon gave me is etched on my soul. Shakespeare couldn't describe it, and I won't try. The rest is like a bad dream. The worst part was that Tia decided that the better part of discretion would be for her to dress in the bathroom. She took a moment or two to decide this. Maybe her sweet little congested organs kept her from thinking straight. I didn't have that trouble: my prick had gone flat, like a blownout tire, the minute those headlights came around and hit me right in the eyes, propped up like that the way I was, on the knuckles of one hand like a fucking gorilla. That missionary position — Oh God! Anyhow, by the time Tia made her move, there was Arnie sitting in the parlor with Sharon coming in from the kitchen carrying the coffee, and both of them staring starkly at naked Tia traipsing delicately through the darkened library beyond, and weaving her way around to get to the bathroom. Allow me to draw the curtain of mercy over the rest of the scene.

Arnie and Sharon were as sweet as pie, and talked a brief moment about the usual polite nothings with Tia, when she finally made her appearance in the parlor with the most utter *sang-froid,* exactly as though they hadn't been staring at her naked a few minutes before with all her clothes over her arm and carrying her shoes. As differentiated from my scumbag father,

380

they didn't ask her her name, or where her family lived, or anything. They were really very sweet to us, and of course imagined that we had already been fucking madly all over the bed and walls. I don't bloody well see how we could've, when they weren't even gone an hour, and were supposed to be gone till past midnight. They did mention in passing that the show in Wilkes-Barre had been cancelled, and their trip had been all for nothing.

Well, not really for nothing. Tia and I certainly had our chance, and gave it the Old College Try. We had lain in each other's arms naked, and I had kissed her lovely body everywhere and more. It seems to me — on trying to remember back absolutely honestly — that I also had *at least half* of the head of my penis well inside of her before those headlights came around and hit us. *Please don't let Tinkerbell die!* It may seem to you mighty slim pickings, remembering details like that, to which I won't absolutely swear anyhow. But that was all the consummated love I had, to mumble over like a faraway aphrodisiacal rosary of memory, with the only woman I ever truly loved — except my mother — for the first forty-six years of my life. I know I've made it sound as though the whole thing was just an adolescent farce, or Comedy of Errors. But how else can I play it? That hour destroyed any chance Tia and I still had left

— maybe it shouldn't have, but it did — to live out the love I think we both felt, and that I know I deeply and truly felt, and felt no other for the next thirty years.

One last detail, also etched forever on my memory. As soon as we humanly could, which was pretty damn quick, Tia and I got out of there, of course. Sharon held the big French doors open for us into the driveway, and just as I was about to walk out second, she said to me with her mouth twisted up into an ineffable *moue* of pretended concern: "Oh, Gershon, there's . . . just one other thing . . ."

"You mean about the money," I babbled. "Forget it. I don't believe in being paid for baby-sitting anyhow."

"No, it's not that," she said, her mouth now hardened into pure, vinegary, unspoken jealousy and spite. "But maybe you better go back to the bedroom and get your shoes?

IT WAS just about a few months after that my sister Matilda had her baby. Matilda's baby was a whole story. She had fallen for one of the fellows she was playing tennis with the summer before, named Joe Malakin, whose family was Latvian or Lithuanian. I

382

think his father worked in the mines. Everybody called Joe "Bonny," because he once had gone to Saint Bonaventure College in some nearby town for a couple of years. He was medium tall and blond and easy-going, and used to make fairly creditable pencil sketches on art paper, some of which he gave to me when I'd see him with Matilda at the tennis courts by Lake Lincoln. I remember an arched doorway and balcony in Mexican hacienda style, which I took to school with me and would dab a bit with my pencil point while showing it around shamelessly, pretending to my admiring friends that I'd drawn the whole thing myself. I had absolutely no morals then about plagiarism, whether of literature or art. If it impressed girls, I'd say I did it. That was all. Mere truth was a wayward creature that didn't matter very much to me when there were girls around to impress.

I must have had a lot of other uncharming habits too, because it appears Bonny had been playing on the courts down at Weston Field the day I went there with young Rabbi Tannenbaum, who trounced me briskly and totally, six-love, six-love. And he told Matilda that I had disgraced myself as a poor loser, yelping piteously at Rabbi Tannenbaum, who was battering at me with fast-served balls as he leaped neatly into the air in his so-unrabbinic shorts.

"Oh, gosh," it appears I had said at one point, "let me at least hit *one* of them, will ya!" That was absolutely unforgivable according to the Scranton Racquet Club rules of WASP sportsmanship. Bonny told Matilda to tell her kid brother to learn to win or lose with a stiff upper lip or else stay off the courts. Although I thought the tennis-players' pretentious gentlemanliness was funny, I decided their rules about not whining were good and tried to play it that way from then on. In fact, I never played any games with the idea of merely winning after that. Not chess — as will be seen — not cards, nothing with bats & balls, not anything. Either it was fun to play, just for the fun of playing, or I wouldn't bother with it at all. Except roulette, but that was years later, I even made up a new rule for chess, when I was playing with some kid I was teaching the game to, that neither the King *nor* the Queen could be taken. That kept them from slaughtering the game by making dumb mistakes early on, and losing their Queen, which I would pitilessly give them back, and go on playing. I later fatally improved that rule. Meanwhile, it put an end pretty soon to things like me plagiarizing John Van A. Weaver's love-poems and signing my name to them, or appropriating Bonny Malakin's Mexican sketches.

384

Well, why make a long story of it? Matilda got pregnant, of course. Girls were always getting pregnant then — it was par for the course. If you made love you got pregnant; anyhow that's what they all believed and it was amazing how often it was true when you consider the mathematics of it: that a girl can get pregnant five or six days at most out of a twenty-eight-day month. There have been an awful lot of girls who let their emotions run away with them just the wrong week of the month. Meaning that ignorance isn't always bliss, not by a long-shot. But bliss is sometimes ignorant.

Except for condoms, which worked pretty good if you remembered to put them on, or could stand them, the things most people were still using then for birth control were rather pathetic, like the girl douching with powerful antiseptics afterwards, which was always too late or even shoved the spermatozoa a little higher up into her womb; or else the man withdrawing before he came. That's been around since the Biblical times of Onan, at least, and requires proud nerves of steel in the man and the controlled timing of a tenth-of-a-second Swiss stopwatch. Few men have either, anyhow not when they have a hardon, and are coming in for their blastoff at orgasm.

385

Few women who weren't rich had such things as a vaginal diaphragm and a tube of spermicidal jelly, and you had to have it fitted by a doctor the first time so what young girl could have that? Nobody could figure out how to work the complex mathematics of the Ogino-Knaus free period, and so nobody trusted it. Even the Catholics, who had no other sin-free system available to them, bitterly called it Vatican Roulette. Punning on Russian Roulette, which is an elaborate duel or duet form of suicide. The Pill was still twenty years in the future. Not invented yet. But there were lots of abortions, all illegal and all dangerous.

I won't even go into the superstitions also being used. Like that if a girl laid on top of the man, or held her breath when the man came into her, she wouldn't get knocked up. Or that if she shook up *half* a bottle of warm Coca-Cola till it foamed, then shot it up her, that would kill all the sperms. It might have given her a thrill, but I doubt it would do more than kiss any sperms. Anyhow, that was the old, Classic Coca-Cola. Your modern, streamlined Diet Coke only kills the very thin, undernourished sperms, so be careful. I don't know what my sister Matilda did or didn't do. All I know is she got pregnant. And my family would've killed her rather than let her marry a blond Christian, a *shaygetz*.

386

How my sister Matilda was able to disguise her pregnancy for the first six or seven months, and especially to disguise it from my mother, is more than I can tell. After all, my mother had five children of her own body and certainly must've known the symptoms. But Matilda was the thinnest person in the family, and she managed somehow for a few months to wear full dresses to work, and to change rapidly into her bathrobe when she got home, on the grounds that she was tired, or going to take a bath, or I-don't-know-what. Anyhow, nobody knew she was pregnant until she was at least six or seven months gone. And then did the fights with my father begin?! — oh, wow!!

I don't believe there was a single evening after Matilda got too plump for her pregnancy to be hidden anymore — my mother was now in cahoots with her towards the end there — when there wasn't some kind of fighting & screaming going on about it. Mostly between Matilda and my father, but sometimes with my mother getting sucked in as well, to protect Matilda. Aside from my father's incessant noisy whoop-te-doo about the "intolerable disgrace to the family," and all that, the main part of the arguments seemed to center around his head-down demand that Matilda must now have an abortion, or as he prudishly phrased it, must "Do Away with her Child of Sin."

Which was the one thing that Matilda was just as head-down about: that she was not going to do.

Matilda wanted her baby fiercely. Her Christian *shaygetz* boyfriend Bonny evidently wasn't planning to marry her, just over a little thing like being pregnant. And I guess Matilda figured the baby was all she'd ever have of his love. She was also obviously too far gone now in her pregnancy for an illegal abortion not to be a real danger to her life. But my father covered that aspect of the problem trenchantly with the repeated wild reply, whenever my mother would try to counter his demands about an abortion by bringing up the matter of saving at least Matilda's life: "That immoral rotten *whoor* would be better off if she was DEAD!! — And so would this family!"

Every time he said it, and with such visible delectation, my mother would blench, her head quivering from side to side in the violence of whatever words she was refusing to say in answer. And she would rush out of the room: into the kitchen if they were fighting about it in the parlor; into the parlor if they were in the kitchen, and into the bathroom — slamming and bolting the door violently — if he was stalking her back & forth torturing her verbally, as was his habit. Us kids often did try to horn in, and make him let her alone — Matilda too — but my mother would just impatiently wave us all away, and keep on serving him back a verbal Roland for his Oliver. Right up until his now-usual climactic "rotten whoor" line about being "DEAD!!" Which struck her to the heart every time, and she would rush away, dynamited. My father pretty clearly liked that, and would strut around, silent and victorious for a few minutes afterwards, glowering and mumbling to himself in proud self-pity.

Eventually, of course, things worked out in accordance with the ancient standard system laid down in the Garden of Eden, or somewhere in its suburbs, by that first sinful unmarried couple, Adam & Eve, at the urgent command of their Creator Jehovah — the very first remark He ever made to 'em, in *Genesis* 1:28, "And God blessed them, and God said unto them: 'Be fruitful, and multiply, and replenish the earth'." And so the time finally came for Matilda's baby to be born, just nine months after that spring night when she and Bonny had enacted their immemorial part.

Everything came to a head one freezing winter night — I think it was in January — when Matilda's premonitory pains of childbirth came to her about eight o'clock at night. I was sitting at the time in the parlor, in my usual uncomfortable corner armchair, trying to read my usual few columns of the *Merriam-Webster Unabridged Dictionary* in two enormous, unhandy

389

volumes; a lunacy I was then seriously engaged in almost every night. Maybe I should've been tatting a sampler in cross-stitch instead, reading *"God Bless Our Happy Home"* in Old English. The screaming & carrying on was especially fierce, of course, that night, as my father realized that this "illegitimate" baby was now about to be born, and *in his house!* Just as I had been born, in that very same house — in fact in the very parlor we were all sitting and shouting — some seventeen years before; also one early winter night.

The noise he was making went on for at least a couple of hours, with him dashing back & forth every few minutes to shout at Matilda and my mother, who had now taken up their vigil in the girls' bedroom, ruthlessly keeping him locked out. I made a side-foray, pretendedly to the bathroom at one point, to check up on how things were going, just for my own peace of mind. I looked out the kitchen window as I passed. It was now snowing slightly. I listened at the bedroom door. Matilda did not cry out at all, when her pains came, but was making some whimpering groans from time to time. I went back to my Webster in the parlor, where my father was holding court with himself in his armchair beside the big floor-radio, which he would turn on unbearably loud if anyone came in to argue with him or dared to answer him back.

390

At a certain point my mother came in and told him flatly that it was now absolutely necessary to get Matilda up off that bedroom bed, and out there to the Hahnemann Hospital nearby. She told him she was no midwife, and Matilda would now have to be allowed some expert care. Sensing his evil opportunity, my father suddenly dashed past her and into the girls' bedroom, of which the door was now unlocked, and started pulling & hauling Matilda off the bed, in her constant bathrobe, and all the way through the house into the parlor. I didn't even realize what he was doing until they arrived in the open portico between the dining-room and parlor, Matilda practically passing out, but still fighting him and struggling to get free.

"Stop it!! Are you crazy?!" My mother was screaming. "She's going to have her baby now — *tonight!!* Are you crazy?!"

"No, *you're* crazy!" he hollered, struggling with all three of us — my mother, Matilda, and now me — trying to get Matilda out of his so-innocently sadistic incestuous embrace. Not the moment for it. But my father somehow dragged the whole Laocoon group all the way to our front door, and tore it open with one hand, shouting these words, which I don't expect I'll forget in a hurry: *"She can have her baby on a garbage-can*

391

cover, in the street!! In the street!!" he kept shouting. *"In the street!!"*

Snow was blowing up onto the front-porch, and a few flakes may even have filtered into our faces through the open door. It was really getting too much. Positively the identical scene from an old silent movie my parents must've seen years before, but I never had, called *Over the Hill to the Poorhouse,* or something like that. In which the stern Abraham-Lincoln-bearded appleknocker father does indeed push his Errant Daughter and her Newborn Child out into the snow! Nature imitates Art, alright, alright; just the way Oscar Wilde said.

I decided things would have to stop. I rushed out into the kitchen to find my butcher-knife to kill him with. The light was on, and before I even got to the kitchenware drawer with all the knives, I suddenly noticed by the table the dark brown painted chair that I knew had one of the cross-rungs loose. I snatched the chair up into the air and ripped it apart by the two front legs like Samson tearing open the jaws of the desert lion. Then, with the ripped-out rung brandished in my hand, I rushed back into the parlor and started whamming my father with it across the head and face like a madman. He let Matilda go instantly, still shouting his chorus, *"In the street!"* I don't remember what I was thinking, except how intensely *I wanted him to be dead*. With my last whack, I got him right across the face and mouth, and knocked one of his front teeth bloodily out and onto the floor. That finished the entertainment.

Can't remember what happened next. My father rushed away, I guess to the bathroom to tend his lost tooth and blood. I remember being disappointed at how little blood there was. I would have loved for there to be a lot more. My mother was still holding Matilda, getting her away from the front door, to sit down on the sofa in front of the big triple bay-window. The same bay-window I was born at. She told me to call a taxi to take Matilda to the hospital, I remember. I found the telephone number and was trying to dial, when I realized I still had the chair-rung in my right hand that knocked my father's tooth out.

Must've fallen completely out after that; probably fell dead-asleep. Emotional crises do that to me the minute they're over. I'm only lucky if I can hang on till then. Angry, and maybe wildly imagining myself victorious, but all collapsed inside. It's just the way Freud says about love & hatred: hating your enemies doesn't hurt you a bit; it's invigorating. It's hating the people *you really love,* or want to love, that breaks you up so badly inside. I imagine that's why divorces are such a ghastly trauma.

By morning everything was over & done with. All Quiet On the East Scranton Front. Matilda's baby had been well & safely born during the night at the Hahnemann Hospital, I think. I was given the word by my mother when she woke me up in the morning. She told me I was to leave work early that afternoon and get to our synagogue, Temple Israel, on Monroe Avenue, for the afternoon-evening prayer, and name the baby. If I couldn't get out of work, I'd go to temple early next morning for the sunrise service, which is what actually happened.

The baby was a girl, and I was to be godfather and name her. My father had rushed off to work that first/last morning and refused even to hear about the baby's birth, or whether it was a girl or a boy, or to have anything whatever to do with naming it. And he would certainly not go anywhere near Temple Israel, to be, as he shouted at my mother, "witness of our family's disgrace, forever!" I noted grimly that didn't give *me* much leeway for disgracing the family in my turn later. I'd just have to do my best.

At the synagogue, Rabbi Arzt told me he understood from my mother over the phone that my sister was not married and that the baby's "putative

394

father" — as he put it grinchingly — was not Jewish. And he explained to me that the baby would therefore have to be named — Judith. — All half-Jewish girl babies are given that name. I think, but I'm not sure, that half-Jewish boy babies are named Abraham, in respect of the Patriarch Abraham having been circumcised by his own hand since not born a Jew. Rabbi Arzt was full of out-moded religiosities like that, which I felt didn't truly square up very well with the modern science and psychology-oriented sermons he always gave. But I noted with pleasure that the secular name Matilda wanted for her baby, June, would fit very well with her Hebrew name of Judith, which means in Hebrew, the Jewess. I was glad later I had stood in for my father as the baby's godfather. Because that baby, known as Cookie-June when she was very little and a long time after, was and is my favorite member of our whole family tribe, except my own wife & children.

I wasn't the only one, either. Guess whose favorite she then rapidly became? My father's, to be sure! And within two months of the night the baby was born — and *not* "on a garbage-can cover in the STREET!!" after which my mother took care of it while Matilda went to work, my father was doing everything he could possibly butt in on, except changing diapers. And that was only because Cookie

395

was a girl, which he stated pontifically would therefore make it immoral for a man to do. Once a hysterical prude, always a hysterical prude. And it looks a lot worse on a man. Awfully cowardly and hypocritical too. His knocked-out tooth was never mentioned, by the way, not even once. When he was told one day, when he came home at noon for lunch, that the baby was sick and needed some kind of shots, he immediately forgot all about his job, got a taxi, and rushed her over to Hahnemann Hospital to do everything necessary.

The rest of the story he told often and proudly about himself. When he saw the doctor stick the hypodermic syringe "into the baby's *flesh*" as he put it, his own head immediately began to revolve, and he knew he was going to be sick to his stummick. Nevertheless, he refused to allow himself to fall out, because he now had the baby in his arms again and was walking through the hospital hall and down the long stone flight of steps outside. His head was going around "like a whirligig," he told us, and he "staggered down the stone staircase hardly knowing what he was doing." Then, when he got to the bottom, he carefully deposited the baby on the very last step, before an uninterested audience of a couple of waiting taxi-drivers, and fainted.

"The human mind," he always added sententiously when telling it — it was one of his favorite lines — "is a wonderful thing." Yes, and so is human play-acting and theatrical hypocrisy.

After that I no longer believed in my family as anything but a bunch of unhappy lunatics; all except my mother of course. God knows she was unhappy too, but she was sane, and worked as hard as a dog to keep her family treading water. And with a special glint in her eye and category in her heart for me, no matter how bad I might be, according to my father's hard rules for everyone but himself. After all, I was her son, her only son; and my tangle with the Intelligence Quotient people had proved to her — if not entirely to them — that she had been right all along in expecting that her only son would be a genius. Even if there was no more real hope for him to be the ambitiously planned "leader in Israel."

ALL I REALLY wanted now was to get away from home — to college, if possible, and as soon as possible. And for that I would need money. I had a pleasant job now in the haberdashery shop, where I was the sweater specialist. This just meant I was the youngest employee and so had the pesky duty of refolding the sweaters after the customers mussed them all up, and then walked out without buying anything. It was considered the hardest job in the store, although really just a walk. In fact, I kind of enjoyed the kinesthetic physical motions of flinging the rich wool sweaters about, and sinking them into the needed folds. Certainly a lot more exhilarating than sticking endless pins back into the unfolded dress-shuts, the appointed work of the more favored older clerk, Shawn, whose racy Irish vocabulary and secret fund of bawdy jokes always left me marvelling.

Because, of course, I was still and already deep into the collecting of sexual slang and jokes and songs, when I could find any; as I had started doing in my second year in high school, at fourteen. Jokes and slang were everywhere; but songs were harder to un-nest. Maybe because the broad, unbuttoned situations people could sing in were hard to set up or fall into; whereas it was easy for any two people to knock off work or play for a minute, to put their heads together and discreetly share or retail the latest dirty jokes. As they were invariably called, though I would doughtily argue they weren't dirty at all, and certainly no dirtier morally than the presumably perfectly clean jokes about cheating and fooling and hurting people.

I always lost those arguments, not realizing, so early on, that people deeply yearned for their dirty jokes to be *good-and* dirty; that they never really laughed whole-heartedly over the halfway, suggestive stuff. How could they? That was the whole point, I now saw. And the whole moral holiday and relief the dirty jokes gave them. Check back to what Freud said: a nice, sinless, presumably harmless way of defying and dirtying and even destroying in fantasy all the people and institutions they really loved, and felt they should consciously respect. Naturally, I was by now deep in reading all the books on psychology I could get hold of. Non-revolutionary socialist revolution now bored me. My sister Ruth had started me off surreptitiously on the real stuff with Freud's *Psychopathology of Everyday Life,* which she recommended I should keep hidden from our father, owing to its "sexy" title.

"Well," I told her, "I've already read Krafft-Ebing's *Psychopathia Sexualis,* about all the freaks. And so have you. I guess I'm ready now for us normal everyday psychopaths."

BY NOW I'd already learned to use a little built-in flattery trying to get their best and deepest-loved jokes out of people. Flattery is hard for me, as I'm basically more the nasty, critical bastard type. But people do like to talk, and like to figure you think they have something to say worth saying. And I found it was often very flattering — to some, not to everybody — to see me actually whip out my little brown leather loose-leaf notebook from my inner pocket (by the heart), and sketch rapidly in a sort of shorthand the bawdy jokes they told me, but not the others; and pin to the wall in full flight some perfect turn of folk-phraseology they dredged up from their almost forgotten childhoods, or even invented themselves: how the hell can you know?

Best of all, I found eventually, was asking people to tell you their *favorite joke*, in any sense of the term. This, I assured them with solemnly unconscious braggadocio at first, would allow me to bat right back at them instantly, like a Reno slot-machine paying off in silver dollars, their entire blitz psychoanalysis. Freud couldn't touch it! Practically as revealing, I'd warn them, as being unwillingly HYPNOTIZED, and subconsciously forced *on the spot* to unveil themselves beyond even Isis' last and Seventh conscious veil. Just straight dishonest advertising, to be sure, but how the jokes flowed into that notebook!

Be assured that not everybody fell for my seductive blitz-psychoanalytic bait. My own fifteen-year-old-daughter stopped yesterday right in the middle of a joke she'd just heard in high school and specially liked, when I warned her that it might tell a lot more about her than it would about high school humor. I very often had that trouble when I was that frank, right from the beginning; and curiously just as often with boys as with girls — men or women. Maybe more often. Girls are pretty darn anxious to give themselves: body & soul. Us men count on that. Whatever the case, or sex, most people fell in quite happily with the evident parlor-game aspect of the fun: *Tell us what you laugh at, and I'll tell you what you are.* Especially when I'd offer to begin with a couple of my own most shocking favorite jokes — and would tell 'em too — and challenge anybody who wanted, to analyze away and be damned! "You show me yours, and I'll show you mine, but don't tell your mother." Come on! — take off them pants!

Trying it out on my family, early on, what was my astonishment to hear my mother tell the two following jokes, as her favorites, both of which she'd heard years before, as a young girl in Rumania, she assured me and my two older sisters, both present as well, though not my father of course. *A girl is told by her*

401

mother not to marry any man whose penis isn't six inches long, and who hasn't got a million dollars. Her favorite boyfriend then refuses to marry her, saying, "Well, maybe I can borrow the million dollars from a bank, but I'm not going to cut the last two inches off my prick to marry any girl!"

But her real favorite, my mother admitted, apologizing for its being so dirty, was this one, into which she segued immediately: *A man goes to the rabbi and demands an immediate divorce, on the grounds that his wife has such filthy habits. "What are these habits?" asks the rabbi gravely. "I can't tell you," the man refuses; "they're too awful to talk about!" "In that case," says the rabbi, "I can't give any divorce. The other party has to be confronted with the evidence." "Oh, alright," the man agrees. "If I have to tell, I'll tell. Every time I go to piss in the sink, it's always full of dirty dishes!"*

I thought that one over a long time — I'm still thinking it over — after dutifully laughing uproariously, of course. The collector has to do what he can to push along the "performance context." And especially, I asked myself then if my mother could possibly not recognize, in the horrible life my father had led her at least since I was five years old and sleeping in the attic, the image of her so plain & simple symbolic statement, lightly disguised as his pissing in the sink and blaming it all on her. Later I also wondered about another possible symbolic meaning, perhaps much deeper

402

buried, when you consider what organ a man uses for pissing. Of herself as the maternal and just recently nourishing sinkful of dishes; and my father, therefore, as pissing not on them, but on her.

With all the love in the world, so much for my mother's favorite joke. My own favorite then was not a bit less bitter, and just as revealing, at least to me. For a long time I refused to analyze it verbally at all. Just fobbed myself off with broad happy-hat bromides concerning ancient Greek theories of humor, with inordinately long adjectives & nouns to match, in order to keep my own mental peace, the little I then had. My favorite joke — who can deny it! — added up to everything I felt about my own home and native-born family life, and why all I wanted was *Out!* This stayed my favorite and bitterest joke for twenty years or more, and successfully drove me off any idea of real marriage till I was a decade beyond where Dante thought he was already, "halfway down the road of this our life." After which, it was replaced as my favorite joke by an even more desperately self-revealing item. But that one, finally, holding out a burning ray of hope!

Here was my own blitz-psychoanalytic joke, after seventeen years of living the fairly standard hometown family-story you've read so far. Neat, sweet & complete, it also sizes up the whole mess in five

403

wonderfully succinct and sardonic final words: *A vaudeville comic, trying out for a job, is describing his act to the theatrical agent. "It's very simple," he says, modestly. "My wife and I come out and shit on the stage, and the kids* wallow *in it." "My God!" cries the horrified agent, "what kind of act do you call* that?!*" "Well," says the vaudevillian, proudly polishing his fingernails on his lapel,* "We *call it* THE ARISTOCRATS*."* Fast curtain on Chapter 12.

CHAPTER 13

ANN ARBOR OR BUST!

TIA'S FAMILY naturally took her with them early that summer to the same beach in New Jersey that I'd planned to arrive at by canoe the summer before. But this time, another young-fellow-me-lad turned up from Scranton: phony, fat Cy Endfield, back from his glorious freshman year at Yale where his rich furrier father had been able to afford to send him. The presumed excuse for his seaside vacation was that Endfield's family might be opening a branch for their store there, peddling mink coats and white fur stoles for autumn wear to tourist females on the main shopping drag at Asbury Park. Who knows?

Endfield gave Tia a big rush, and as his family was stenching with money he took her everywhere. But he did not try to make love to her, in any physical sense, as Tia assured jealous me in her letters, because all he really wanted was some decorative young mammal on his arm to give him *class*. Sometimes she wondered, she said — clearly when she felt horny — whether he wouldn't find a Russian wolfhound on a leash just as satisfactory. He also very much wanted to beat my time with her, being fanatically competitive with me, always, and knowing as everyone did that I loved her madly. He therefore spent most of their evenings together squiring Tia around to restaurants and expensive entertainments, and all the rest of his time with her, as she explained, talking about high philosophical matters. I could hardly believe this, but fervently hoped it was true. While obviously not homosexual, Endfield had a cold and manipulative *sexless* quality about him that no one could fail to observe, and a mocking theatrical phoniness that had marked him early for acting and the motion pictures. Both Kennedy and I assumed, without knowing anything about it, that masturbation was his favorite sexual act. It was very clear — even to Cy — that his cold passion for cards-&-coin magic and prestidigitation was the key to his character, and that he never actually would or could love anyone but himself.

Endfield was now soon to blossom out as a sophomore at Yale, essentially a snazzy eastern seaboard college for rich boys, and sophomoric he was. Nothing was of importance to him now but tiresome card-tricks and high aesthetic and socialistic talk in the

406

vaporous vein of Oscar Wilde's *Soul of Man under Socialism* and other soft-focus radical gab. In this he thought of himself as emulating the poet Shelley, a century before, getting thrown out of Oxford at the age of nineteen for his inflammatory pamphlet on *The Necessity of Atheism*. As religion didn't seem to have much zip anymore in the twentieth century, Endfield's imaginary revolt centered more around economics. This sort of airy radicalism squared rather poorly with the crude vulgar bucks in his petit-bourgeois family background, based, as I had the unkindness to point out to him, on peddling the pickled skins of dead vermin and ermine to the rich, to decorate their females. A pure slice of "conspicuous consumption" right out of Veblen's *Theory of the Leisure Class*; which had become my bible after Bellamy, and of which the elegant sardonic style — by a poor Midwest Scandihoovian carpenter's son — was all my delight.

Like all the *révolté* college dilettantes I knew then, and was later to know in France, Endfield was also — at least for show — quite gone on all the latest fad books and tempest-in-a-teapot literary and artistic controversies being plugged in the *New York Times* and *Tribune* in their competing book review sections. At the moment there was Thomas Mann's *Magic Mountain*, and *The Fountain* by Charles Morgan, for starters, now

407

replacing Thornton Wilder's pipsqueak-philosophical *The Bridge of San Luis Rey*, which the various book clubs were still pushing. Also a whole slew of highly faddish British novelists and short-story writers, such as John Cowper Powys in his *Wolf Solent* (snobbishly issued in two volumes for no particular reason), most of whom seemed to be drooling on about impotence lightly veiled as fashionable homosexuality, or the reverse.

And of course all the endless volumes of Marcel Proust's *Remembrance of Things Past* and Henry James, covering the identical subject matter. Plus some priceless *precioso* named Julian Green, an American expatriate living in France who purportedly wrote all his drearily groping works in French and then translated them back into English himself. Thus going Oscar Wilde's *Salomé* one up and one better, since Wilde had secretly needed Pierre Louÿs to ghostwrite the French original of *Salomé* for him, and then himself "assisted" his spiteful boyfriend and nemesis Alfred Bosie Douglas, to translate it back into English. It was all very refined.

I tried to read some of this snobbish prinkle-prankle stuff to keep up with the literary and philosophical program, with jargon to match, that Cy was shoving on Tia, but it was just too ethereal and too vaguely written for me to wade through. "Like fucking

408

a half-frozen jelly fish in a bucket of lavender snot," as I remember commenting to him in my juvenile humorous vein. Adding a few snide sidebars from Gilbert & Sullivan's *Patience* to the same effect. Of course I was not able then to pinpoint it as just the homosexual *beau parler* and empty dithering all this ephemeral literature so evidently was, but I was also not to be intellectually intimidated and told them both flatly that this shit was not for me.

I got back a rapid, bloated note, in Endfield's usual big-talking Negro minister style, bawling me out tastefully for my vulgarity and tastelessness, which he assured me he was carefully pointing out to Tia. At first I planned to wipe my ass on this and send it back to him, but decided he would try to get me in even worse with Tia for it if I did, so I contented myself with wiping my ass on it, and flushed it down the toilet. That don't change things, but you feel better.

As opposed to the fairy-tale where the little boy says that the Emperor's "new clothes" are a fake and a fraud, and everybody listens to him; all I have gotten all my life, for refusing to inhale and succumb to all this fad gubbidge in snob literature and mock modern music and art, that Endfield was trying to peddle me then at second-hand, was to be told that I was a hopeless vulgarian. I guess it's true too. Anaïs Nin certainly kicked me out of her bed on the same aesthetic grounds just a few years later. But for Tia's benefit I was able to cold-cock the argument this time by replying that I had no more patience for modern fictional authors, and would be reading nothing but Shakespeare for the rest of the summer. I figured that even Endfield didn't have the nerve to bad-mouth that.

My worst blunder was when I told them that the only two recent books I had really liked were Thomas Wolfe's *Look Homeward Angel,* which was the obviously autobiographical story of a young man very much like myself trying to find his intellectual niche. (This Endfield stated was utterly immature and poorly written.) — and Lion Feuchtwanger's *Power,* which was the expurgated American title of a magnificent historical novel that came out first in Germany and even in the British translation under its true title of *Jew Suss.* About the Jewish court financier Oppenheimer in the eighteenth century who ended up hanged on a special gallows higher than Haman when the German duke protecting him fell dead suddenly of a heart-attack one day.

Although just as Jewish as I was, Endfield told me flatly that mere Judaism was not a worthwhile subject for a book anymore, adding pointedly that *he and Tia* — who was also Jewish — felt that for any

410

book to be worth its while today, it had to concern itself not with eccentric individuals and outmoded religions but with *humanity*. In fact I thoroughly agreed with him or them but when I replied that I couldn't see how Thomas Mann's sexless convolutions in the higher altitudes of a Swiss tuberculosis sanitarium would hasten the Future of Humanity, Enfield stated that I was merely too dumb and coarse to understand the symbolism involved. The sanitarium *was* humanity, he explained in a rather impatient but quite lengthy letter, and we were all sick unto death. I wanted to answer that I didn't feel a bit sick, except over his big-talk letter, but I went along with the gag and said I agreed, but why keep reading about peculiar sexless people going around in the barrel like that? What was our plan for *action?*

As can be plainly seen, I was a real tribulation to him, since obviously Endfield and I were really struggling silently over Tia. Her brain, that is. Not her body. There he was, right on the premises by the oceanside, with the books and the shows and the snooty restaurants and taxis all the time; while I was desperately trying to fight him with a couple of 3-cent postage stamps and my already ink-stained Bar Mitzvah yellow fountain pen, to get him off my girl's front porch and snag her back to me. Not easy; and my bad

411

character made it even harder as I'll roundly admit in a minute. The only reason I was writing to him at all, as will be understood, was that Tia couldn't receive letters directly from me, and the only contact with her I could have all summer was via phony, fat, finger-twiddling, attitudinizing, verbigerous Cyril Endfield.

I tried at least to get things away from the tuberculosis and impotence of Mann and Powys, and back into the erotic groove. And I sent Cy a copy of James Branch Cabell's *Jurgen* to give to Tia for me. At least that had some openly symbolized sexy passages about virile two-handed swords and glistening caverns, and hiding the swords in the humid caverns and whatnot; and was not about the well-rotted and slowly dying humanity we all presumably deplored but were supposed to be avidly reading about all the time. I also sent her in the same package a lovely illustrated edition of Anatole France's *The Revolt of the Angels*, which had some elegantly erotic passages where the flirtatious Frenchwoman in her high but bulging corset tries with her guilessly straying hand to seduce her guardian angel. Endfield refused to give Tia the books, on the admittedly valid grounds that I was "patently trying to seduce her on paper," and also refused to be our letterbox anymore.

Meanwhile, it appears he was not as anesthetic as he seemed or wished to be thought, for he also talked to her a great deal about me, as she told me later, mainly about how loud and uncouth and undesirable I was, which again nobody can deny. Running down the opposition, as I had tried to run down Manny Grossman to Gwen Schwab, seems to have been a principal tactic among us young swains. This always tipped our hand that we were competing for whatever young lady was the audience to our animadversions on the other guy. It took me years to learn that this seldom or never works, and that the only reason it seemed to work so well with Gwen is because she was the one who was doing the competing — with Tia. The real thing, I find, to cut out another man with a girl, is to get the girl alone in a warm parlor, bedroom or bath, or cool woodland glade, wrassle her down onto the hearthrug and tear off her bra and panties with your teeth. No reference need be made to the vulgar competition. Out of sight, out of mind. All's fair in love and war.

When Tia got back home, nearly a month before Endfield did, he wrote her a long series of letters for the next month, all of which she showed me as they arrived, or read me over the phone, in which he continued to anatomize me ruthlessly. All the letters

413

referred to me under the secret code of "Juliet" — code name for "Romeo," Tia assured me, in respect of my loving her — also *with feminine pronouns to match,* in all references to me. Why that? Because Tia's mother would try to get to the mail every morning before she did, and opened all her letters to make sure I wasn't writing to Tia or getting any secret messages through. Endfield was really doing a great job for me, keeping me the main subject of their elaborate correspondence as "Juliet" this way, but I still didn't appreciate it.

Tia and I managed to see each other twice more, evenings, at our old trysting-place on the cliff over Stipp's abandoned quarry. She assured me that Cy had never touched a hair of her head or anywhere else, and was not really interested in girls at all, only in vapid talk. We didn't make love on the ground, because Tia said she was afraid of rolling off into the quarry, but we did everything else we could. Actually the idea did pass through my mind again fleetingly that it might solve everything if we rolled over the cliff by accident, when we were coming, and died together beautifully. Tia read my mind. We'd been through the whole thing the year before, anyhow, about that cliff over the quarry; but we had nowhere else private we could go to. Tia also had lots of guts hidden behind her

414

China-doll front, and refused to be intimidated by my unspoken threats.

She was of course still strictly forbidden to see me, and the ladies' club spy-service her mother had set up like a new Sir Francis Walsingham or Cardinal Richelieu was still operating by telephone against us. They say one woman likes to help another woman get fucked, but these biddies certainly didn't act like it. I admit they had all been warned I was the head of a dastardly ring of Lackawanna County white-slavers — at the age of seventeen — doubtless operating with canal-boats in deserted mine shafts, like in the *Phantom of the Opera,* so maybe they were just trying to do their motherly duty. But when I couldn't see Tia I became frantic and aggressive, against her as well as everyone else. I would even write wildly nasty and violently obscene letters to Tia, sometimes insulting all the parts of her beautiful body, especially not forgetting her buttocks and genitals, and even her breasts which were in truth all my joy and delight. But I had the good sense, at the same time, never to pass any of these epistolary monstrosities to our old faithful letterbox, Mildred, to give Tia; and I destroyed them all. All but one.

The final handwritten letter I did unfortunately send through in a moment of mild insanity, covering

415

the girl I loved with verbal sadism and filth on some poppycock pretext or other — probably just jealousy or frustrated bile — including, for openers, a whole alphabetical anti-litany of insulting and obscene adjectives just by way of stylistic display. Tia properly refused to take it seriously, and gave the letter back to me quietly the next time I saw her, assuring me that the dirty words hadn't shocked her at all and that she understood that I was half crazed with frustration. I almost sank to the floor weeping, at her forgiveness, like the modern folktale about Patient Griselda and the husband who tears the dishes off the banqueting table on a bet with a friend to find out who has the most patient wife. I still have that letter — to my shame — and it is truly horrible. I wish I could say that it taught me a lesson, but it didn't, and I still sometimes do exactly the same thing in words, and worse, though I never again committed such an outburst to paper.

Since music has charms to sooth the savage beast, or breast, Tia then kissed my eyes, and to prove she had really forgiven me she laid my head against her breasts and started humming the Beethoven *Moonlight Sonata* which she had been learning on the piano to please me, but that I had never been able to hear her play. I thought my heart would burst. Her tiny little Oriental heart-shaped face, with the black widow's

416

peak coming down sharply toward her eyebrows, shone down on me angelically in the moonlight that night over the old abandoned quarry on Colfax Avenue. It reappeared often in my dreams, exactly the same, for years afterwards. I could sketch her face perfectly for you now. That would be the last time we would be together as lovers, but I didn't know that then.

There are situations in life that one cannot describe. Too close. Too involved. Too prejudiced. Too hard to stand back and take a calm and a sensibly appraising look. Too tied-up and tortured in and by it. We've all been through that. Well, this time I hardly need to describe it. Luckily for this record of my tormented youth, of the girl whose love I'd lost for good & all, the religious faith that never meant much to me and that I had now discarded forever — at the deeply mature age of seventeen — along with the timid and secret approaches to the *Talmud* and *Kabbala* that were to be my first internalized escapes into the heavily populated empyrean of empty scholarship; I have a witness! An impeccable, irreproachable witness, who carries his, er, testimonials proudly before him as he goes — and I do mean proudly.

This is an authentic letter, one for the book! — Typewritten, folded, sent transcontinental through the

417

U.S. mails, received and read — I don't know how seriously — and then snatched from the burning disinterest of Time, then suddenly waved before my astonished nose some thirty years after its date (August 8th, 1935) by the young Hollywood writer to whom it was written: Israel Shapiro, known preferentially, though not to fame, as Paul Jarrico. Well, the Scottish ploughboy-poet Robert Burns asked the gods *the gift to gie him, To see himself as others see him.* This is how others saw me then, at seventeen, or a year or two older, in some of the longest, worst spelled epistolary sentences ever written:

"Two years ago I reached a certain point in my personal education and I was vastly pleased with myself and content that I was prepared to enter and participate in any, all, good, bad, intellectual, radical, babitty, sham, society into which chance might thrust me. I looked back, vastly proud, at the Education of Cyril Endfield. In the year and a half which had just passed, I had learned a new language, seen a new world, passed the horizon of "unthinking", crashed through the pall of the everyday into the new life which was conscious, alive to the perrenial [*sic*] issues which change the flux of our meager existence, which had books, and three — even four or five — syllable words sliding glibly unselfconsciously from rolling confidant tongues, and the parphenalia [*sic*] of culture with music and art (painting) and the metaphysics of science, and the polysyllables of the psychological jargon which so neatly pigeonholed the inception, genesis, and resolution of the innumerable conflicts impinging on this new life, and more, a certain new freedom as the doldrum stupid superstitions in which we were so carefully reared fell before the gloriously naive iconoclasm and the overassured agnosticism, and the whole vast important battle against "mores", the rebellion, the clarion call-to-arms of all these new intellectual forces in defense of the acquired world with its uncustomary customs, its poses against poseurs, its childish superiorities, its exoticism to the outside, its incredible overconfidence, its hypersensitivity, its emotional hysteria, its self-flagellations — it was new, novel exciting this burgeoning of the intelligence, but soon I had read enough books (and had *encountered* as many more) to carry on an enlightened conversation, and heard enough

419

music to recognize the Fifth and Caesar Franck's First, seen enough productions to speak (but hurriedly so I could not be put to task) about surrealism or Picasso's absinthe drinker, and I could prettily synthesize these things with ten-letter abstractions, giving an impression of integration which of course never did, nor still does not, exist. And so, without regret, in fact a little relieved from the somewhat excessive burden, I awarded myself the degree and considered my education finished. The Education of Cyril Endfield.

"For the past two years I have done nothing, have read only those few books which the sheer pressure of shame of ignorance has forced me to, have bothered to look up no more than two or three (no more) words in a dictionary, and have only responded to the vast cultural possibilities of my environments to the degree that there was compulsion from without. Only the saving urges of an ego which refused to be neglected has made me keep face. O I cannot say that I was slipping back to the unthinkable-of-worlds, for an alert consciousness which was kept in constant turmoil by unceasing cogitation alternated by moody introspection or phantastic imagery was the one gift-irrevocable from the new life, but I was slipping into that comatose lethargy, that crude complacency of spirit, which maintained to my eternal satisfaction that knowledge was not knowledge until I knew it, that that which I did not know, nor could not dedeuce [*sic*] from what I saw was not worth knowing, in short, that I was sufficient unto myself and could afford to curl up and eat, sleep, and fornicate until my capacities for such things were exhausted. But during this whole period of great deep-rooted unrest was fulminating and it finally crystallized in a wild orgy. . . of undeviating rigidity, "party line", and a fury of physical and intellectual activity in still a newer world.

"With the coming of summer, and the return of sanity, or the old insanity, and I again started my education where I left off. And so it was, with the old joy of discovery, endeavour, that last night I dashed happily to the library to use the dictionary for identifying the twenty five (odd) words I have picked up in my recent reading. Words I had encountered innumerable times before, and have disdained

421

to trouble myself with. I had just finished entering them in a small notebook when Gershon walked in. Earlier in the evening I had made arrangements to meet him. We went home and a few minutes after we arrived Jim Kennedy arrived. It seems that poor Gershon is still tremendously troubled by the girl (Tia), and last night he went into a bitter tirade against her insufficiencies, my heartlessness, Jim's heartlessness, and his own soulfulness, climaxing the effusion with a bitter denunciation of Cyril, and all that was wrong with Cyril, and with a declaration that he would no longer see me. It was intensely amusing listening to him so audibly punctuating his sentences, inserting innumerable parenthesis, apologising [*sic*] for himself, his thoughts, his past mistakes in so obvious a fashion and at the same time denying the apology, qualifying every other sentence, explaining, reasoning, rationalizing, convincing himself while trying to convince us, doing everything with the same intensity, same brilliance, same vituperative paranoia, same verbosity, on the same high plane of intelligence — as he would have one year ago or two years ago. The great spiral of the universe involuting to the soul of Gershon in a mighty distortion, in an incomprehensible perversion, to the soul of Gershon, the lost soul, lost within himself, crying for itself, beating (torturing) itself, looking from without itself into a mazed, not quite distinct world. Throwing to the four winds, for whoever is so good to listen, tremendous generalizations, hasty but completely assured evaluations, dismissing the obvious, the important, and divagating into the microcosmic, the spectacular, the subtle, the subterfuges of Freud-Adler-Jung dynamic psychology, the sub-consious, [*sic*] knowing all and everything but himself, lost, lost, with compass, without the guiding moss on protective trees, swathed in a brilliant panoply opaque from within transparent from without, struggling, fighting for preservation, for a source of salvation, denying, denouncing, damning with mightily eloquent imprecations the entire scheme, order, credo, of the lives which have thrust him in this dark lost spot. And the most one could do was to look on pitying, knowing too well that a proffered hand of help would be scorned, denigrated by a soul which knows no motivations but its own.

"And then, with a cloying poorly invoked anti-climax, he turned once more to [Tia], heaping a vast abuse on [Tia], which by its sheer intensity became complimentary, lauditory [*sic*] for the effort behind the derogations. Finally, with the homecoming of my parents, he left, I suppose for ever, probably cursing himself bitterly in later hours for this last revelation to an unsympathetic audience. So the passing of Gershon."

[Wait! Wait! Don't Stop Here!!! Don't Go Away Satisfied!! Now the Ending: — Ed.] "I see no chance for my coming to California this summer. My father needs me here for a few more weeks, and besides he has not paid me and I have no money. The growing consciousness of these vast impediments to doing what I want most to do has been a bitter pill which I have refused to swallow until this late moment. But there are more summers, and unlike love affairs, a friendship can persist despite this entire fatuous, half-unreal business of trans-continental letter writing. Your own letters are marvelously precious to me, a voice

424

from the hidden lands of my desire, but sometime, as now, I feel that these which I write are meaningless, incoherent, and better unwritten. I ask myself 'What do I tell him which he does not know?' How can these secret woes concern him? Can he be pleased as the receiving-pot for the drain from those carcinomal accretions which grow on me from the irritations of dreary Scranton? What can he think, as, time after time, he must suffer the vomit, the fecal dregs of an unsatisfied perhaps wandering mind?? . . ."

GREAT ending, that peroration, isn't it? Although that "wild orgy of... undeviating rigidity" may not've been as erotic as you might think. But considering the preceding pages of stuff about me, I guess I have to assume that those final "carcinomal accretions," plus of course the fecal dregs and vomit of the "perhaps wandering mind," at least partly include me. Friends like that you can obviously stick up your ass. But I owe a debt to Jarrico for saving and showing me the thing, even if many years later: it's a lulu. As promised, I never went back to Endfield's house, and didn't see or hear of him again for years, and then only by accident. Every time I ever saw him was an unpleasant experience one way or another, though I accepted it at first as part of my education. I've known several other people like that — he-male & she-male, either or both — but I now no longer have any educational excuse for hanging around with them, so I don't. Not anymore.

Endfield's conversational style maybe wasn't as fruity and verbigerous as his epistolary — !! — but it was bad enough. It's not a stylistic question. He never had a good word to say about anything or anybody that wasn't the latest "in" thing, and always delighted personally and particularly in bringing me down, if he could. I am very vulnerable to ugly-souled, jealous people. Who isn't? To me, losing Endfield was good riddance to real bad rubbidge. I'm sure he felt the same about me with perhaps a tinge of regret at having lost so wide-open a conversational victim, and with such agonizingly sensitive cuticle. So the passing of Cyril.

I had a couple of other friends, of course, but I was sorry to miss out on seeing Jimmy Kennedy anymore, those Friday nights. And to hear his great wild brags and lies — I hope — about his red-hot sex-jags with Sidonie, my former wet-dream girl, and the half-dozen presumably almost as incandescent wenches who then replaced her in Jim's stories as time wore on. That was really the main thing I missed about those adolescent bull-sessions in the Endfields' cushy parlors, which often dragged on with Coca-Cola and sometimes Crème de Menthe till four or five in the morning. And then there'd be the long walk home and continuation of our talk, because Kennedy lived up on the South Side near me. All uphill, and often along rainy or snowy streets in the bitter cold, but wonderfully steamed-up with Jim's detailed sex reminiscences — to which I can't do justice without notes — but which had always bored Endfield ragged, and were therefore mostly reserved for the walk home, as men among men, not prestidigitators!

Another important thing Endfield's house had offered, which I would certainly miss, were all the expensive new books his family could afford to let him buy, instead of waiting months for a turn at them at the public library. Mostly faddish shit, of course, as I've already said, but there was the occasional magnificent one: the last great one I remember was Hervey Allen's *Anthony Adverse*, which was infinitely more, and much better written, than the usual best-seller trash on the department-store lending libraries' shelves. Those were evidently manufactured by paid eunuchs, for idle housewives to dream over; and so were the cookie-cutter produced murder-mysteries on the same shelves, for their tired husbands' little soporific (or aphrodisiac?) bucket of blood at midnight.

The Endfields could also afford to subscribe to the several classy magazines I'd devour there, though Cy would never loan me anything but bound books. I was very impressed and influenced by the short-lived *American Spectator,* the last editorial swan-song of that greatest of all American literary coteries, witty and urbane: the two best critics, H. L. Mencken and George Jean Nathan, and James Branch Cabell, reigning author in the semi-erotica line at the time, as in *Jurgen,* but as lathe-turned and hand-chiselled a lapidary artist in prose as could be imagined. This first came out as a gargantuan, oversize newspaper, getting progressively smaller with each & every issue, till it finally collapsed for lack of discerning readership — like mine, to be sure. Fortunately, the editors then got out the one & only *American Spectator Yearbook,* reprinting most, but not all, the best pieces: a truly regal feast of modern literature, incredibly almost forgotten now.

At a much lower, and therefore infinitely more popular and successful level, they had another subscription, right from Number 1 on, to the then-new "men's" magazine, *Esquire* — it's still running and unwanted, like an incurable clap — imitating the

428

notorious Samuel Roth's men's magazine, *Beau,* a decade before, but we knew nothing about that then. *Esquire's* printed text was theoretically very masculine and vaguely naughty, for a grownup male audience fixated with flashy clothes and cars. But in fact it was lumped together monthly out of hopelessly second-rate pieces thrown them by fashionable male authors briefly in the news, who enjoyed banking the heavy cash *Esquire* was able to offer. Naturally, everything was basically expurgated and coy, in a mock-manly fashion that would have been ludicrous if it weren't so disgusting in its gutlessness, even to us horny adolescents sneaking peeks.

The only truly virile part of that, and all the imitative "men's" mags for decades to come — *Playboy, Penthouse, Lui,* and a dozen others, also including those exposé-style imitations — though admittedly in a merely front-projecting symbolic sense, was the concentration on fast automobiles. This *macho* overcompensation had already starred in Marinetti's fascist *Manifesto of Futurism,* in 1907, where it was perhaps too frankly coupled with war, homosexual love for other men, and total contempt for women even as sexual tools. The best cars ever shown in *Esquire* were an unforgettable series of swooping aerodynamic designs in Bakst ballet style, by one Russian expatriate,

429

Alexis de Sakhnoffsky. But eventually his splendid 1930's art-deco approach to aerodynamics was applied only to airplanes and interplanetary target-practice, disguised as rocket transportation, and never more to cars after World War II. Consider the ugly, truncated, blocky, hopeless, sexless and zipless refrigerators-on-wheels all the car-manufacturers of the world are peddling today. Where are you now when we need you, Alexis?

Esquire's presumably bold and sexy cartoons, printed in full color, were the one most famous thing and novelty about it. But they left me cold, as being only one glossy notch above the similar deluge of lightly off-color comic cuts in the much bawdier college-humor and folk-humor magazines being published then all over the country. Like *Captain Billy's Whiz-Bang,* a leftover, as its title indicated, of soldier bawdry from World War I; and the *Smokehouse* (polite for: *Outhouse) Gazette.* And the never-to-be-matched or even approached *Broadway Brevities,* an only slightly laundered smut-sheet and whore-&-homo tabloid for sale on all the newsstands in New York in the roaring 30s, at the bottom years of the Depression. Only the canny *Inland Printer* typographer-editor, Earl Emmons, had the sense to collect a file of the incredible *Broadway Brevities* while it ran; and that set — which I had the

good luck to inherit and the ambition to complete —
appears to be the only set known to exist today, with a
couple of duplicate numbers I presented to the Kinsey
Library at Indiana.

The most famous cartoons in the men's mags,
were and still are of the glacial and epoxy semi-nude
girls posing in their negligees, as first drawn for *Esquire*
by one George Petty, in the slick, over-decorative
glossy style of the movie musical-comedies with Busby
Berkeley costumes and mechanically revolving back-
grounds. I hated all that *ersatz* crap, always with white
telephones reminding me of enema-can tubes. My
favorites were the sexual situation-humor cartoons,
boldly drawn and swashingly colored in freebooter
style by the two American Daumiers of the period:
Peter Arno, who later became my friend, and the
Negro artist, E. Simms Campbell.

Campbell specialized in drawing juicy, near-
naked blondes for wish-fulfillment subscribers of all
races. Someone also wrote and published in *Esquire* an
incisive and seminal article that alerted American music
collectors for the first time to the importance of saving
at once the great but disprized flood of Negro jazz and
blues records of the 1910s and '20s, already massively
disappearing. There were a few jazz-buffs, to be sure,
but nobody had noticed until then that this was valid

431

folklore, and of a very powerful kind. All the music libraries and archivists were still busy recording nothing but American Indian tribal dances and hillbilly ballads by surviving oldsters, except for one brave soul at the Library of Congress, Robert W. Gordon, who was then kicked out for his pains, his recordings immediately being turned over to a media-wise Texas college professor, John Lomax and his ballsy son Alan. But Gordon fooled them, and took his records with him to the University of Oregon, where they still are in part. None of it was ever published, of course.

Two much greater European Daumiers then, and far more savage than Arno in their satire, George Grosz and Alexander King, fortunately emigrated to America when the Hitler decades were just beginning, and had their own incredibly virulent cartoon magazine, *Americana,* which appeared in New York for only a year or two in the early 1930s, also at the bottom of the Depression. It is the highpoint of unexpurgated satirical art anywhere in this century, and I'm sad to say I don't know if a single set still survives, or where! This at a time when millions of Americans were instead delighting only in the weak advertising parodies and pantywaist nonsense of George Delacorte's new humor magazine *Ballyhoo* and its even more tepid parodic imitators for decades after. Descending finally

432

in the 1950s to comic-book format and pictorial crip-crap in the proudly hysterical but, alas, totally unfunny *Mad* magazine, far inferior to its contemporary, the *National Lampoon,* which was apparently begun by a talented gang of really hip and non-pantywaist Harvard men.

I met the almost-legendary Alex King several times in banal social situations, competing for a girl, but never had the wit to recognize in the soft-spoken, grinning and subservient smoothie I was introduced to, with tiny Charlie Chaplin moustache and absurd neckties, the same powerful artist and immigrant drug-addict whose acidly satirical brush-&-pen in *Americana* (sometimes signed "Nord Ley," to avoid overpopulating his magazine) had so long been my delight. Still today, most people who've ever heard Alex King's name don't realize that he was anything but a vaguely 1930s book-illustrator, specializing in over-drawn Negro faces, and the big boss's picture-editor and witty idea-man on *Life* magazine; then becoming a popular tall-tale radio & t.v. raconteur concerning his fabulous life, toward the end of his career.

Art in America: a very great artist is turned into a "media personality," with the payoff in megabucks, while his art wholly dries up and is forever after

433

forgotten. The same way you now hear Vivaldi's *Four Seasons* (but never much else of his miraculously rediscovered output) mostly on mood-music recordings in public toilets. King's delightful but purposely superficial autobiographical volumes, especially *I Should Have Kissed Her More* — or somewhere — tell much, but by no means the most crucial parts of his story. *Kissed* concerns itself with the titillatingly expurgated record of some of his cuter love-affairs, carefully *cuisined* to suit the t.v. audience's delicate sensibilities about straight sex, or straight anything else but crooked crime and bloody violence. King's *Mine Enemy Grows Older* tells a lot more, though again not all. So also *May This House be Safe From Tigers*. Try them. Elegant sociological homework.

Yes, I had other friends then, aside from my cold, fat, over-intellectualized enemy, sophomoric Cy Endfield. In particular, those years and after, there were Bob Sewall and his inseparable friend John "Gee-Whiz" Brown, both of whom were a year or two older than me and had peculiarly repressed typically Christian characters that I didn't much care for, or always respond to, but beggars can't be choosers. At least they were both planning to be writers, as I was, though I wasn't yet entirely sure I wouldn't do the world more good as a psychologist. The rabbi business was by

434

now one hundred percent dead for me. They shared John's operating jalopy of 1920s vintage, which meant I could be moving around with them adventurously weekend nights, instead of sitting, endlessly *talking* past midnight with sedentary, highly verbalized friends like Endfield or Mel Cantor, or myself. Adolescents *talk* too much and fuck too little, anyway.

Sewall and Brown also shared a girlfriend — who sort of went with the car — a strange creature with mousey hair and burning eyes named Darlene Matthis. She was an early groupie whose original target had been John, who played saxophone, rather woodenly I thought, in a small white-jazz trio in Dunmore, Saturday nights till very late. Darlene had this delusion about herself that she was a *grande amoureuse* or nymphomaniac-in-bud, or I don't know what, which Bob and John naturally encouraged her to go on believing. She was generally in the car with us wherever we went, and right on till near daybreak. Then we'd end up at her place, a sort of dark, cavernous parlor with an old-fashioned square Tiffany lamp-cover all in heavy blobs of colored glass tike a church window dominating the dining-room table. At that hour her mother was always safely asleep upstairs, we felt sure, and we could do anything we liked if we didn't make any noise, with one kooky nautch-girl as our joint harem.

The parlor and dining-room communicated through an open double doorway with a wooden overhead bar, on which was strung a floor-length fringe of dark brown beads alternating with ugly yellow amber ones. This gave Darlene and either Bob or John a simulacrum of privacy when she took them on, alternately, on the parlor sofa, while the alternate stud or swain waited his turn talking in low tones with me — always the odd-man-out — under the Tiffany lampshade. Doubtless as a concession to keeping her mother asleep, Darlene never made a sound when she came, though she did writhe and thrash around a lot, with them as *her* two-man harem.

I thought this odd, especially for a nymphomaniac, as both Tia and Sharon and most of the other girls I'd been intimate with before then, even to the degree of finger-firkytootling, always did quite a bit of moaning or at least passionate giggling from the minute I started. I never took a turn on Darlene. I didn't want her. Her cold and somehow spaced-out lasciviousness disarmed and disgusted me. She reminded me a lot of Jeanie-With-the-Dark-Brown-Hole, the twelve-year-old girl in my public school who took on all the boys in an old packing-case under her

436

front porch; with creepy Shaver, the local child homosexual, out drumming up customers for her, so he could watch. I also didn't want to watch Bob and John alternately at work on Darlene's ass.

For excuse — oh, I had to have an excuse, all right — I'd explained carefully that I was still desperately in love with the exotically beautiful Tia, and therefore totally impotent with anybody else. This wasn't quite true, but it served the purpose of excusing me from stud-duty, and having to wet-deck in on either or both of my friends' semen. I did think vaguely of maybe humping Darlene *first* one night, in order to avoid the buttered-bun vaginal atmosphere that didn't appeal to me at all. But at the last minute I couldn't get a hardon, and everybody laughed at me. But that did prove I'd been telling the truth — maybe more than I knew — about Tia.

One night when Darlene wasn't with us, we ended up, only the three of us for a blessing, at Sewall's house up in Hyde Park. His parents were away temporarily and we could play Sewall's jazz records pretty loud if we liked. We sat in the kitchen eating snacks out of the ice-box, with the two of them drinking beer, something I then believed I disliked and found bitter, though I thought wine and liqueurs were great — and classier too. I heated myself a glass of

437

milk on the stove, while they razzed me. Sewall was telling us about his father, a mild-mannered mailman who had been caught, years before, in a raid on an unauthorized whorehouse. John Brown lived in a second-story apartment downtown under just such a whorehouse, which communicated with his bedroom through the air-shaft: he had no other window. You could hear the ten-minute customers talking to the middle-aged whore — almost continuously, it seemed to him — while they undressed partly, and fucked her. Always talked about work and the mines and unemployment and all that. Never about sex. I wondered if they were all crazy or if it was me?

Scranton was always a big whore-town, Allentown too, owing to the large immigrant mine- and factory-population; and prostitution was legal or at least tolerated in certain specific back-alleys, but not in unauthorized apartments around town. Sewall's father had been caught with a bunch of other men in a raid on just such an unauthorized joint, which of course had to pay off regularly to the cops, just like the equally illegal speakeasies under Prohibition, but apparently hadn't done so. He was arraigned and put on the police-station blotter with some other men, the ones who hadn't bribed their way out of the rap in the police-van. This made his misadventure public property, and he was then blackmailed about it for years by a small local, ostensibly "crusading" newspaper — crusading against speakeasies, blind-pigs, and prostitution, that is — published in Scranton or Wilkes-Barre nearby. The whole newspaper was apparently hardly more than a blackmail set-up, particularly their purity crusade.

They set up this unimportant little pitiful story in a few lines of type, but didn't print it. Instead they sent a galley-proof to Mr. Sewall, telling him flatly that this was going to be published the following week in the Scranton local-news column, and that they were sending him the proof for him to corroborate! Naturally he phoned them immediately, to beg them not to publish the story, which would certainly have cost him his post-office job and probably his laboriously-earned retirement fund too. He was told by the editor over the phone and later in person — not in the typewritten warning letter, you notice — that newspapers only ran stories like that to fill space in the paper not already taken up by advertisements, and that advertising was every newspaper's real business. The two cents the public paid for the paper hardly even covered the manufacturing cost. That was true, too. If, therefore, he'd fill up the same space instead, with a small, anonymous "COMPLIMENTS OF A FRIEND" blind

439

announcement, selling nothing and saying nothing, but taking up a couple of column-inches in the paper, the scandalous story incriminating him would not be run. In other words, straight journalistic blackmail.

Presumably all the other identifiable men caught in that, and godnose how many other police raids, were also offered the same golden opportunity, at column-inch prices matching their affluence or poverty. Because there were always a couple of columns of these "complimentary" blind ads in every issue, always in various large-&-or small framed sizes. They kept blackmailing Sewall's father this way every week for years, even though by now his misadventure in the whorehouse raid was long-since far in the past. What did they care, they warned him, when he eventually tried to cancel his weekly Compliments-Of-A-Friend little bordered ad. If he had the crust to cancel his ad, and ever stopped paying, they said, they'd immediately run the story without date-line, for its "news value." Did it all the time, so pay up! He paid up, for all the rest of his employable life. Now you know about half-ass American crooked journalism, in both small and big towns. And there are plenty of even simpler cash payoffs, without any ads. But European, Near-Eastern and Latin American journalism aren't a damn bit different. — Worse, if anything.

440

To show you just how juvenile we still were, all in our late teens, Bob and John and I once decided to have a penis-measuring contest to sort of round off the evening. Although the parlor was deserted and Bob's parents were away, we went upstairs to his bedroom for this fairly ancient adolescent ceremony — at least as old as the Beggar's Benison secret society in Scotland in the seventeenth century — I suppose so no early-morning passer-by could see us from the street through the parlor window. But who knows? When I say *we* decided, it isn't actually true. The whole thing was Sewall's canny idea, since he knew he'd be pretty sure to win, and shame us with his sausage-sized nine-incher. John and I, both modest six-and-a-half inchers (well, *going* on seven), had to concede defeat, while Sewall whirled his monster-sized wanger around the air, in a little victory-dance, with a nasty little shit-eating, I-told-you-so grin.

But just to show you how Nature often wastes her best gifts on the ungrateful and the unworthy, and incidentally to cast a suddenly blinding light on the unplumbed depths of Bob's personal life and problems, he then decided to show us that his quarter-yard-long champion penis was sensitive only to sexual pleasure and insensible to pain. A hard thing to prove. But he valiantly, or kookily, got a large darning needle

441

from his mother's comequick sewing-necessary, which he went all the way downstairs and back to find. Then he proceeded masochistically to tease out half-an-inch of thin purple capillary from the veined skin at one side of his prick, and dangled it before our horripilated eyes and noses, claiming fraudulently it was a nerve, not a capillary, and that proved he felt no pain!

Bob also said he had privately practiced the same trick on his penis "nerve" several times before. I believe him. It reminds me terribly of Mark Twain's little-known story "My First Lie" about how, as a boy, he had taken the part of the fraudulent medium or shill for a carnival mind-reading hypnotist, or similar, and then tried to persuade *his mother* to stick pins in him, as the hypnotist had done, to prove he felt no pain. His mother wisely refused. The hypnotist had already apparently given him a sufficient habit. But then, Twain was — then or thereafter — a textbook masochist case, as it pleased him to document to the hilt in another obscure but even more translucent autobiographical piece, about how much he truly enjoyed going to the dentist for painful tooth-&-gum scraping, which he recommends to everyone. Black humor? — Maybe. I'm not sure. Short men often turn to masochism.

But Twain's autobiographical incident with his mother is far more interesting and significant, because it shows the real and dreamed-of female source for the masochistic pain and domination he wanted, and the childhood prototype of those dominant female mid-Victorian lady editors, bear-wardens, and wives Twain sought for, married, and submitted to all the rest of his life. When he wasn't out crudely chasing underage girls, as a white-haired, white-suited, and therefore wholly pure old geezer or gentleman, finally getting caught, doubtless red-peckered with one such teen-aged young lady — he called them his "Angel-Fish Aquarium" — 'aving a bit of houghmagundie in the bushes, somewhere fittingly in the Virgin Islands. And being put out of his misery under massive sedation when shipped back home to the U.S. in disgrace to hush things up. The whole story is there, for him-who-runs to read, in Hamlin Hill's lacerating biographical study of Twain's last ten years, *Mark Twain: God's Fool,* including a photograph of Twain and the rather well-developed young "Angel-Fish" in question, in their bathing-suits. Who Murdered Mark Twain?

NIGHTS when Darlene was with us were a lot less unpredictable and abnormal. The jazz music wasn't as good, though, at John's saxophone job, as on Bob's phonograph record collection at home. I didn't much like instrumental jazz anyway; only vocal blues. Those were the nights we couldn't have Bob's rare and precious Bluebird and Okeh and Vocation and Brunswick ten-inch jazz records to listen to: the Victor and Columbia companies' "race record" labels for colored persons in de outhouse, as opposed to the same companies' other, larger, *human race,* or white audience, records. Instead, we would sit around a little brass-bound marble table, drearily nursing our required one glass of flat beer or Coca-Cola, in that small, smoky, lowclass beer-joint backroom, lost somewhere out in the wilds of Dunmore, P.A., while John played semi-pro saxophone with his three-piece white band, plus whorehouse piano which was the best part.

I just suffered through the tired, flabby, imitative white-jazz stuff. John was my friend, after all. But what was great would be the occasional Negro singer who'd sit in, to pick up a couple of bucks and table-offerings for a stint of blues singing or guitar. Never will I forget one husky-voiced woman baritone, not monstrously fat and awful the way most Negro blues- and opera-singers were then, but thin and tired

444

and pretty fierce-looking under tons of slathered-on lipstick and makeup. She was surely a lesbian, because with the drinkers' encouragement — they all knew her except me — she sang an unusually unexpurgated version, no doubt the original of the polite clean-up in the books, of the old New Orleans pimp-song, "St. James Infirmary Blues," about the whore who's died of venereal disease:

> Ah went down to St. James Infirmary,
> Saw mah bah-HAY-by layin' there;
> She was stretched out onna table,
> Wid her tits — an' *cunt* — all bare . . .
>
> Let'er go, let'er go, god-*DAMN*-'er!
> Whe-hayr-eveh she-*HE!* may be;
> She kin look dis whole worl' oveh,
> But she'll neveh find a *(spoken:* hot-fuckin,' tit-suckin') *MAN!!* like me.

Lesbians were supposed to be a rare phenomenon then, but I was struck by the searing sincerity of her masquerade. I could feel her voice burning up the air when she hit that last line, calling herself the *MAN!!* she identified with to her very soul.

445

That wasn't the first folksong I'd ever noted down, right on the premises, nor even the first bawdy one from a woman or girl. But it surely was an eye-opener to me as to how little authenticity and passion are left, after the folksong popularizers and anthologizers get through, with the songs the singers really sing. I heard it sung again, thirty years later, even more laceratingly, by a coed who had just sold her illegitimate baby for adoption.

I remember another night with all three of them. Silent "Gee-Whiz" John and Darlene and Bob — and me just tagging along as usual — helling around that night late, after John's saxophone stint in Dunmore, in his beat-up old black Chevrolet touring-car with the canvas top and open sides. We must've been somewhere up around Olyphant or Archbald by then. Every once in a while we'd park in some dark street, and John and Bob would climb over and be sitting in the back seat sharing Darlene, both sucking on her nipples together, and one or the other feeling her cunt in the dark. And her with her dress-bodice pulled all the way down, and me in the front seat prissily not partaking, on the excuse of being in love elsewhere. Besides, she only had two nipples. And pretending to be laughing at them all.

446

Darlene visibly, and gesturally — then and finally verbally and perfectly frankly, since we were all too damn dumb to understand, wanted all three of us to make love to her together that night. Not by turns, as they usually did, but all three of us at once, so she could Experience Life To The Full!! Bob and I were pretty much willing to give it a whirl; me for scientific purposes, of course, for my study of kissing, now enlarged to cover sex-postures and technique. Or it may even have all been Bob's idea. But John was just too shy to pull out his cock, *and* be able to get it stiff with two other men present, and pitch into whichever of Darlene's palpitating holes would be left for him, in the queen-trio or quartet she was so hot to try. Later he explained that he didn't think the back of a Chevy was the right place for acrobatic double- and triple-decker sandwiches of that type. He also mumbled something about "What about the come-stains all over my back seat?"

"Come-stains, my ass!" I assured him haughtily. "In a situation like that, we all give Darlene a hot-shot, right to the heart. She swallows everything, or we kill her!"

Macho me, always posing as so goddam know-it-all and tough. A hot-shot meant without any condoms, and no pulling out! It's a word that hasn't

447

been around much lately, but it'll be back soon, what with all the crafty recent Moral Majority media-mindwash about everybody dying of AIDS. Condoms oughta have a terrific future now, if only somebody could figure out how to make real money out of them. Just condoms is penny-ante stuff. Maybe combined with six delicious flavors in vaginal jellies, or tongue-tip models for AIDS-scared, yellowbellied cowards who'd rather suck each other off obscurely through pasted-down "Crotchguard" rubber sheets than just decently die. Or combined with vibrating rectal plugs in Jacuzzi whirlpool baths, for straight narcissists. After all, who wants to go on living — or fucking either, for that matter — in a world of none but hypothetically diseased lovers? Work on that aspect, willya? Bigger phagocytes!

My friend John just grinned at me and mumbled "Gee-whiz!" — always his best line, but I hated it — with his usual hang-dog grin down one side intended to cover his thin upper lip, about which he was very sensitive. He said it was caused by the saxophone *embouchure,* and was even planning to grow a moustache. So was I, but not to cover up anything. Hiding and apologizing was for losers, I knew. I even had a dead, blackened incisor right in the front of my mouth, but I wasn't ever going to let it cramp my style.

Or to make me smile sideways, *titsa-de-bitsa,* instead of laughing right out in a roar, *hupcha-de-hupcha!* That's what my Uncle Joel, Baron Von Teufelsdreckh, had taught me, and that's what I learned.

John also always had a small packet of Three Merry Widows or Trojans or some other rubbers discreetly stowed in his inner pocket. "Sold for Prevention of Disease Only," the package said. I was never willing to wear one of those in my life, after I tried one on, except maybe once. And that was a lamb's-gut fishskin, so called, with a little blue tape for tying it on at the base of your prick so it wouldn't slip off. That was supposed to be more elegant, for a highflying sport like me, than mere rubber. Thinner too. I couldn't really understand John's over-modest, silent, underplayed ways, that Bob Sewall also pretended to believe in. It seemed to be part of their *goyish* mystique, to act like hip but inadequate wimps. "Tight upper-lip. . . Pip-pip, stout fella!. . . *Beau Geste* forever!" One thing I knew for sure was, girls didn't appreciate recessive, self-effacing guys like that. Not normal girls. But I also didn't realize at all how close I had come to acting like just that kind of guy with Tia, myself.

Not all my friends then were as childlike and normal as Bob Sewall — Mark Twain. Some of them,

449

homosexual or otherwise, very definitely wanted to lead me in the paths of unrighteousness. It wasn't too hard to do, either, considering that I always lacked money. I was earning a wage then in the Scranton Dry Goods haberdashery shop for almost the first time in my life, but I was certainly pissing it away faster than I earned it — at the munificent new government minimum for all full-time workers, of twelve dollars and ninety-five cents for a forty-hour week. That missing nickel, to make it a full thirteen bucks, was cleverly withheld to prevent you from falling into some higher bracket where you'd eventually have a legal right to some matchingly higher bracket of retirement pay or social security (hoo-hah!) or maybe a nickel bag of peanuts, what with the inflation, some fifty years later when they'd kick you out to pasture.

MY MONEY mostly went for books in Stück's secondhand bookshop, and even at the new-book counters in the big Rexall's and Liggett's discount drugstores downtown, where there were always tablefuls of cheaply-printed remainders and plate re-issues of all the splendid sex classics that had come out in beautiful editions in New York in the 1920s in

English translations. We called it laughingly Liggett's Library of Applied Pornography. These books came out right through till the bottom of the Depression, when all the best sex book publishers like Covici-Friede and especially Horace Liveright had gone bust. Their printing-plates had then fallen into the hands of their creditor printers & binders, and little *schlock* remainder houses that became rich and big on other publishers' mistakes and misfortunes.

I was in addition spending a disgusting and ridiculous amount of money, setting up the mildly alcoholic drinks for Mel Cantor and Tia and myself, on our triple-dates, with me as fifth wheel or He-Who-Gets-Slapped, long after Andreyev: He-Who-Pays-the-Check — for some other guy to kiss his girl. Anyhow, I was broke all the time. I even got Mildred's father, who was a job printer, to knock me out two hundred tiny one-line bookplates in Old English type: "GERSHON E. LEGMAN." I never used most of them, having become G. Legman meanwhile. Saved problems with people who still wanted to call me "George." And the more money I made, the more things I wanted to waste it on, like everyone else. I even wore a monogrammed grey silk muffler then, the fringe like a *tallis;* also a snap-brimmed felt hat and grey suede gauntlet-style gloves, of which I carried one in

451

my left hand, though I had no idea why. I got it all at discount on my job. In my mind I think I believed I looked pretty much like those debonair movie-actors Ronald Colman or, more particularly, William Powell who played *The Thin Man* opposite my dream-consort, Myrna Loy, or the incredibly lovely and Oriental-looking Merle Oberon — prosaically born somewhere outside the Orient, I had to admit — who looked even *more* like Tia.

One day, just after 6 p.m., when I got out of work and came into Stück's bookshop, a tall young man was arguing with him about something, but they both shut up about it the moment I walked in.

"Don't I know you?" the young man said to me abruptly, to change the subject I guess. I studied him a minute.

"Sure," I said. "You're the son-of-a-bitch eagle scout that shot off that gun in the dark the time you were telling the ghost story at scout camp, around the bonfire, and all us little cubs shit in our pants!" Gil Sheldon was his name, I think, the bastard!

We both had a good laugh over that, and walked out together to have an ice-cream soda at his expense, to make amends for that unexpected gunshot. When I asked him why he'd been arguing with Orvie Stuck, he looked at me sharply and then laid out on the

452

soda-fountain table where we were sitting a small book, cheaply bound in cloth. It was entitled *The Town Bull,* and the merest flick through its pages showed me at once that it was highly pornographic, though I wasn't too sure what a town-bull really might be. But I could guess.

"Orvie wouldn't give me a buck for it," he said disgustedly. "Everybody knows a book like that's worth twice as much. You want to buy it?" he added negligently, as I kept thumbing through the pages. A town-bull had to be a guy who fucked all the girls in town, just from the few lines I'd caught, full of graphic descriptions of spouting pricks & cunts: like a dream come true.

"I'd like to," I admitted. "I sure would. But I haven't got any money. I've got to stick to things for a quarter, right now. Half-a-buck is my top."

We both knew, of course, he wouldn't sell it to me for anything like that, but he offered to show me where he got it. He said the guy who ran the place would lend out dirty books like that for a quarter over the weekend, from Friday to Monday, or ten cents a night. I wondered why I'd never heard about that before, and also why neither my sister Ruth nor I had ever known that Orvie also regularly handled the real stuff, if he did. Well, live & learn. And I hurried along

453

by the side of my new mentor, who seemed to be about twenty years old, and so tall and handsome and blond it was absolutely a crime. Just the way I'd remembered him from years before, at scout camp up at Duck Pond, telling that great story about the benighted traveller who sees the white hand creeping at the foot of his blanket in the strange wayside inn, and grabs his gun and *shoots* the white hand *(BANG!!!)* Only to find that it's his own foot.

The place we were going to was nominally a magic-and-novelty-shop down on Penn Avenue, somewhere that a bookstore had no reason to be, I thought, surrounded by hat factories and wholesale butcher-houses like the one my father once worked for. My new friend disposed of his book quickly, under the counter, and disappeared even more quickly with a new one in his scuffed paper bag. He gave me a brief handwave and knowing smirk as he left. He was very upperclass and handsome, but I still didn't like him. The proprietor of the magic store immediately offered me the same *Town Bull* for two dollars, which I told him I didn't have; but I offered to rent it for the coming weekend for the announced quarter. This also fell through when it turned out I couldn't just *rent* the book, but would have to pay down the entire two-dollar price, and would get a dollar seventy-five back when I returned it on Monday.

I tried to argue; gave him my name, assured him I was totally honest, and promised I would even bring the book back next day, which was Saturday, so he could rent it out again, and pay him down now the full twenty-five cents anyhow, for trusting me. We were still discussing this — me kind of desperately, and him cynically and cold like a smalltime crook, and with his mouth curled down at the corners — when another customer walked in. I thought to myself, "This is just like it was at Orvie Stück's," and immediately addressed the new customer, whom I didn't know from Adam, boldly demanding that he should assure the proprietor that I was honest and should be trusted without a deposit. Just on my honest face.

The newcomer was as ugly and dark and grubby, and even a little misshapen, as my eagle scout friend had been tall and handsome and blond. He didn't even glance at the title of the book on the counter, under discussion. "Y'ever read a book like that before?" he asked.

"Sure, lots of times. My sister and I read them together."

"Your sister and you?" he repeated slowly, plucking his nostrils outward with a thoughtful thumb

& forefinger. "You're a real character, aint'cha? Let 'im have the book, Joe," he told the proprietor. "If he don't bring it back, I'll make it good. He looks honest to me." He handed a small, heavy-looking square package across the counter, carefully wrapped in brown paper.

"Okay, Doc," said the proprietor, slipping my gnome-like friend a ten dollar bill, which he folded meticulously and slipped into his vest-pocket. The proprietor then handed me *The Town Bull* after slipping it into another well-used paper bag.

"I'll sure bring it back," I assured them both now, with victory and the book in my grasp. "I'm writing a scientific book on sex technique," I added proudly. "Books like that are my research."

"Wel-l-l!" said the gnome, on a rising note. "You and I ought to know each other better. I'm working on a book on that too."

Then we walked out together, and the couple of blocks back to the courthouse square, where I'd be catching the Petersburg trolley home. My new benefactor, the gnome, was very charming and candid, for all his evidently mocking air. He told me his name was 'Doc' Rankin — "Everybody calls me 'Doc'," he said — and he was a veteran of World War I, and a professional artist. I understood.

456

"You do the drawings for those books, don't you?" I said.

"Only the good ones," he replied, with his lips pursed in an amused smile. "Care for a drink?"

"I'm too young to get served liquor," I admitted; "but I'll be glad to have an orange-juice while you knock back a beer."

This made Rankin laugh out loud, and we went into a restaurant-bar right across the street from the trolley-stop. It was Chris Colovos' Twin-Grill, I suddenly realized then, where my father had once worked years before, as manager, until he got crushed by the huckster's truck out in the back-alley. Well, he wouldn't be there now, to spy on me.

We both had orange-juice. "I don't drink much," Rankin explained. "I was wounded pretty bad in the war," he said. "In a wheel-chair for a couple of years."

"Yes," I said eagerly. "I know a little about that. I was kicked out of high school last year for distributing pages of *The Horror of It,* to protest against war. A man I know told me it was even worse on the German side. They lost their whole young male population."

"Izzat so?" Rankin wanted to know. "Serves the dumb Heinies right for listening to Kaiser Bill. I

457

was kidding about being an artist," he went on suddenly without any transition. "I'm only a cartoonist. I do the squeezers. You know — the little comic books, with the people out of the funnypapers." He slipped me a small vertical pamphlet out of his jacket pocket. "Here, get a load of this one; but behind the menu, huh?"

I disguised it rapidly behind the menu and gave it a swift but intense once-over. I had seen others like it, but only eight pages long, and squat and flat. This one was a tall sixteen-pager with little extra pictures and remarks in the margins: a sort of *de luxe* comic book, of a kind I had never seen before. I tendered it back to 'Doc' Rankin reluctantly, but he just gestured that I should keep it and stick it in my pocket. I immediately determined mentally that I'd start a collection of squeezers at once. That had to be what was in the wrapped package Rankin had slipped the magic-dealer and been paid for. I'd concentrate, of course, on the tall ones with the remarks and little extra drawings in the margins: much more room for fun & jokes.

'Doc' Rankin; I wondered why the 'Doc'? Just an honorific; he couldn't be a real doctor with practically that dese-dem-&-dose accent, and his strange, dark, gnomelike look. And why in Scranton?

Well, everybody has to live someplace. A few years later, in New York, his secret printer-publisher, Louis Shomer, told me that Rankin was generally called 'The Indian,' and that I was to call him by that moniker too, and avoid using his real name. The couple of hopeful sex-scholars and historians who've applied themselves in more recent years to the squeezers, and the low-level but graphic sex education they formed for us thousands of desperately-searching adolescent American kids, have been struck by the enormous output of Rankin's erotic comic-books, and his unmistakable crude and graphic humorous style, of the kind used by advertising artists in the 1910s; and have tried to peg him with the hopeless new moniker of 'Mr. Prolific.' Good God! — What next? Oh, mock scholarship, what sins are committed in thy name!

Rankin clearly enjoyed my tense appreciation of his art. "I'll be goin' on poses pretty soon," he said; "like I told ya. You know — 'The Swan Dive', 'The Whirling Basket' — the works. I'll leave one at Joe's store for ya. I'm waiting now for a friend of mine, to eat supper. He's a *real* artist! He can draw rings around anything I could ever do. Name of Laurent Stracke — ever heard of him?"

"I surely have!" I replied, all excited. "My sister and I have a book with weird pictures by Laurent Stracke. He's really *great!*"

"Tell me more about your sister," Rankin asked. "What's she; a twin?"

But at that moment a person who could only be Stracke came in the door and limped directly over to our table. He was not only a cripple, dragging a gimpy leg as he walked, but he was so diminutive and frail in appearance that he made the gnomelike Rankin and only medium-tall me look like giants. And when he sat down, his torso was even smaller than you'd have expected, his face barely peering over the tabletop.

"Young admirer of yours, Larry," said Rankin heartily. "Wants to meet ya!"

They immediately invited me to have supper with them, man-style, but I knew my mother would never forgive me if I didn't come home for her standard *gefilte-fisch* and boiled chicken on a Friday night: the Sabbath eve. Stracke scratched his address hurriedly on a bit of paper, and told me to be sure to come and see him immediately — the next night, Saturday, if possible. And he'd show me some of his greatest new drawings, to illustrate H. G. Wells' *When the Sleeper Wakes,* which he'd just finished and would

460

have to send off to the publisher in England on Monday. And then I'd never be able to see them till the book was published.

Saturday evening, seven p.m., I was there. Stracke's address was on lower Adams Avenue and very close to my former high school. He met me at the downstairs door, and hurried me up to his room limping excitedly. It hardly looked like an artist's studio, but it did have an upright easel and several big elephant portfolios of his drawings leaning against the walls. The new pictures he showed me were indeed wonderful, and in his best weird style, though I didn't quite see how they'd illustrate *When the Sleeper Wakes,* a book I myself had read. Stracke then explained that his next job would be the illustrations for Shakespeare's *Midsummer Night's Dream* and *The Tempest* in one *de luxe* volume. His real trouble though, he said, was getting the right kind of models. Particularly for Ariel — half-boy and half-elf.

"What would you say to posing for me?" he asked, and from the audible tremor in his voice when he said it, I immediately understood that I'd been fooled again. Stracke had to be just another Dolgoruki: out to fuck me in the ass. Or to suck me off. Hard to know, looking at homos, what their specialty was. They were all the same, really.

461

"I'd pay you, of course," he was saying. "Union rates!"

To my own surprise, I agreed, assuring him I wouldn't want payment — maybe just one of his drawings — and would be doing it out of admiration for his art.

"That's, ah, *nude* — you understand," he quavered.

I understood. And I took off all my clothes and stood taking some stupid pose as he directed me, pretending that I was Shakespeare's Ariel, but naked as a jaybird's ass.

He grabbed a large oblong plasterboard and practically threw it onto the easel; then hoisted himself up on a high, rotating stool of wood, fixing his twisted leg into the footrest bar, and sketching wild lines with motions like lightning flashes, peering at me from behind the big board. It didn't take long for me to notice that, with his other hand, he had taken out his prick and was jerking it slowly and methodically, partly screened behind the easel. I was staring at him too, observing the very strange way all his fingers were encompassing the head of his prick, all facing his ripped open pants-fly.

Suddenly he jumped down and hobbled over to where I stood. "Are you going to let me put it into

462

you?" he begged intensely, his voice very low and almost cracking. "Over on the bed. I'll pay you, y'know."

"No," I said. "Don't pay me. You're a great artist."

He fox-trotted me over to his big double-bed fast, his arms and body unexpectedly strong for a tiny twisted cripple, I remember thinking. I did not resist him in any way. He pushed me down on my side, facing the wall, and draped himself clumsily in back of me. To my surprise he kept jerking his prick with one hand, and then, just as he was struggling to push his hips forward and fuck me, suddenly he shot all over my buttocks — just a couple of tiny, hot drops.

"Arrggh!" he half-snarled, half-shouted. "Arrgh!! Arrgh!" And then he fell back on the pillows, panting, and seemed to be struggling for breath.

"Are you all right, Mr. Stracke?" I asked. I was worried. He looked as though he was about to die.

"Arrgh!" he barked again. "Arrgh!" But this time a little more quietly. "Call me Larry, will you?" he begged.

While I was dressing he offered me the money again: a five-dollar bill. But I assured him I wouldn't take it, and repeated that what I'd really like would be one of his drawings. I looked at his purported drawing

463

of me on the plasterboard on the easel. It was just a couple of spasmodic chicken-tracks. Pitiful. I told him diplomatically I wasn't that vain, and would be satisfied with one of his ordinary drawings. While he was rumpling quickly through his big elephant portfolios to find something suitable — not worth more than five dollars, I assumed, and maybe less, when you consider what a fiasco his attempt at buggery had been — I was thinking of Dolgoruki, his neighbor just down the street.

I supposed they lived there right near the high school, to pick up the available boy-ass easier. And inveigle them to their studios with their marvelous cackalanny bullshit stories about music and art. And I was remembering too what my mother had said that time, about Dolgoruki wanting to get me drunk and alone with him in a hotel bedroom, somewhere out of town. And me being so dumb that I wanted to go. And then that poor Rosanna Trimmler, begging me to come to visit her in Moscow, P.A., so we could roll in the hayloft together and she could prove to me that no girl could ever be nicer to me than she could — love or no love.

In fact, the drawing of his that Laurent Stracke gave me was a real masterpiece, all wild and flowing lines in his best arabesque style. Not one of Stracke's

464

saccharine children's book illustrations, but something really beautiful and weird. The homos naturally always go for children's books, of course, like Rojankovsky later, though *he* was certainly no homo. You have to see his wild erotic work to understand. I didn't feel a bit like a prostitute walking home up Vine Street that evening. But years later, when I had to sell Laurent Stracke's drawing for money to eat, for Beverley and me, then I realized that I had indeed prostituted myself.

TO MAKE it possible to keep seeing Tia, even if not alone, I asked our mutual friend Mel Cantor, who after all had known Tia before I did, to take her out a couple of times each week; me to sneak in later on their date. Jimmy Kennedy had been doing this for me until he tried to betray me by kissing Tia in the taxi home (with me paying to get the driver to slow down: *Le Cocu Magnifique!)* when Tia got slightly drunk one Thursday night on *crème de cacao.* What ever became of those so-called strict Pennsylvania laws about selling intoxicating beverages to minors on the balconies of fashionable evening barrooms, I can't imagine. Then Mel took over. He would appear at Tia's house early in the

465

evening, flatter the ass off her mother — something he was astonishingly good at, Tia reported — and they would then ankle out with the family's gooiest blessing. No doubt congratulating themselves on her escape from the local adolescent white-slaver, me. Often I'd be able to make my surreptitious appearance later, and meet Mel and Tia on the discreet mezzanine of our favorite bar near the post office on Courthouse Square. And of course I happily paid all our small restaurant checks, trio theatre tickets and the like, out of the small fund of money I was saving up from my current job as a haberdashery salesman, to pay my first semester's tuition at college. If my mother hadn't saved out half my pay, I'd never have got there.

They say people learn from their mistakes, if they won't learn any other way, but I never did. I always kept making the same mistakes over and over — big ones too — especially when it involved trusting or loving someone. I dunno: I must be the easiest person in the world to brainwash and swindle, anyhow about all the unimportant froth other people are always anxious for me to do or buy, or not to do. I've at least tried to save out a couple of the big central things for myself — Emerson's "work I believe in, somewhere to live, someone to love" — but those weren't mistakes.

It was all wonderfully surreptitious, tripledating secretly, and it never occurred to me that Mel might try to steal back Tia's affections for himself, after having dropped her two summers before. When it became clear, though, that he was indeed trying to steal her, I had to pretend to overlook it, as I was now almost wholly dependent on his help to get to see her at all. I also sensed — this is something I do a lot of, and I can't explain how or why, but I always trust these silent messages I get from people much more than I ever trust anything they say — I sensed that he was only competing with me for mastery over the girl we all knew I loved, and that he didn't really want or love Tia now except maybe as a triumph over me. Cy Endfield's sexless squiring her about had certainly been so intended, as we all understood when he kept writing letters vilifying me after she had already left him. Those bitterly critical "Juliet" letters made his real purpose only too clear, not to mention the intentionally castratory feminine pronouns endlessly woven into the letters to *cut me down*.

Mel and Tia and I had long since agreed that we would save our money for a year and then all go to Oberlin college together, out near Cleveland somewhere. While I was working in the haberdashery department of the Scranton Dry Goods, Mel had a

467

very lousy job in a refrigeration plant down in the wholesale meat district, where the chemicals were affecting his eyes badly. We begged him to get another job, but it wasn't so easy, and as he cared a great deal about going to college too, the way his older brother had done, he wouldn't give up the job. Mostly what I cared about was to be able to keep on seeing Tia, no matter where. I did not consciously have any other ambitions or plans. But Oberlin was fine. It had been famous as an important station on the Underground Railroad just before the Civil War, smuggling Negroes out of the slave states and up to Northern Canada and freedom. It had a reputation now for being a very good place for over-bright kids who couldn't ever fit into the usual educational routine slots, which I had realized by now to be my case.

However, Oberlin did not live up to their Underground Railroad reputation, and sent me a pained letter after they got my transcripts, pointing out that although I had an outstanding scholastic record in all the schools I'd ever been to, I also had been in every known kind of trouble in each & every one of them. This included my brash record of presumed Communism, on *Suppressions* magazine to be sure, one-shot as it may have been. They decided they *"did not feel*

468

I would be able, therefore, fully to utilize the Oberlin Experience."

The letter was a real pious puker, all in that piss-elegant style, instead of just a plain, manly No. They did say they were impressed by my I.Q. record, but they bad-mouthed that too by adding that the I.Q. was not, in their estimation, as important at Oberlin as "adaptability," which is what I had thought the I.Q. tests tested for. But I guess they were right: I was clearly not their man. That left the University of Michigan to go to, at Ann Arbor near Detroit, as it was a big state university that never refused anybody with a good record — the dumbbells were shunted off to Michigan State College at Lansing — and the tuition was low. Besides, it didn't seem very far on the map from Oberlin, Ohio, where Mel and Tia had been accepted immediately, and I wrongly figured I'd be able to hitchhike out to see her every weekend. And that's what I was going to do. The whole college and education *shtick* had ceased to mean anything whatsoever to me when it became clear that I would still be separated from the girl I loved so very much, and now with a heavy, persistent tone of hopelessness.

In September, Tia and Mel went on to Oberlin together by train. The term began a few days later at Michigan, and I planned to hitchhike as my

469

haberdashery-shop money was already pretty thin after laying aside the modest sum demanded for tuition. I sent on my pressboard trunk full of drugstore reprint erotica and clean shirts and underwear by railway express, and carried only a black cardboard bookbag by way of light luggage, on which I had lettered in white paint the traditional Pike's Peak pioneers' challenge or avaunt: "ANN ARBOR OR BUST!"

I was still not very sure in my mind where the hell Oberlin was, except that I knew you had to go through Cleveland to get there. Disdaining any maps as supererogatory, I made my way with hitched truck-rides south, through the snob suburbs of Cleveland, getting further and further from Oberlin all the time. I finally realized I was on the wrong track when the signs began mentioning Akron on ahead, and I banged on the little back window of the truck I was riding in and got the driver to let me off at the next gas station. There I finally broke down and got a map, which set me right.

Ever since then I've been partial to maps and diagrams whenever it's a question of finding or placing something or somebody somewhere, and I now always cheerfully admit that I'm a deef, dumb & blind Croatian cretin whenever anybody starts *explaining* me in a helpful way that I should go two blocks left and

470

then three miles around to the right — that's north —
and then two miles etc. etc., but not till I'm at the next
crossing by the church. Not the one with the big spire,
but with the pillars out front. Frig that! Draw me a
picture.

The man in the gas station who gave me the
map, for which he would accept no money, had a
marvelous twangy accent and said he came from
Indiana himself and knew how easy it was to get mixed
up "in all the Heightses around Cleveland. You
shoulda hadda turned there while you were still in
Cuyahoga county," he told me. I shoulda hadda turned
somewheres because by the time I got to Oberlin and
managed to find Tia and Mel through the registrar's
office, I could see I was about as welcome as a
hippopotamus turd in a punchbowl. They didn't
exactly tell me to get lost somewhere, but the message
was plain. I was just incapable of accepting it.

When it came near evening, Tia simply
disappeared after giving me a big sisterly kiss on the
cheek, and stating that she had to go to her room to
take a bath. Mel and I sat there a while longer talking
in the local malted-milk palace — students were not
allowed to drink alcohol publicly, except at football
games, and I don't know if Oberlin even had anything
so vulgar as a football team.

471

Mel made it as plain as A-B-C that he wouldn't be able to put me up that night on the floor of his room, as I was taking for granted. I reminded him that this was only a side-trip for me, and that I'd be hitchhiking the very next day to Ann Arbor, but that wasn't good enough. He clearly wanted to be rid of me *right away*, and finally admitted that he and Tia had a private date for that evening. This wasn't going to be like back home, he told me with a shit-eating grin. "Two is company — three is a crowd, you know," he ended.

I must have looked as wiped out as I felt, because he asked me if I wanted another malted, and while I was drinking it he explained to me laboriously that he and Tia had discovered on the train that they were now in love with each other *again*. And that I couldn't expect to hang around with them when they were just rediscovering each other again, *and* et cetera, et cetera. But of course I should certainly come back to visit them in Oberlin *once in a while*, as I was threatening to do, but only occasionally of course, to share their happiness "in a friendly way."

In fact, he said, he knew he was speaking for Tia as well, when he asked me *like a friend*, that if I did come back to see them *occasionally*, I wasn't to stand around looking miserable like a dumb ox that's been struck on the head with a sledge-hammer — by his two best friends, which Mel neglected to say — because it somehow soured their newfound *happiness*, now dating since their train ride to Oberlin. Did I understand?

I could tell exactly what that prick was going to say before he even opened his mouth, just by the sweetly forgiving shit-eating smile spread over his map, and the unusual gesture he then engaged in of offering to pay for the second malted milk. Because Mel was always, would be to the end of his life a phoney, no-talent guy and a frantic cheapskate and freeloader — intellectually and every other way — greedy to grab everything from everybody, all the way from cash to cunt and back, though he could never imagine that anybody had the wit to notice his crude parasitism except himself. The thought came to mind, I remember, even as he was sitting there expatiating on their newfound *happiness:* "I'll bet he thinks Tia is rich on account of that Essex sports car her father drives, or whatever the hell it is. That's why he wants her back now."

But I sat and said nothing, and listened in perfect silence to every word, savoring the dull pain of it like an arrow through my heart, and thrilling helplessly each time he happened to pronounce Tia's name, though he referred to her very precisely as

473

Esther — also missing all the music of that name. I knew that the pain I felt, listening to his true-happiness-and-friendliness clatfart, would turn from dull to unbearably sharp as soon as I'd be alone, so I matched his own mock-contrite sweetness with my own deeply understanding smirk, line for line, like a veddy British stage comedy.

"You want Tia to be *happy*, don't you?" he challenged me finally, to sort of clinch things, still a bit unsure of his victory. I should have killed the son-of-a-bitch then & there, I know, but I was young. And instead of getting up and leaving with the proper hearty handshake, as expected, I suddenly began arguing with him.

It was all crazy, I told him desperately. How could he be in love with Tia now, when he was telling me hardly a week before about this passionate affair he was having with the wife of a mathematics teacher at one of the business colleges in Scranton, who happened to live next door?

"That wasn't love," he said coldly. "That was just sex."

"Well this isn't just sex either," I cried! "I'm all the way in love, right up over my head and call it curls!" And how could she be in love with him, I

474

asked, when just aside from me she was dating Cy Endfield all summer at the ocean resort?

"I gave her my permission for that," he said even more coldly.

"*You* gave her your permission?! Well, *I* gave her my permission too! Maybe she didn't need *neither* of our permissions."

"Love is a wayward thing," Mel began explaining broadly, but I cut him off. I'm sorry to have to admit that I went on ungallantly to mention that Tia and I had been pretty intimate physically ourselves, and that our affair wasn't the sort of kaffee-klatch flirtation with foolosophy and sub-virile literature that Endfield had been treating her to. I didn't go so far as to say I'd really laid Tia, because I never had; but certainly I left it to be understood.

"Don't try to kid me, Gershon," Mel said flatly, speaking for almost the first time to me now in his natural voice. "I slept with Esther for the first time last night, and she was so tight it was practically impossible to get in. And then when I did get in, she bled all over the place."

That was the mortal blow. I had no more to say. I stumbled away, wordless, my face frozen in a pretendedly disbelieving wiseguy sneer, but I knew perfectly well he was telling the truth.

475

THAT NIGHT I slept behind a billboard on the highway somewhere, with the black cardboard bookbag for a pillow. Rides were very hard to get. All the cars were big — too big — the kind rich people drive. Rich people won't ever give you a ride unless they plan to exploit you sexually or to offer you a job as their gardener, or both. Like in *Lady Chatterley's Lover.* In the morning I was up early and hitching on again toward the University of Michigan. I ate nothing: my stomach felt as though I had breakfasted on poisoned rocks. My little white-painted sign that I kept holding up to the drivers' view on the side of my bookbag — ANN ARBOR OR BUST! — seemed to have lost its magic charm. Almost no one would pick me up. Not even truck drivers. On a stretch along Lake Erie, somewhere near Sandusky, Ohio, some son-of-a-bitch appleknocker driving a farm truck gave me a brief lift and then set me down on the highway in the exact asshole of Nowhere, with the cars whistling by at sixty miles an hour, while he turned off onto a side road. They'll do it every time!

476

"Well, son," he said cheerily, before disappearing from view, "I guess ever' little bit helps, eh?"

I must have been stuck there in the boiling sun two hours or more, with my thumb and bookbag sign held up, but no one would stop or was planning to stop. I was getting groggy in the sun. I had no hat and nothing to drink. When the cars I hailed wouldn't stop I would curse after them with a Cheshire cat grin, putting my thumb down at prick level and shaking it at them, or sometimes I'd give them a big mock bow. On one such bow I pitched forward onto the pavement, and was sitting there wondering what had happened, with my head spinning, when a motorcycle suddenly stopped by me.

I assumed it was the state troopers, but it was just some guy on a cycle who had seen me fall. He took me up in back of him on the saddle-seat, chocked my bookbag between his knees, told me to hold on tight to his pants belt, and zoomed off. Just a few minutes later he turned down on a side road by a big barn. I was saying to myself, "Oh God! not another of those *every little bit helps,* is it?" I was ready to cry, or to kill him. We got off the cycle, which he trundled into the barn, saying to me, "Wait there. You can drink the soda in that bottle if it ain't too flat." I drank it. To

477

my total stupefaction he immediately reappeared, pushing out of the barn a small airplane of the cockpit type.

"I can take you as far as Toledo," he said. "Hop in. I gotta get a piece for the motor, but I think we'll get there all right."

We got there fine, and I hitched the rest of the way to Detroit and Ann Arbor in a grinning daze, thinking to myself that I was probably the first and only person in the world who'd ever hitchhiked a ride in an airplane, and from a laying-down position! That was in the days before evacuating refugees in helicopters was common — after having machine-gunned all their relatives for weeks from the same helicopters. I still feel grateful to that young man, who was undoubtedly drafted into a job as a murderous mad-dog Marine or Army bombing pilot when the war came, three or four years later.

Hitchhiking is usually a mess, and dangerous too, especially from homosexual truck drivers and homosexual cowboys — also cops — of whom there must be thousands, though the folklore is that those are the most virile guys. But sometimes you actually do meet a wonderful person hitchhiking, usually the lonely ones who want to talk to you to keep from falling asleep at the wheel. Never the loners who want to listen to continuous rock & roll on the car radio. Louis Adamic has a long short story — really oral history before tape-recorders — called "Girl on the Road," in the anthology *This Is My Best*. That story says it *all*. It's a true masterpiece of underplayed pathos and realism that Gorki would have been proud of.

There was quite a contingent from Scranton at the University of Michigan that year. The first one I ran into was Teddy Weiss, I think. Weiss had a grand emotional speaking voice, and never talked about anything but his destined career as a lawyer: the perfect choice. There was likewise Joe Bernstein, whom I knew well from Hebrew school and Central High, and who later offered to publish my books in Paris, but never did. Both he and I got this idea of going to France from his older brother, who'd just come back from studying medicine, with a chunky, square, smuggled-in copy of Joyce's *Ulysses* — I can still see the floppy light blue paper covers — that he bought in Paris and brought back. That was the copy we all read. After all, it was obvious: if Joyce's and D. H. Lawrence's "unpublishable" books could be published in Paris and Italy, and to hell with censorship; so could mine. All I had to do was to get there. But it took me another twenty years.

479

There were also a couple of girls from Central, and my distant cousin Erwin Rothman, whom I couldn't abide because people said he looked exactly like me, except that he wore his hair ludicrously slicked down. Family chromosomes or no, people who look exactly like you are evidently stealing your identity, and I hated him. I'd see Rothman sometimes, studying earnestly by his window, late evenings when I'd be coming down the hill from pissing my time away playing chess at the Michigan Union. And I would stop and glare at him without his knowing, and would say to myself dubiously, "Why, I don't look a *bit* like him. Do I?" And I'd sinfully wish poor Erwin dead, as he sat there — not me! — grinding greazily by his midnight oil, for all the world like Byalik's poetic "Ha-Mathmid."

After I'd found a boarding house in Ann Arbor that had an old upright piano I could use in the hall downstairs and got myself signed up at the University, plus the School of Music which was what I really cared about most, I saw that my money wouldn't last more than another two months. I'd always known I'd have to work after hours to get through college, and I swallowed my shame about exploiting my Judaism and turned up to ask for a job at the Jewish Students' Center. This was being run, of all people, by Rabbi

480

Heller, the dynamic modern parson who for years had officiated at the Reform synagogue in Scranton where my father taught a syncretistic Sunday school on the side.

Heller welcomed me with open arms, like a lost sheep in the fold, and all the more so in that the religious pigment — if I may so express it — of the Jewish Center at Michigan was a lot closer to Jewish Orthodox than either our family's Conservative or his Reform. But of course religion wasn't the main thing; what was important was getting the students to come there for whatever reason: ping pong, chess, girls, anything; and not lose all their Jewish consciousness. Jews can't ever really become Christians, for all their *goyishe* name-changes and Christmas trees "for the children." They just become White-Negro passers — *sub-goy* chow-mein consumers, Hungry-O's, media nothings — and they and their children hopefully fade away into the hostile host-population.

Whatever the religious hue, they had me in a blue-&-white silk *tallis* and beautifully embroidered *yarmulke* skullcap the very first Friday night, singing a loud if unenthusiastic benediction over a glass of sacramental wine — "The Wine so SWEET you can cut it with a KNIFE!" I writhed at my own hypocrisy, but I would have reneged on a lot more than my atheism to stay close to wherever Tia French was.

It was hard to make friends with anyone there, or at college, nor did I try at first. I was still all churned up inside about having lost the girl I loved. — Oh, I knew I had lost her now! Everybody knows you can't heat up an old affair. No sense even trying. Too sad. And I spent hours berating myself, sometimes aloud, when I should have been studying, for not having realized that no one could hold onto a passionate girl like Tia unless you made love to her. Just the way my Uncle Joel said.

I had really lost her, I told myself, that night when we were in bed together and naked, and her legs already open and twining; and that damned Sharon and her cuckoldy husband came tearing into the driveway with the headlights blazing on us through the window. Damn them both! And then that other next-to-last last chance with that blanket roll brazenly under my arm at nine in the morning, only to have Tia tell me that she had started menstruating again. "So who the hell cares?!" I raged at her, and at myself for listening to her. "It's all part of being human, isn't it?" *Through Mud & Blood to Glory!* — Mud or blood, fire or flood, *Legman Rides Tonight!*

How could I have been so *dumb*, I berated myself a hundred times; and all along? When here it was me — me, myself & I — that was finger-diddling Tia every time we had a secret minute together. And sucking her breasts, and doing everything I knew or could invent to get her wildly ready — and then never coming through! There was such a thing as "respecting" the girl you loved, but not way too much like that! And all the hints she'd given me, when I thought back: and yes! we should be making love instead of just talking about it; that yes! if my father and her mother were going to claim we'd done it already then we certainly ought to do it. But instead, I kept talking how we should wait till we had a place to go where it could be *beautiful*. What flesh-&-blood woman was going to stand for that kind of tergiversation, worthy only of phony, foolish, impotent Wolf Solent. Damn fool that I was! Damn *FOOL!!* Nowhere to go, nowhere to go, nowhere to *go!!* That had been the whole thing, wasn't it? Or at least my whole idiotic excuse.

And now that there *was* somewhere to go, in towns where no one would know us or give a tinker's damn about what we did, it was that stinker Mel who had crudely busted in and plucked the fruit I had ripened so hotly with my love. And why was it, I

483

wondered too, that I was always so brisk and ready —
Up Their Flue With a Screw or Two! — when it came
to fucking & sucking little girls in cellars and rusty,
dusty old mills; and Johnny-on-the-spot every time she
honked the horn for twiddling the clitoris of a
flibbertigibbet young married woman like Sharon
Grossman: front & back and upside down, the whole
fucking palette — pardon my bitter jokes! But when it
came to sweet, adorable, dark-haired Tia with her
melting eyes and juicy lips, in the two long years I'd
known her I had never made unadorned love to her
even once. Never actually made plain & simple love
even one single idiotic time to the girl I adored.

True to my fated life-lines, I had now instantly
become the Official Troublemaker of the incoming
class at Michigan, and was later to be blamed *in absentia*
for everything that went on there in the way of campus
Communism for the next umpteen years, including
being the Grey Eminence and presumed inspiration of
the Weathermen decades later, even though I had
managed to get thrown out after five months. That's
the way it is, being a legend. Three-quarters myth, and
one-quarter total mystery! Actually, the catalogue of
my real crimes at that period is very clear in my mind.
The main element was that I hated everybody and was
brokenhearted over Tia. My basic crime was that I was

484

struggling to combine the uncombinable: an overwhelming sex-problem and total heartbreak.

Although I know it doesn't look good for my record as a juvenile Don Juan, the truth is that except for the fiasco with Gwen on her front porch on Tia's graduation night, and that year-long fling with Sharon Grossman, I never once touched or even looked lustfully at another girl except maybe Darlene Matthis, in the whole two years since I'd fallen in love. In love with Tia French, at first sight — the way coal goes into cellars! — With her wearing that garnet-colored dress with the neckline going from side to side. Just like Dante and Beatrice, only worse.

Of my unimportant freshman peccadilloes I will concede that there were a minor few. I do recollect, at Michigan, mischievously and indignantly busting up the required first-week Hygiene Lecture for all of us incoming freshmen, in which we were direly warned, with colored slides *in terrorem*, against sex, unwanted pregnancy, and venereal disease. The freshperson girls were given a similar brain-washing at Oberlin, Tia told me. I had jumped up angrily and gave a rousing counter-oration from the floor at the end of the lecture we had to endure, pointing out to the tight-assed faculty lecturer and my co-freshmen cohorts the self-evident truth overlooked by the Declaration of

485

Independence, that we had come to the University of Michigan, the pride of the Wolverine State, "to *learn to be* MEN, *not masturbators!!*" This brought down the whole house of unwilling he-virgins in wild applause. The lecturer had not said a single frank word of that or any other type, all the while he was grinding off on his gruesome and spectacular colored side-show slides of twisted peenies and running syphilis sores. I also seemed to remember shouting, over the riotous applause and catcalls of the rest of the freshmen: *"And what makes you think all the girls at Michigan have venereal disease?!?!!"*

This was really craftily running around the official position's earthworks, as I knew they were really only trying to warn us against the presumably diseased townie girls, and the greasy-spoon waitresses and plain two-buck prostitutes in Detroit nearby on Saturday nights. And certainly not against Nice Freshman Girls whom nobody was expected to get a chance to fuck at all. The lecture then broke up, with me giving an impromptu counter-lecture outdoors on birth control methods that work, with half the boys listening to me enthralled and the fraternity jock-types hooting and razzing with a thumb-&-forefinger twisted up to their mouths, which surprised me greatly.

486

That same week, the bulletin boards announced that there would be an evening dance for upperclassmen and their dates in the Michigan Union gymnasium-ballroom, simultaneously with Hell Night for the freshmen, in which us subhumans were traditionally warned by word of mouth that we could expect to be depantsed by the sophomores if we dared to show our snivelling noses anywhere on campus during the hours of the dance. Just for the hell of it, I decided to respond to this challenge with what I thought of as Aesopian subtlety, on the self-castratory style of the fox-who-lost-his-tail; but which I now see was a lot closer to the important neurotic life-game strangely overlooked in Dr. Eric Berne's *Games People Play,* which let's call YCFMIQ, or "You Can't Fire Me, I Quit!" In an even rougher personal version, this became my own psychological attitude toward regular employment for years.

I talked a bunch of other freshmen, of whom I was now a sort of honorary ringleader since my bold vindication of our sexual rights at the anti-sex lecture, into leaving their pants at home that night and wandering around the campus *pretending* they had already been depantsed by sophomores. We couldn't get into very much trouble that way, I pointed out, since we would have already pre-empted the sophomores' announced Hell Night punch. So what more could they do than chase us? We gathered, pantsless as planned, right in front of the Michigan Union where the upperclassmen's dance was taking place, with guys & girls going into the building arm-in-arm, and got a big stare and giggle each time we were noticed.

With one other brave henchman, I then decided we should attack the fortress and invade the Union itself. At this point all the others faded away, but the two of us trudged right in, looking pained and stupid, and made a long, helpless fuss at the front checkroom desk, where the upperclassmen and their girls were leaving their coats. We explained that we had been depantsed — gesture at our own bare legs and jockey shorts under our jackets, since we purposely wore no coats — and had been told by the sophs who depantsed us that our trousers would be waiting for us at the checkroom desk. So kindly hand them over, we insisted, staring brazenly at all the girls and their escorts standing nearby. Eventually I left my henchman doing this yeoman work, telling him to go away after each demand and then come back even more insistently every fifteen minutes. This would mean a new male/female audience and further shock-value each time, and that's what we were after.

488

Looking for bigger game, or call it a wholesale audience for my softcore flashdance, I took advantage of a lull in arrivals at the dance — it had already been on an hour or so — and insinuated myself up the staircase and into the almost completely darkened library on the second floor which was full of armchairs and even sofas. I'd been told reliably that this would be turned over to the dancers and their partners for necking purposes: the Passion Pit, it was called. Inside the door as I came in, I found all the electric buttons controlling the library, right on the wall, hand-high, and I immediately punched them all vigorously, turning on every bloody light in the place suddenly and with blinding effect. Tableau!!

The feminine screams, as the necking couples tried violently to extricate themselves from each other, would have satisfied all the cruellest impulses of Gilles de Retz or the Marquis de Sade. And there I stood, akimbo in my pantsless, pretended innocence, looking like a sort of unexpected Robin Hood in doublet & shoon (only), while I delivered my prepared line in a loud, plaintive voice:

"Has anybody here seen *my pants?!*"

Two upperclassmen projected themselves on me with miraculous speed — probably members of Carle Aldren's football squad, I mused, as they picked

489

me up bodily and flung me out the door into the hall. I knew I richly deserved it. As I flew through the air I could hear one of them grating, "I'll *get* you for this, you green-assed piss monkey."

I went back to my room, grinning and vilely satisfied with myself. My henchman had disappeared. And I wrote in my big, leather sex-slang notebook: *"Piss monkey, green-assed,* pejorative term, Univ. of Mich.," with a cross-reference also indicated for *green-assed,* when the time would come to transfer my materials to index-cards for alphabetizing into the grand *Dictionary of Sex* I planned. I also made a few longer folklore notes on depantsing as a form of mild sexual hazing. But it turned out later that I hadn't understood my pejorative term at all, and that *piss monkey* and *green-ass* were both really highly pejorative terms that all the upperclassmen used for freshmen, especially when beating their asses off and intimidating them verbally at fraternity initiations. At Texas Aggie, which had the most brutal and terrifying initiations and Hell Weeks of all, the frosh were called piss heads — politely in the printed college catalogue, "wetheads."

The one thing I didn't write down anything about was my own peculiar deportment, which might've been worth a line or two in my notebooks even then. How did it happen — I forgot to ask

490

myself — that I was accepting the symbolic castration of being stripped of my pants in the very act in which I told myself I was defying it?   In fact, nobody had depantsed me but me.   Nay, worse and further, how did it happen that here I was — me! — suddenly turning the lights on all these harmless college students doing nothing more than allowed, and even institutionalized heavy necking and light petting, in premises set aside for them and lights purposely dimmed so they could do it?   Wasn't that awfully similar to what the father I hated so much had been accustomed to do to my sisters, Ruth and Matilda, when they brought their dates into the parlor late in the evening for a goodnight hug & kiss, or whatever more they wanted?   So how come now it was me playing the part of High Moral Censor?

Well, I explained to myself Jesuitically when I finally did get around to asking me these inconvenient questions, that wasn't exactly what I was doing.   I wasn't there to peek at *them* — I'd sworn off peeking that time I made Ruth cry about "The Afternoon of a Faun."   I was turning on the light suddenly to make them look at *me*, pantsless as I was, and so triumph over the upperclassmen's Hell Night harassment by a sort of moral jiu-jitsu, where my victorious attack took the form, merely the form, of falling on my ass.

491

I guess I convinced me, all right, but it does seem strange, especially the moral jiu-jitsu part — that "soft-yielding" Japanese art still around under the names of judo and killer karate for aggressive Western hepcats in canvas pajamas. For here I was, ostentatiously becoming *just like* my father and doing what he would do, while telling myself that's how I was fighting him! Everybody knows Oscar Wilde's one and only really famous line, that nasty and untrue thing of obvious homosexual S. & M. intent from *The Ballad of Reading Gaol,* that "Each man kills the thing he loves." His better line, that "Nature imitates Art," is very deep indeed, but only intended as a witty reversal of Seneca. What was bothering me now, though, was the much worse reversal that seemed to be happening to me, and takes up where Wilde left off: *"Each man becomes the thing he hates."*

After the incident of me turning on all the lights in the Passion Pit, I was a marked man. Anything that happened on campus was unquestionably my fault, and was laid at my door even if it wasn't. When somebody looked up the formula for making gunpowder and left a batch of it in a laboratory drawer in Chem/Physics class, which a lab assistant then innocently opened the next morning and got his arm blown off, I was given the third degree for

492

hours at the university Dean's office, and then only let go for lack of proof. In fact, I hadn't done it, and don't know and never did know a damn thing about chemistry, which baffled me completely even in the simple inorganic form. Less than a month later another wiseguy — according to my theory, the same amateur Erostratus — threw a big chunk of sodium into the Michigan Union swimming pool from the balcony, fortunately when nobody was there, for the fun of creating a noisy explosion. I was at the Union that night, but not in the afternoon when the explosion happened. Third degree again; proved my alibi, hands down; and was let go with a solemn warning that the *next* time —

"But I didn't do it *this* time!" I protested.

"You did it, all right," the Dean said disgustedly. "We just can't prove it. And *last* time you blew Hendrick's arm off. And we can't prove that either." And he turned away from totally-innocent me in impotent loathing, muttering something about having to give me the benefit of the doubt. *Malus lex.*

WHAT BROUGHT me out of my tail spin, to the degree that I ever really came out of it at all, was

493

playing chess. The elegant aggressions and sublimated killings of this ornately lethal war-game just suited my inner emotional plight and I'm surprised I didn't take up boxing instead. I might even have done so, but since that was the ploy or reaction of the Jewish anti-hero of Hemingway's *The Sun Also Rises*, not to mention Firpo Bull-Nigger Abe, my Atlantic City friend ten years before, and Sidney Franklin, Hemingway's own Jewish bullfighter friend from Brooklyn, I got the feeling that such vulgar physical overcompensations were getting played out, so I stuck to chess. I may've said earlier that I'd never again play games vulgarly to win, after being called to order on the proper stiff-upper-lip mock-British way of losing at tennis. But chess was an exception. The truth was, I wasn't playing to win; I was playing to kill. I understood perfectly the not-very-well hidden meaning of the game, as gentlemanly murder according to rigid rules, and that was what I wanted.

Eventually I dropped part of my loser pose altogether, and instead of getting the job I planned as a student janitor or some other shit-lifting menial chores to earn my tuition, I grudgingly accepted a little vertical mobility on the social scale and became the semi-official cantor — not yet rabbi — at the Jewish students' synagogue and clubhouse. Rabbi Heller, who

494

preached no sermons of any kind, being strictly an administrator now, was ecstatic about my ritual singing and *dovening*, me rocking piously back & forth on my arches as I sang; and the lachrymose and almost visible fake-piety with which I chanted the *Kiddush* prayer over the sacramental wine on Friday nights. Heller was so impressed he even went out and rustled me up an engraved silver goblet to do it with in fitting fashion, instead of the mere glass kitchen tumbler I had to use at first. I was really disgusted with myself every instant I spent in the Jewish Center, pretending to be a psalmodizing God-flunkey again. I felt about like the little mermaid at-land in the Hans Christian Andersen fairytale, who has to pay for the human feet she's bought by magic in order to be with the prince she loves, by cutting out her tongue, thus loosing her beautiful voice, and by feeling at all times as though walking on knives. This is a much more profound parable than O. Henry's cheap paradox plagiarism, "The Gift of the Magi," about the mutually-pawned man's watch and cut-off woman's hair. The mermaid's fate was also mine, every time I burst into song in my best voice over that silver goblet. Like the mermaid's every step, I felt as though I were walking on knives of dishonesty with every note I sang.

495

Fortunately, I was only on duty at the students' synagogue Friday nights and Saturday mornings. I refused to teach Sunday school, disguised as a "Jewish interest discussion group," and to walk frankly that far in my father's footsteps, as Rabbi Heller was anxious for me to do to give him his weekend off. I had signed up at the School of Music to continue my piano lessons, but found I couldn't do any practicing evenings in my rooming-house because everybody else was doing homework. They would drag me bodily off the piano-bench, claiming that my tinkling at the keyboard disturbed their studies. I myself never did any school-studying, which now meant nothing at all to me. Having lost the girl I loved and not wanting any other, I truly felt I was half-dead, a zombie.

Nothing and nobody interested me. And I lounged sullenly through my classes all day, drank endless chocolate malteds compulsively and began to put on weight though I'd always been thin. Most evenings I spent at the Michigan Union, which was a sort of recreation center for students the Greek-letter snob fraternities didn't want, or who didn't want the fraternities. There was a swimming pool and a gymnasium, which doubled frequently as the ballroom for student dances, and a so-called library upstairs without any books, mainly used with the lights out —

as already seen — as a passion-pit for students who wanted to neck with their dates the nights the balls and proms were going on downstairs. And that was about it. But the main lobby downstairs was fitted up with half a dozen chess-tables and chairs grouped around them, and that was where I found my salvation, as I didn't have to speak to anyone to sit down and play.

I would slouch in, and over to the reception desk, and ask for a chess set in its sliding-top wooden box with a wordless gesture, and then sit down at a table and set up a game and wait for someone to slip into the seat opposite me. The good players didn't like me because I played very badly and aggressively, sometimes knocking the pieces right off the board with a savage snap when I took a pawn or a rook. The poor players didn't like me either, but they had to play with me, because nobody else would take them on.

I was mad to win, and slaughtered the poor dubs like a killer shark. I never spoke: just grunted "check" and "mate" now & then. These easy victories began to disgust me fast, and after a while I stopped knocking the pieces off the board. But I now maliciously insisted on playing a new form of the game that I invented, where you have to *take the king* as the final move! This drove the other players out of their minds. Even the experts used to group around my

497

table when a mate was close, just to watch with beady eyes when the king died. Meanwhile complaining vociferously about my "goofy" new rules. But compulsively staying to watch, you can betcher ass.

"If you don't like 'em, don't play 'em!" I'd snarl, more to myself than to lousy voyeuristic hypocrites like that. They were like the mass audiences at bullfights and prizefights and the guillotine — now crime & horror t.v. Their weakling consciences told them they ought to say they hated it, but they were heavily mesmerized by the idea of death and cruelty, which added up to *power and sex* in some perverted way in their minds. And they *had* to watch. I should have sold tickets.

Playing to the audience now, I even started once again knocking at least that one last piece, the king, off the endgame board as my final move. But this took my already nervously exacerbated audience right over the edge of their repressions, and I got into a couple of fistfights that way and had to stop. Fistfighting, as with Hemingway and Bull-Nigger Abe, was the chess of clods, I knew. My one little change in the rules had come too close to the unconscious and historical meaning of the game — with its "check" and "mate" the Persian words "shah" and "mat," meaning *Kill the king!* — And eventually no one would play with

498

regicide me. No one but one Negro youth who I taught to be a cracker-jack player by means of my consciously cut-throat long-killing Oedipal approach. He and I understood what my new form of the game meant.

We met one rainy night when a bunch of us were stuck under a portico waiting for the rain to stop. I was beginning then to come out of my mutism and took it upon myself to give a private "Fuck Whitey!" pep-talk to this young Negro student hanging around the edge of the group of whites yearning to be accepted. I assured him, while the rain poured down around us, that no white man was ever really friends with a Negro, nor the reverse; and that improving race-relations was all balls and the only part anybody really enjoyed about it was the secretly hate-filled miscegenation. I told him that what he ought to do was what the boy-genius Paul Morphy had done in the 1850s — to learn to be a great chess-player and then *grind down* all his white opponents over the chess-table with a totally and infuriatingly gentlemanly aplomb. I omitted, of course, to tell him what eventually happened to Morphy: how he had turned paranoiac when the English champion refused to meet him and get trounced, whereupon Morphy went mad and died of apoplexy.

Despite the fact, as I insisted, that we as white & black were enemies to the bone, I offered to make a truce with him long enough to teach him to play chess — I don't believe he had ever touched a piece before — and get him started on his nefarious career as the *Black Morpheus,* and I am afraid that's exactly what happened. He clutched at the idea with a fierce delight, and put up with all my patronizing and nastiness until he learned to play well enough to beat me every game. Then he would lightly and with a deliciously crooked smile announce check & mate by knocking my king rolling to the floor. Communication is always better without words.

Of course, I would never pick it up and neither would he, and we'd sit and grin at each other like two man-eating sharks chewing off each other's pricks in the sixty-nine position, our eyeteeth bared, while pretending to love each other like asshole buddies. He also taught me how to rap hands together in Negro hepcat style with large, askew arm-gestures, which we agreed was only the vulgar African jungle-bunny equivalent of chess, in the way of mock-combat.

This young man, whose real name I never knew then — we called him Doctor Joe — suddenly appeared again briefly in my life, writing to me when my book *Oragenitalism* was first openly published in

500

1969. He had long before discovered the anonymous first edition of 1940 (my first book) of which he had somehow procured, by inside pull, one of the very rare copies seized and not destroyed — so they said — by the police, and was using this for years as the secret basis of his success in seducing and pleasing white women. He was not exactly writing to me about that, since by a marvelous coincidence he hadn't at first realized that his former white chess teacher and companion was also the unknown and pseudonymous author of his Bible of cunnilinctus. That sort of spiked his little red wagon, but he didn't know it.

He went to some trouble, however, to describe in disguise his complicated sexual life, which now specially included miscegenational white/black orgies and voyeuristic wife-trading, in which he would join at the end by sucking the white man's semen out of his wife's vagina in order to absorb in this way his lighter-skinned rival's mystic "strength." His letter then ended, after some long discussion of his many chess victories over astonished white players, who "couldn't believe a black man could beat them," by confiding to me that he was now a clinical psychiatrist in a rich San Francisco suburb. And that he had spent the last two years of his college career at Oberlin, where he became the lover of my former girlfriend Teresa French, when

Mel Cantor and another later lover got through with her. He felt this would be of interest to me to know.

This teaches us the meaning of the Arab proverb, that if you nurse a frozen snake in your bosom, when you have revived it with the heat of your body it will bite you to death. Like that ugly avenging angel, Young Mordaunt, in Dumas' *Twenty Years After*, who is really the arch-evil Milady's illegitimate son, out to get the Three Musketeers for having first married and then murdered his mother. You never know, sometimes, what an idle jest will do.

What I found so curious about Doctor Joe Morpheus' delayed-action revenge, as the clinical psychiatrist he purported to be, was that both in the personal and chess-playing parts of his letter to me, and in his descriptions of his highflying private sex-games with white women, he was so completely unconscious of his towering self-hatred as a Negro. As he saw it and gloated over it, what was so specially humiliating to the white men he beat at chess was the "blackness" of the man who beat them, not really that he was just a better chess-player. I thought our original contract at Michigan had made that vengeful point conspicuously clear, yet here was this highly intelligent man who had gone through half a lifetime completely overlooking it. As of course do all black boxers and

Olympic champions who exult in their basket-ball court and running track victories over whites.

Morpheus really went pretty far in this direction of dangerous racial self-humiliation — something like eating shit in public to prove the white boss is under-nourishing you — in the part he later played as the "Negro Rapist," in the sexual charades or home theatricals that accompanied his black/white wife-swapping orgies. Hundreds — perhaps thousands — of Negroes have been lynched for the "Negro Rapist" stereotype that Morpheus was willing to sink to, just as a preliminary spice for his neurotic fun & games with white couples. It is exactly the same with his attempt to freeze my soul with the knowledge that he had also put his "big black cock" into certain mucous pelvic tissues of the girl I once loved. Implying further that he had also turned her over to other of his Negro friends for whipping and more of the same, by scamming her into believing that this was her socialistic "duty." To make up for the evil that other whites have done to other blacks in other centuries. This too, I assume he felt, would especially hurt me. Guard on your Queen!

What was the real triumph over me here, that Morpheus was so anxious that I should know? Was it simply that his cock was black and big, and mine (presumably) a mere pinkish brown and not as big? Or that what he had done had somehow dirtied and defiled the girl I loved, and therefore me, *because* his cock was black. Are black cocks really any dirtier than white ones? Can't they wash? Or is their "dirtiness" built-in, racial, inexpugnable? My friend in Paris, the Negro novelist Richard Wright, and another writer, a black French pimp I knew there too, both assured me that to them fucking a white woman — they were both married to white women — meant "pissing up the ass of the whole white race!" Mere physical gorilla glory, fellows. Better stick to chess.

THE "Oberlin Experience" had turned sour for Tia sooner than I ever could have thought, and worse, owing to Mel Cantor's unfailing pretention and competitiveness. On my next rather diffident visit to them in Oberlin he was a lot happier to see me than I expected. As he explained it all to me, the first day in Freshman English everybody had to write a short placement theme on a chosen topic in a list of about twenty the young professors all gave, such as "How I Spent My Vacation", "Why I am at College", "My Pet Peeves", and so forth. This was standard practice

504

everywhere. Mel took the only topic that wasn't wholly insulting, which was "Women Writers," although he didn't know a damn thing about the subject in any historical sense, as he was frank to admit. He managed to fill up several sheets, however, with knowing references to, and appreciations of George Eliot, George Sand, Aphra Behn — whom he had never read — Mary "Frankenstein" Shelley, and all the American women poets like Emily Dickinson and Edna St. Vincent Millay that I'd been reading aloud to him and myself all that early summer, out of Untermeyer's big anthology, to furbish up my loneliness.

I never found out why the young professor included a feminist subject-choice like that among the freshman placement topics, decades before Women's Liberation got to be news. It must have been a favorite of his, though, 'cause the next time Mel showed up for English class, he was told he was excused and to come instead to the professor's home Thursday nights for a seminar. A dozen other eager kids turned up there too, mostly boys, and it was no doubt a lot of fun — especially not to have to sit through Freshman English 1: gerunds, exercises, etc. All they had to do was to write a theme on any subject they wished during the week, and then turn them in each Thursday night, when the young professor would read aloud those from the week before and have the students criticize them without knowing who the authors were.

The professor particularly enjoyed making each of the authors part of the game, by inviting them straight-faced to criticize their own themes anonymously. Mel always went along with the gag, which I agreed with him was very fine, and would tear into his own themes violently when it came his turn to criticize, while the other students would try to shush him and complained about his unfairness to the unknown writer. Mel eventually wrote an end-of-the-term theme which he showed me proudly, called "Our Seminar," in which he described everyone's character and abilities in very flattering terms including his own and the professor's. It ended, if I remember rightly: *"Then there's Cantor. Our seminar is a quiet pool into which everyone puts his feet. When Cantor puts his foot in it, there's no more pool."* Well said; but I wonder if it wasn't more a pious hope than a reality.

Aside from his big feet — or maybe the metaphor was pebbles and a big rock thrown into the quiet pool — Mel was unsatisfied with this Thursday night paradise right from the beginning, because his Tia had not been promoted to the seminar group. One of the only two times I hitchhiked back to Oberlin to

506

see them, he told me he felt humiliated, or more likely it was Tia who felt that way, to think of her tooling along with the dumbbells back in Freshman English 1. I think what he really wanted was to show off how pretty she was, and that she was now *his*. He did everything he could to convince the professor that Tia belonged in the seminar, and built up her writing ability to the skies until the professor finally gave in and invited her. I knew Tia a lot better than Mel did, even though I had to admit he was sleeping with her and not me. And I tried to caution him that her real gifts were all emotivity and sweetness — like Sylvia Sidney who always suffered so beautifully in the movies, whom she also looked a lot like — and not really intellectuality. But Mel wouldn't listen, and accused me out-of-hand of crude anti-Marxist patriarchalism. Phrased more modernly, I was marked by a statement like that as a prototypical, rotten, male-chauvinist macho pig.

Mel also pooh-poohed me haughtily when I asked what would happen if Tia *didn't* make the grade in the seminar, and was sent back to Freshman English 1. How would she *feel*, I asked, if maybe the day came when she had to walk *back* through the door into the class of ordinary dumbbells, in her little white sacrificial dress, *if* things should happen to turn out that way? She would die of *mortification*, is what! I told him I'd

507

had lots of letters from Tia, and although I loved her desperately I knew she couldn't write anything *but* letters.

For all my emphasis and over-emphasis, Mel wouldn't listen a damn bit, and I didn't have the heart to do more than warn Tia indirectly on that trip, in the vaguest possible way, urging her to bust her beautiful little moon-shaped ass writing some *really* great themes. She lasted two Thursday nights. Everybody was wowed by her prettiness, to be sure, with the defender of women's rights, Mel, presenting her on his arm like a lightly veiled nautch-dancer. Then the professor pitilessly sent her back to freshman gerunds. I've been told that Tia's writing improved since, to adequate; but in those days even I had to admit she couldn't write for beans. Now *I* was the one that was humiliated when she got dropped out of the seminar, not to mention Tia. I was furious at Mel for his clumsiness, and could have killed him when he wrote me about it. He seemed quite calm, though he admitted Tia was very, very disappointed. But, he assured me, she'd get over it. "Anyhow," he ended airily, "she's taking up tennis now." My Tia, a female sports jock?! Never!

Though I had no way of knowing it, Tia was being shaken then by a much worse rejection, which I think changed her for life. It would have changed me.

508

And she eagerly accepted when I wrote to her halfway through the term to say that I'd bought three tickets for her and Mel and me — just like the old times! — to hear the Budapest String Quartet at the Oberlin auditorium. I'd seen their schedule pasted up in the Music School, and used up my last money on those three reserved tickets and the luxury of train fare, this once, to get my ass to Oberlin before the concert started.

At that time I believed that I hated *all* string quartets, and not just Beethoven's last six — which I *still* hate. But this was the only concert I could get three tickets for, all seated together. I had really wanted to hear the Don Cossacks instead. Tia sat between me and Mel, and I shamelessly held one of her hands in spite of his disapproving side-glances. I also kept hold of her upper arm with my other hand underneath, jamming my knuckles hard into the side of her sweet breasts. She made no effort to stop me, and let me do what I liked.

They played Schubert's angelic *13th Quartet in A-minor*. To heartaching me, it was exactly like a door opening into Heaven. Holding onto Tia with both hands that way probably helped the music too. Fortunately, they did not follow it up, as I've heard the Budapests do since — none of whom were ever in that

509

city in their life, by the way, all of them being Russians — with Schubert's ghastly and neurotic *14th Quartet,* with its frightful shrieking strings, supposed to be wonderful merely because of the sadistic nickname someone stuck to it, of "Death and the Maiden."

Like the tens of thousands of people who placidly watched the Swedish movie, *Elvira Madigan* some years later, in which a man shoots to death the woman he presumably loves — an obvious but depraved symbol for their implied sexual intercourse, to be sure — while the soundtrack defiles the exquisite Hesitation Largo from Mozart's *21st Piano Concerto.* As it was, that night, the concert at the Oberlin Auditorium with all my fingers grimly sunk into Tia's soft flesh was the highpoint of my musical life, a lost Shangri-La I looked back to yearningly for many years after.

Tia's own life was becoming much grimmer then too. She was accustomed to my idolizing her, and accepted it as the proper homage to her winsome beauty and charm. But she was not prepared for Mel's type of sudden neurotic rejection, and even worse his snide manipulation of people. I did see Tia one more time, and never again, when I got kicked out of Michigan not long after for stealing a typewriter, and stopped off at Oberlin to kiss her goodbye — forever,

510

as it turned out. She didn't tell me a single word then of what happened, and of course I was delighted that Mel wasn't there to spoil our last goodbye, and didn't concern myself with anyone but Tia. Our goodbye kiss was very chaste — I preferred it that way too, as I had planned it in my head, not in my balls — and ended formally with me declaiming by heart the superb farewell-forever from Shakespeare's *Troilus & Cressida:*

> And suddenly, where injury of chance
> Puts back leave-taking, justles roughly by
> All time of pause, rudely beguiles our lips
> Of all rejoindure, forcibly prevents
> Our lock'd embrasures, strangles our dear vows
> Even in the birth of our own labouring breath
> —
>
> We two, that with so many thousand sighs
> Did buy each other, must poorly sell ourselves
> With the rude brevity and discharge of one.
>
> Injurious tune now with a robber's haste
> Crams his rich thievery up, he knows not how:
> As many farewells as be stars in heaven,
> With distinct breath and consigned kisses to them,
> He fumbles up into a loose *adieu,*

511

And scants us with a single famish'd kiss,
Distasted with the salt of broken tears.

Whereupon, the horses of Diomedes being ready, the two lovers part forever, each to their separate infidelities.

What had happened I found out about only a long while later, when Mel and I got to know each other well again for a while in New York. It was just as I psyched, and had told him that first time at Oberlin, the morning after he bragged about deflowering Tia the night before. It was all a fake — Mel didn't love her at all. He had met an older woman in Scranton that summer whom he really preferred, named Zhenia, the one he had told me was just a sex-affair. And she'd suddenly arrived at Oberlin in the middle of the first semester looking for Mel. They'd been having this red-hot affair all summer — exactly like mine with Sharon Grossman — unknown to any of us then, and especially to his family, since she was their next-door neighbor. It had all started with Zhenia being maternal and sympathetic about Mel's eye-troubles and headaches caused by the chemicals at the refrigeration plant he was working at. And very soon she was holding warm compresses over his temples and the bridge of his nose, every evening in the Cantors' kitchen, and later in her own. This was an "old Alsatian remedy" from her European past.

Zhenia was very soon ready to abandon her husband, Willis, a low-voltage wimp and wet smack — according to Mel — and only good enough to get her out of Europe, where they'd met on his one & only vacation abroad, bicycling through northern France and Belgium with a graduate student group of superannuated he- and she-virgins. Willis had now accepted an uninspiring job as assistant professor of mathematics at an obscure upstate New York college, in some one-horse lake town where Zhenia correctly assessed that living would hardly be much of a thrill for a cultivated European woman. Since she was already having this affair with Mel, her husband clearly wasn't satisfying her, and life at Finger Lake would surely very rapidly add up to: Who's to be my next affair? Otherwise it would be more like being buried alive.

By way of necessary subterfuge she claimed that she was passionately interested in classical & modern architecture, and that Finger Lake's Burgwitz College (431 students) did not have a sufficiently high-ranking school of architecture to suit her. In fact it had none at all. But things had taken her a certain amount of time before she could break loose from her manipulated wimp-ass of a husband, without actually getting a divorce, so he would continue paying her bills for a while at least. She was theoretically going to get herself a degree in Architectural Aesthetics, and at the best college for it anyone could find, which just happened to be where Mel was going too.

Zhenia arrived at Oberlin later in the term, with her fabulous collection of sexy gloves, dark stockings, *terrific* underwear, and expensive exotic perfume, to go on with her perfectly honest amour with bouncy young Mel, under the aegis of the ancient and noble art of Architecture. While plump, good-humored dud husband Willis, sloughed off painlessly in the Finger Lakes region of Upper New York state, came through exactly on schedule and as programmed, playing the standard unvirile chump and unwitting cuckold; and of course dutifully paying all the bills. This was distressingly similar to the low comedy I had hassled myself into all the preceding year, paying for the drinks at after-dinner bars for Tia and her various best-friend dates, standing-in — as I fondly imagined — for myself.

In France this would be considered a comedy situation. In America it had all the makings of tragedy for everyone concerned — except Mel. Tia was allowed only the part of the Innocent Victim. My part, if I had been there, was slated to be that of Rescueron-White-Horse, as I saw things; but really much more of the Patsy or Uncle Charlie, in the life-game of LMCAHOYSUC, or "Let Me Cry About Him On Your Shoulder, Uncle Charlie," which an incredible number of women have tried to play with me all my life, offering me only their unenthusiastic erotic baits, or tepid leftovers from the *other* guy, to make me willing to play. This is really a sort of cutrate supportive psychotherapy, with the payoff to the hedge-psychoanalyst in warmed-over pussy. In this case, I didn't even get that much satisfaction, as my star chess-student, *Black Morpheus* or Doctor Joe, skidded in on a wet deck to do the job.

Like all European women trying to get to America, and getting there, particularly since the Second World War, Zhenia knew how to pour on the sex till the hair flew off your head. That was not what she was really like, as I learned later when I met her again in New York, but that was the act she put on. Since it's very well understood among all European women, by some kind of secret international female freemasonry, that red-hot sex-jobs are the only kind of women repressed and pussy-whipped American men really yearn for — and it won't be you, you lying son-of-a-bitch, that's going to tell me any different! — these highly neurotic but intensely practical female

Conquistadoras start telephoning their pubic powerhouse or Sunday scrotal sex-punch the minute they sight the Statue of Liberty.

As the *Europe on Five-&-Ten Dollars a Day* guidebooks all negligently forget to mention, most of these women are totally frigid, absolutely icebound; but will put on a wonderful act for you, including a steamed-up mock orgasm with ululating shrieks that will blast the windows right out of your bachelor apartment. IF you can afford to simultaneously stuff their assholes full of gold. John Updike asserts in one of his *Rabbit-stew* sex novels, that this type is now endemic in America as well, but I have never sighted any native examples, possibly because I don't have that many South African gold-pieces to play around with wrapped in safe-sex condoms, and don't live in Bucks County.

Any birdwatcher caring to do further study on the type here described will find plenty of them, both domestic & imported, on television and especially in the movies and on the fast track in the business world today. The far-famed-&-frequently-married Gabor sisters, all of whom snagged off millionaires, including their widowed mother who came with them from Hungary as coach, were the first crack regiment of merely *ersatz* imitations or simulacra of the breed to hit

516

America right after the war. But the Gabors are much more elegant and richly reserved than the twisting, attitudinizing type I mean. Play it cool!

One now often encounters in professional life in America and abroad a new and less satisfying native type of loveless mock-female, known as *Super-shicksas* or men-with-cunts — I believe I may have married one or two of them in my romantic search for intelligent women, and the more fool I! — who frankly refuse femininity and may also compulsively sport men's haircuts and clothes, right up to & including grungy green sneakers and/or Harris tweed jackets in small boys' sizes. These pathetic Elektras, though not quite lesbians in transvestite disguise, often admit or *almost* admit to their frigidity and super-muscular inability to feel any love or sexual passion, which is the true measure of their "female" castration. Eventually, their "New Chastity" sex-act does not go over too well with normal men. And they mostly find themselves after a couple of years of peddling their *shtick,* proudly paying their own bills, and observing bitterly that the really coarse Hollywood sugar is still being grabbed off by the shameless fake-feminine types whom they feel too much gentlemanly honor to attempt to imitate. Never do they observe that both they themselves and the fluffy blonde gold-diggers they think they despise are

517

floundering helplessly in the same treacly mora$$ of orally-oriented egoi$m and materialistic greed.

Both sorts naturally specialize in high-class fellation and are often artists at it, desperately trying to clear the speeded-up action out of their overfucked but, alas, anaesthetic cunts. This can certainly be fun, if you have the nerve to face their occasional midnight avatars during their menstrual periods — especially if they nervously *miss* them, being almost invariably early menopausers, thin, virilistic, small-breasted, and embroiled in nervous anorexia and a perpetual diet — when they are suddenly transmogrified into fang-bearing furies of the Screaming Spiderwoman or Vera the Vampire type. It takes a braver man than me to want to kiss & make up by means of fast-food fellation or even a rapid sixty-nine at that point. Just don't forget your Swedish steel penis-case, brother.

I never met Zhenia Trimble, as she was now called as Willis's wife, but once then at Oberlin. I also didn't realize then that she was my friend Mel Cantor's secret passion, and assumed she was just a fascinating aspect of the campus scene. When you shook hands with Zhenia on first being presented to her, she would take your hand in both of hers and hold it with overflowing sincerity and sentimentality right between her heavily décolleté breasts — against The Heart, that is. She would then do a sort of slow emotional wiggle or unconscious hully-gully of the shoulders and haunches, coming upwards at you with a soft rotary motion like frame-by-frame bumps & grinds. Meanwhile murmuring throaty compliments with a lot of trance-like lip motions, about all the wonderful things she'd heard about you, or would dream up right there on the spur of the moment. Like a lot of people on the make — all sexes: male, female, and *demi-caractère* — Zhenia was a total believer in the persuasive power of flattery and the verbal cocktease.

Faced with the battery of Zhenia's plunging neckline, wriggling pelvis, and invitingly soupy lipstick smile and flattering lies, you could feel or imagine you already felt all her sphincters closing lushly over your marvelling eyes, nose, mouth and more intimate anatomy; while the rest of your senses — if you still had any hanging loose — were invaded with the imaginary frangipani-laden pussy-juice flowering lusciously around you in the air. Everyone within twenty yards could hear the brass sewing of your fly-zipper zinging like an overstrung harp, or was already ducking the flying pants buttons, as the case might be. Zhenia would then come in for her unfailing smash finish in the instant-ensorcellment department, and would hit you amidships with her best and most profound under-the-eyelashes, half-horny, half-poetic, wholly ineluctable bedroom look that you could pour on bread like liquid peppergrass honey. She was, or purported to be, so erotic a self-starter of truly extraordinary caliber, that she left man or boy no option — if he had two balls bulging between his legs and wanted to keep on feeling like a man — but to start grabbing at the hem of her panties, as she presumably wanted, right up to the crotch.

Zhenia trotted out all this erotic armamentarium on every male person she met, including me; and Mel told me that some of the older professors were tremblingly frightened of the way she came on so strong. The professors' wives at Oberlin were apparently ready to import a team of Mafia hit-men to knock off Zhenia, or at least ship her back in a box to her point of origin in Luxemburg. There was also some question of getting her legal husband Willis to invite her back to Burgwitz College in Finger Lake, New York, where he didn't know what he was missing. A friend of both Mel's and mine told me that their French professor, who had gone the same route as poor Willis, and foolishly married an Italian *contessa* after World War I and brought her back to Oberlin, had stated to him coldly that only totally frigid women overacted like Zhenia in public, and warned him that he should try to save his friend Mel. I wonder though. I don't think Zhenia was frigid. Just coming on too strong.

Four or five years later I met Zhenia again in New York at her request, to play LMCAHOYSUC with me. Remember? — that's "Let Me Cry About Him On Your Shoulder, Uncle Charlie," the particular and signifying life-game or Nemesis of my own life. I dunno why. Maybe because I'm such a sympathetic and understanding cuss, not really likely to rape anybody myself, but with such irresponsible male friends, whose moral and marital deficiencies are All My Fault. Some of Zhenia's corny sex-comedy had quieted down by then, and I actually liked her quieter style very well, though I did not exploit the situation sexually in any way and never even took her head literally on my shoulder. The truth is, I was afraid of her, and what might come *next*. Zhenia was extremely cultivated in many ways which did not surprise me, but a real psychological mess. She taught me a lot about architecture, though, and color-combinations.

She and Mel had been living together quite amicably for three years, after she went back to Willis long enough to divorce him. She had discovered through a friendly lawyer that New York State law, and perhaps the laws of most other states, allow a woman

521

to divorce a husband who doesn't want to divorce her, using the standard hokum grounds of "mental cruelty" — which can mean his asking her to go down on him, or him on her! — and to force him to pay all the costs of the divorce, plus ample monetary support for the rest of her natural life or until she remarries.

That was why she hadn't ever married Mel, who still didn't have any definite employment in view. Anyhow, Willis was still supporting her, not Mel, who she said was *not* the affectionate person she had thought he was at first, and really needed a mother, not a wife. In the end she had been profoundly hurt, after she finished putting Mel through college on Willis's money, when Mel eventually threw her over on short notice for a couple of adulterous side-affairs, as she called them, and a soft life married to an heiress.

It was very clear to me that Zhenia's intention in coming to see me in my hall bedroom, monastically furnished with bed, books, and a typewriter — replacing the bell, book & candle of other monasteries — was not just to get news of Mel and brood over her sadness about him, but to hook up with some other simple-minded young sex-nut, namely me. That's the whole trick about the "Uncle Charlie" game, and why Uncle Charlie always has to lose. I was positive that Zhenia would give an absolutely Grade A performance

522

in bed, but I was also positive that it wouldn't be anything *but* a performance, and who wants that, especially if it means buying into the life of an obviously very neurotic woman?

I certainly couldn't fault her for anything she had done, except maybe the way the divorce had been so profitable to her — and to Mel: the part she was bitterest about. She had fallen in love with Mel, whether just sexually or every other way there is, and she had left her husband for him. What else had I been doing with Sharon? That's the Law of Love, and no man-made law or woman-made law can ever change it. Don't you know that song about "The Gypsy Laddie"? — *But tonight!! she sleeps on the cold, cold ground. By the side of the Black-jack Gypsy-O!* Even the parody is pretty powerful and immutable, where *(Fast, stamping rhythm): The Lady of the Manor was a-dressing for the ball, When she spied a Hieland Tinker lashing piss against the wall. With his great big kidney-cracker, and balls the size of three, And a YARD-and-a-half of foreskin hangin' well below his knee! — Hangin' down!! Swingin' free!! And a YARD-and-a-half of foreskin, &c.* I'm not suggesting that that's how Mel was outfitted, nor her either. But that's the way it always works, call it love or call it sex.

One thing was sure: on first meeting Zhenia in Scranton, Mel had gone over like a tenpin under the onslaught of her hot sexjob come-on. He and I were just two bright seventeen-year-old-boys, fresh out of ankle-high sneakers, short pants, and high school. Zhenia was thirty-five or more, and admitted to twenty-eight. Although, as I say, I have absolutely no first-hand idea what she was like in bed, Mel visibly preferred her yohimbine-charged act to Tia's winsomeness and simple lack of prudery, and her normal erotic willingness. I imagine that, by comparison, Zhenia's pelvic offering felt more like hurtling through the Simplon Tunnel on an electrified eggplant. All you had to do was *hang on!* Seventeen-year-old Tia obviously could not compete on those grounds.

Since I'm telling the truth, I should mention that I was sorry not to dare to risk finding out what Zhenia was really like in bed, after all that build-up. But I knew she wanted to get her hooks into me, bad, now that Mel was gone, and I was afraid. I suppose I still might have proved virile enough — *scared stiff*, and all that — but at that point it would only have been in the interests of science; and curiously enough that's something I've never done. Not even once, and that was with a bulldyke Lesbian twice my age who had me cornered, and announced the entertainment by asking me in her deep, booming baritone-contralto: "Legman?

524

How do you feel about buggering women?" Answer: The less said the better. Anal erotism is more appreciated than you think.

So now we knew. Mel's newly discovered or warmed-over sudden soufflé of love for Tia, which had closed the door forever on my chances of beginning again with her, away from home and the surveillance of her family and mine, had really been just a spy-story front, behind which he was to continue carrying on his amour with his secret love, Zhenia, at Oberlin. Tia never told me a word of this, or even hinted at it in our few letters later. But Mel explained it all quite shamelessly to me, one winter day in New York, describing himself pathetically as having been a "victim of passion" — like me. I guess that was to keep me from throwing any stones.

The whole thing had evidently been willed by Heaven, and Mel couldn't fight it, because there was some mystic or occult sympathy or an Elective Affinity (long after Goethe's *Werther*) between Zhenia's life-lines and his own, owing to the three matching letters in their names: Melvin and Zhenia. Tia's name, after all, did not match with Mel's for more than one letter, whether as Esther or Teresa. And husband Willis's did not match Zhenia's as well. I pointed out that, in that case, my name had *four* letters that match up with

Esther, and three even if we called her Teresa. But for some occult reason I was thrown out at second base, anyhow.

All this came strangely from the mouth of an embryonic Marxian-Socialist philosopher, thinker, and writer like my friend Mel, who did not hesitate to remind me scathingly that Lenin had said that "Religion is the opium of the People," when I took the job as *shammus* at the Jewish Student Center. But Zhenia had made him see the Higher Truth of horoscopes, name-ology, lucky numbers, amulets, and even, I do believe, hexes, surrealism, and all the rest of that outworn and *démodé* but luxurious mental trash. He's not the only one, either. In over-intellectualized France, it's practically the state religion.

I wouldn't say Mel went the whole distance, except to humor her along, but he did go pretty far. I even seem to remember one period there when he was playing around with the childish noughts & crosses of pitifully piddling Professor Rhine at Duke University — a person and place alas never noted for anything else but this soft-focus, let us say, self-delusion concerning presumed "thought-transmission." But it turns out that Rhine was just a piker, in the way of Southern Collegiate Comfort for the grieving and the needing-to-believe. Comes now one Professor Raymond Moody,

526

dynamic, young (44 years old), and rather sappily sincere-looking, of the Department of Psychology of West Virginia College, Carrollton, Georgia — you've heard of it by now, haven't you? — who feels that millions of us have experiences of Approach To Death, especially children (a low blow, that), where we float in luminous form over our own stretched-out bodies, and are sucked up into a "black tunnel" at vertiginous speed, finally to See The Light, which transpierces us and fills us with Religious Love and Understanding for *everyone*. Onward! There's even a pop-song about it in the works: Paul Misraki's "Open Your Door To Me!"

It appears my friend Mel had got hooked on mental trash of this type, though more "scientific" and slightly less pathetic and womb-return gooey, by reading the now-forgotten *Mental Radio* of our one-time idealistic Utopian knight, Upton Sinclair, then foundering into occultism and politics, and soon to blossom out secretly as a wartime government courier and spy — also after the war. He too is not the only one. Spying for the government is quite a large profession in America and abroad, since World War II, on the admirable style of Joshua's spies against innocent Jericho, Sir Francis Walsingham's against the Jesuit spies of Armada Spain, Cardinal Richelieu and

Louis XIV; and since then the less-well sanitized Russian Cheka and Okhrana and the K.G.B. Not to mention the brilliant and heroic British "secret chambers," and their Classified Intelligence; now in the U.S. too, in our own FBI, CIA, and NSA — usually and purposely overlooked, though the most enormous, far-reaching and tentacular of them all. Our innocence is gone.

528

Made in the USA
Middletown, DE
21 April 2017